Becoming a Teacher Researcher in Literacy Teaching and Learning

Designed to facilitate teachers' efforts to meet the actual challenges and dilemmas they face in their classrooms, *Becoming a Teacher Researcher in Literacy Teaching and Learning*:

- Provides ba____round information and key concepts in teacher research (What is it? How does it relate to qu____tive and experimental, quantitative research?)
- Covers the t____er research process from the initial proposal to writing up the report as publishable ____sentable work
- Presents the ____s of inquiry—the "how-to" strategies of collecting data, analyzing the data, and writing ____ teacher research study
- Illustrates a ____ of literacy topics and grade levels
- Features 12 2-1 s by teacher researchers who have gone through the process
- Helps teach____ ____derstand how knowledge is constructed socially in their classrooms so that they can cre____ the kinds of instructional communities that promote *all* students' learning

Addressing the importance of teacher research for better instruction, reform, and political action, this practical, engaging text emphasizes strategies teachers can use to support and strengthen their voices as they dialogue with others in the educational community, so that their ideas and perspectives may have an impact on educational practice both locally in their schools and districts, and more broadly.

Christine C. P ____as is Professor Emerita, Curriculum and Instruction, University of Illinois at Chicago.

Eli Tucker-Ra ____ is Research Scientist with the Chèche Konnen Center at TERC.

Tc

Becoming a Teacher Researcher in Literacy and Learning

Strategies and Tools for the Inquiry Process

**Christine C. Pappas and
Eli Tucker-Raymond**

With

Tara Braverman, Shannon Dozoryst,
Meg Goethals, Katie Paciga, Cindy Pauletti,
Nicole Perez, Catherine Plocher, Dawn Siska,
Kristen Terstriep, Libby Tuerk,
Courtney Wellner, and Sandra Zanghi

Routledge
Taylor & Francis Group

NEW YORK AND LONDON

First published 2011
by Routledge
270 Madison Avenue, New York, NY 10016

Simultaneously published in the UK
by Routledge
2 Park Square, Milton Park, Abingdon, Oxon OX14 4RN

Routledge is an imprint of the Taylor & Francis Group, an informa business

Typeset in Bell Gothic and Perpetua by
Keystroke, Station Road, Codsall, Wolverhampton
Printed and bound in the United States of America on acid-free paper by
Edwards Brothers, Inc.

Library of Congress Cataloging in Publication Data
Pappas, Christine C.
    Becoming a teacher researcher in literacy teaching and learning : strategies and
    tools for the inquiry process / Christine C. Pappas, Eli Tucker-Raymond ;
    with Tara Braverman. . .[et al.].
        p. cm.
    Includes index.
    1. Reading (Elementary) 2. English language—Composition and exercises—
Study and teaching (Elementary) I. Tucker-Raymond, Eli. II. Title.
    LB1573.P195 2011
    372.607′2—dc22   2010026908

ISBN 13: 978–0–415–99620–4 (hbk)
ISBN 13: 978–0–415–99621–1 (pbk)
ISBN 13: 978–0–203–83609–5 (ebk)

SUSTAINABLE FORESTRY INITIATIVE
Certified Fiber Sourcing
www.sfiprogram.org

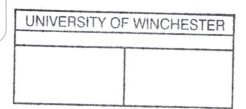

Contents

CONTENTS

Preface

Although teacher research has become more common and accepted in educational research, it is still the case that the *voices* of teachers are often silenced or not taken account of in the discourse of reform. Their ideas, their expertise, their experiences are neglected or not sought out regarding better practices for literacy teaching and learning.

In this book, we talk a lot about teacher voice, relying on Bakhtin's notion of *voice* as "speaking personality, the speaking consciousness" (1981, p. 434). Voice, here, is a perspective that always enacts particular social values by addressing, or being in dialogue with, other voices (Cazden, 1992; Wertsch, 1991). A major aim of this book is to provide research strategies for teachers to support and strengthen their voices—their speaking personalities, their points of view—as they dialogue with others in the educational community. *Becoming a Teacher Researcher in Literacy Teaching and Learning* gives them tools to address the challenges they face in teaching, as well as offering them ways to share the findings of their studies. In doing so, they also have the potential for *being heard*, so that their ideas and perspectives may have an impact on educational practice both locally in their schools and districts and more broadly (Freeman, 2010).

Teacher research is the *systematic, intentional inquiry by teachers* into their own school and classroom work (Cochran-Smith & Lytle, 1993). It is meant to foster an *explicit* awareness of teachers' practices; it represents opportunities to become *reflective practitioners*. It offers ways for them to think about who is and is not learning in their classroom and consider what to do about it. It helps teachers to create a classroom context that encourages equitable learning by figuring out why their best intentions may not be realized. Teachers are often asked (or "required") to engage with a range of reform efforts. Teacher inquiry is a way for them to study these new ideas and their own students for themselves so that they can critically evaluate them. Moreover, in the current climate of standardized evaluation, teacher research enables teachers to develop alternative assessments that more directly guide instruction for children.

The purpose of this book is to help teachers (or pre-service teachers) to conduct inquiries about the literacy teaching and learning in their own classrooms—including learning how to write up these studies so that their voices can be heard by a broader educational audience. This does not mean that all inquiries should or must be written up and submitted as a conference presentation or to a journal for publication. However, we hope this book, besides offering teacher researchers ways to systematically reflect on their work—and contribute their voices more locally—provides writing-up strategies for those who do want them.

This book is designed to be used in a university course, but it is also written so that teachers who are not affiliated with any college or university will also find it helpful. It covers important aspects of teacher research: creating the inquiry question; planning the inquiry; composing letters for obtaining informed parent permission and consent; developing a preliminary literature review on an inquiry topic; carrying out ongoing data analyses via data summaries based on cycles of inquiry; formatting various data findings in inquiry reports; and so forth. It also provides examples of papers by twelve teacher researchers who conducted their inquiries several years ago in a literacy teacher research course that we (Chris and Eli) team-taught. Other useful information is also provided in appendices, as indicated in the section "Overview of the Book" (p. ix).

WHO WE ARE

Chris Pappas is currently Professor Emerita at the University of Illinois at Chicago (UIC), where she taught Master's-level literacy teacher research for twenty years. Many of the strategies covered in this book are ones that evolved in teaching this course during this period. Over the years, she has also been involved in university–school action research projects, collaborating with teacher researchers to study together teaching and learning in their classrooms. These experiences have also influenced the ideas found in this book. One project involved teachers exploring ways to take on collaborative styles of teaching literacy to their children who came from diverse ethnolinguistic backgrounds through study of their classroom discourse (Pappas and Zecker, 2001a, 2001b). Other projects consisted of examining with urban teacher researchers how to create and implement integrated science-literacy units to foster children's science understandings and generic science discourse (e.g., Pappas, Varelas, Barry, & Rife, 2003; Varelas, Pappas, & the ISLE Team, 2006). Finally, Chris is coauthor of a textbook, *An Integrated Perspective in the Elementary School: An Action Approach* (Pappas, Kiefer, & Levstik, 2006), which features and illustrates how teachers can do inquiry as part of developing and implementing integrated units.

Eli Tucker-Raymond is a Research Scientist with the Chèche Konnen Center at TERC, a nonprofit math and science educational research organization. As a graduate student at UIC, he team-taught the literacy teacher research course with Chris and then taught it on his own. Eli's dissertation, "MEDIAted: A collaborative action research study on critical media literacy" (Tucker-Raymond, 2009), was a collaborative action research study, one that involved three middle school teachers and himself learning how to integrate critical media literacy curricula into their classrooms. Subsequently, he has been involved in several collaborative action research projects with teachers. For example, in one project he, together with a seventh-grade teacher and her class, investigated how broad issues of globalization, such as international transmigration and privatization of goods and services, impacted students on a daily basis (Tucker-Raymond & Rosario, 2009). In another project, he and three teacher researchers created an after-school program for fifth graders that integrated scientific inquiry and media production aimed at developing students' understandings of locally relevant and globally meaningful water issues such as water quality, access, and rights.

Twelve teacher researchers who took the course that Chris and Eli team-taught and who agreed to include their papers for these book are Tara Braverman, Shannon Dozoryst, Meg Goethals, Katie Paciga, Cindy Pauletti, Nicole Perez, Catherine Plocher, Dawn Siska, Kristen

Terstriep, Libby Tuerk, Courtney Wellner, and Sandra Zanghi. These teachers taught a range of literacy topics to students in K-12 classrooms. One of them taught a pull-out program and two were literacy coaches.

This book is not about the course that Chris and Eli taught and the above-named teacher researchers took as students, but we use their work and voices to illustrate the strategies that teachers may employ in their inquiries. As indicated above, the collaborating teacher researchers did their studies during a semester course, and therefore their projects had usually lasted six to eight weeks when they wrote them up. They may have continued them after the course, but the examples here are the ones that were conducted during this course time frame.

OVERVIEW OF THE BOOK

This book consists of four major parts. Part One covers background information on teacher research more generally: What is it? How does it relate to qualitative and experimental, quantitative research? It also covers chapters on the initial plans or first steps of inquiry on literacy topics more specifically: finding your inquiry question about literacy teaching and learning; creating a proposal to outline possible ways to collect data on this question; and developing a preliminary literature review of some of the major ideas from theory and research that can inform the conceptual framework for your literacy study, as well as offer instructional strategies to try out in your study. In addition, it covers the ethical features of teacher research and how to write forms for obtaining informed consent for your literacy inquiry.

Part Two consists of chapters that provide the details of inquiry—the "how-to" strategies of collecting data, analyzing these data, and, finally, writing up your study. A range of data collection methods are discussed, including how to conduct case studies and use focal students in inquiries. How to analyze the qualitative data gathered in teacher inquiries is covered, plus how to create data summaries as a means of analyzing data in an ongoing way. Finally, approaches to writing up your inquiry as a publishable text are presented: crafting a lead beginning, reporting a finding, and then structuring the whole paper.

Although we use examples from the work of the above-named twelve teacher researchers in previous chapters, the chapters of Part Three provide the results of their studies as written up for the course. These papers cover a range of literacy topics (e.g., vocabulary strategies, reading and writing workshops, independent reading, word identification strategies, literature circles, read-alouds and small-group discussions, peer writing conferences). These studies were also conducted in different grade levels, from kindergarten to high school classrooms.

The Epilogue presents further reflections and possibilities to summarize the importance of teacher research for better instruction, reform, and political action.

Finally, three appendices are included: Appendix A is a general peer conferencing form that can be used for gaining feedback on the various writings that teacher researchers may compose during the inquiry process; Appendix B covers citing conventions of the American Psychological Association (APA) to follow when submitting manuscripts to journals, conferences, or other publishing outlets; and Appendix C provides reminders on grammatical and other language usage for teacher researchers to consider when writing up their inquiries.

Three major features have also been incorporated to help you use this book more easily and effectively. The first feature is foregrounding questions at the beginning of each chapter to highlight important ideas to be covered in them. The second feature is notes to offer additional explanations regarding an idea, or provide further information on a topic. Finally, throughout your inquiry process, seeking collaborative feedback from other teacher researchers (other classmates if you are using this book for a class, or other school or network colleagues if you are not) is beneficial (Burns, 1999; Cochran-Smith & Lytle, 2009). Thus, although you may undertake an *individual* research inquiry, obtaining others' perspectives enables you to refine and elucidate your own viewpoint and voice about what is being studied. As a result, we include possible various experiences in which to participate with others, to be found throughout the book and at the end of chapters ("suggested activities").

In summary, this book is meant to facilitate teachers' efforts to meet the actual challenges and dilemmas that they face in their classrooms. The strategies herein are intended to support or scaffold their journeys in teacher research on literacy topics, including how to write up, *with voice*, their inquiries for a wider audience. These tools are offered to help teachers understand how knowledge is constructed socially in their classrooms so that they can create the kinds of instructional communities that promote *all* students' learning.

REFERENCES

Bakhtin, M. M. (1981). *The dialogic imagination: Four essays by M. M. Bakhtin* (M. Holquist [Ed.], C. Emerson & M. Holquist [Trans.]). Austin, TX: University of Texas Press.

Burns, A. (1999). *Collaborative action research for English language teachers.* Cambridge: Cambridge University Press.

Cazden, C. B. (1992). *Whole language plus: Essays on literacy in the United States and New Zealand.* New York: Teachers College Press.

Cochran-Smith, M., & Lytle, S. (1993). *Inside/outside: Teacher research and knowledge.* New York: Teachers College Press.

Cochran-Smith, M., & Lytle, S. L. (2009). *Inquiry as stance: Practitioner research for the next generation.* New York: Teachers College Press.

Freeman, G. (2010). On being heard: Ten strategies for classroom teachers. *Democracy and Education, 18,* 40–46.

Pappas, C. C., Kiefer, B. Z., & Levstik, L. S. (2006). *An integrated language perspective in the elementary school: An action approach.* Boston: Pearson Education.

Pappas, C. C., Varelas, M., Barry, A., & Rife, A. (2003). Dialogic inquiry around information texts: The role of intertextulality in constructing scientific understandings in urban primary classrooms. *Linguistics and Education, 13*(4), 435–482.

Pappas, C. C., & Zecker, L. B. (Eds.). (2001a). *Teacher inquiries in literacy teaching-learning: Learning to collaborate in elementary urban classrooms.* Mahwah, NJ: Lawrence Erlbaum.

Pappas, C. C., & Zecker, L. B. (Eds.). (2001b). *Working with teacher researchers in urban classrooms: Transforming literacy curriculum genres.* Mahwah, NJ: Lawrence Erlbaum.

Tucker-Raymond, E. (2009). *MEDIAted: A collaborative action research group on critical media literacy.* Unpublished doctoral dissertation, University of Illinois at Chicago.

Tucker-Raymond, E. & Rosario, M. (2009). *"Can I talk about oppression?" Making space for history in students.* Paper presented at Conference on Latino Education and Immigration Integration, Athens, GA, October.

Varelas, M., & Pappas, C. C., & the ISLE Team. (2006). Young children's own illustrated information books: Making sense in science through words and pictures. In R. Douglas, M. P. Klentschy, & K. Worth, with W. Binder (Eds.), *Linking science and literacy in the K-8 classroom* (pp. 95–116). Arlington, VA: National Science Teachers Association.

Wertsch, J. V. (1991). *Voices of the mind: A sociocultural approach to mediated action.* Cambridge, MA: Harvard University Press.

Part One

Defining, Planning, and Starting Your Teacher Research

This part of the book covers the first phases of teacher research. Chapter 1 defines teacher research and offers rationales for such inquiry; it describes the nature of teacher research, placing it within the umbrella of qualitative research by distinguishing this approach from quantitative research; and it outlines the validity and reliability aspects of qualitative teacher research. In this chapter and subsequent chapters in this part of the book (as well as the rest of the book), the *voice* of the teacher researcher is emphasized. Chapter 2 covers the first, critical step of teacher research: identifying your research questions. It discusses a range of strategies for finding your inquiry questions, including the role of initial fieldnote-taking in this process. Chapter 3 describes how to plan your inquiry—how to create a research proposal, decide on possible data collection techniques to use, and consider the potential ethical issues in your study, including how to prepare participant permission/consent forms. Chapter 4 involves developing a preliminary literature review for your study. It presents strategies for finding, reading, and writing about the published work of others on your inquiry topic in ways that enable you to retain your voice as a teacher researcher. It also shows you how to follow APA (American Psychological Association) citing conventions in composing this literature review.

In the above chapters, when relevant we use examples from the work of our collaborating teacher researchers to illustrate aspects of this early phase of teacher inquiry. Moreover, we offer suggested activities that provide a means to incorporate feedback from a colleague in these early experiences of teacher research.

Chapter 1

So, What Is Teacher Research Anyway?

- What is teacher research exactly?
- How does teacher research relate to quantitative and qualitative research?
- What do concepts of reliability and validity have to do with teacher research?

WHAT IS TEACHER RESEARCH?

Teacher research can be called by different terms, for example *action research*, *teacher reflection*, or *practitioner research or inquiry*. In this book, we mostly use *teacher research* or *teacher inquiry*, although we may sometimes refer to these other terms. Also, although the book centers on teacher research on aspects of literacy teaching and learning, this chapter provides background on teacher research more generally.

Teacher research enables teachers to explore the underlying assumptions, biases, values, and ideologies that are inherent in their curriculum and pedagogies. Teachers are seen as knowers, deliberate intellectuals who constantly theorize about their practice as part of practice itself. Although the purpose of this book is to help beginning, novice teacher researchers, Cochran-Smith and Lytle (2009) argue that teacher research develops a worldview and habit of mind that they call *inquiry as stance*. Such a perspective is a way of knowing and being in the world of educational practice that is found across educational contexts and teachers' professional careers, one that connects them to other groups and social movements that attempt to challenge inequities that are perpetuated by the educational status quo. Thus, your individual beginning efforts in conducting teacher research on literacy topics, which we hope this book facilitates, represent some of your early steps in this lifelong journey of professional inquiry.

In the Preface, we defined teacher research as *intentional, systematic inquiry* conducted by teachers in their classrooms or schools that privileges their own voices and points of view (Cochran-Smith & Lytle, 1993). It is *systematic* in that there are ordered ways of gathering and documenting information or experiences in written form (or other multimodal ways such as video images, pictures, or drawings), as well as recollecting, rethinking, and analyzing classroom events. Although useful insights can always be gained through more spontaneous teaching–learning activities, teacher research is an explicit, *intentional*, and planned enterprise. Finally, it is *inquiry* because it emanates from, or generates questions about, classroom events, and involves teachers' reflections as they make sense of their experiences. As such, teacher research is similar to what Langer (1989), a scholar in "positive psychology," calls *mindfulness*: paying attention, consciously looking for what is new and different, reconsidering what we know by questioning preconceived ideas. Mindfulness, thus, is the essence of teacher research, one that promotes a distinctive way of knowing of teaching.

Rationales for Teacher Research

Another way to define teacher research is to outline some of the major reasons for it. That is, what are the benefits of teacher inquiry?

- Often, teachers are required to implement school-, district- and state-initiated reform efforts. Yet, the proposed reforms do not address the agendas and prior knowledge of the given teacher on the topic, and therefore, because they are context-free recommendations, are not always successful or sustained. Teacher research asks practitioners to investigate the practical issues or concerns that arise when teaching within a particular social context; it enables teachers to better understand the concepts and ideas of the curriculum as they relate it to particular circumstances. Thus, teacher inquiry helps teachers to implement and sustain reform curricula.
- Teacher research enables teachers to analyze all kinds of data. In addition to their consideration of their students' standardized test outcomes, teacher research offers the opportunity to gain insight into the features of student learning as it takes place, thereby making possible reflective, data-driven instruction. It can yield insight into the educational experiences of students from diverse ethno-linguistic backgrounds. It allows teachers to identify their own characteristic ways of interpreting students' behavior, so that they are able to discuss their ideas with students, parents, and other school personnel. It helps teachers to envision complex systems of concepts and data (formative and summative), and situates them in an ongoing and evolving teaching–learning process.
- Teacher research is a way for teachers to come to know their students in more intimate, human ways. It brings teachers closer to their students, not only as learners but also as people. In doing so, it enables teachers to better recognize and teach to their students' strengths. By focusing on puzzling concerns or tensions in practice, teachers can better think about how their teaching is or is not reaching the people in their classroom.
- The curriculum is always changing, always requiring new concepts and understandings for teachers and students to learn. The best teachers are those who can change and adapt, those who have an inquiry stance toward teaching and learning. Moreover, good inquiry consists of explorations with no predetermined correct answers but with answers that are questioned again and again as new perspectives are utilized.
- Finally, teacher research does not merely improve the lives of participants in the present or near-present. It also contributes to the long-term intellectual and professional develop-

ment of the participants and to the general knowledge base in the field. The practice of research cultivates tools and habits of mind necessary for effective teaching, thereby making them empowered professionals. And, because teachers include particular contextual information in their research, others can evaluate the relevance of the findings to different situations.

Cycles of Action Research in Teacher Inquiry

In teacher inquiry, teachers engage in spirals or cycles of observation, reflection, and action for the purpose of developing their own understanding and improving their practice and student learning. Wells (1994) outlines the four recurring major activities of this action research:

- *Observing*: making systematic observations of particular, relevant aspects of classroom life to determine what is actually happening.
- *Interpreting* these observations by reflecting on why things are happening as they are. For both things that are working well and those that are not in the situation, teachers attempt to discover the factors that seem to be responsible.
- *Planning change* by constructing hypotheses for what changes might bring an improvement for the unsatisfactory aspects of the current situation. They consider how one or more of these changes might be undertaken and plan how to implement it.
- *Acting out* the planned change. They try out a new way to approach their practice.

Integrally related to these components of teacher research is the teacher's personal theory. A teacher's *interpretative* or *conceptual framework* is critical in teacher inquiry, for it informs and is formed by the cycles of action research; his or her theory becomes a *living theory* for practice (Whitehead & McNiff, 2006). Adopting a mindful, reflective stance, teacher researchers make the connections between theory and practice more explicit. Their theories are grounded by their practice, and vice versa, and in this reciprocal process teachers are able to develop a more conscious understanding of the underlying basis of their actions.

Subsequent chapters in this part and the next expand the above cycles of action research, including how considering the ideas of the work of others—theoretical and practical ones—supports the teacher research process.

TEACHER RESEARCH AS A QUALITATIVE ENDEAVOR

Teacher research falls under the umbrella of qualitative research.[1] It is "qualitative research conducted by insiders in educational settings to improve their own practice" (Zeni, 2001, p. xiv). Thus, comparisons of qualitative research versus quantitative research offer further clarification of what teacher research involves. A major goal of qualitative research is to study and understand the research from the inside, via what is called an *emic* perspective (Burns, 1999; Schwalbach, 2003). Moreover, this view argues that what happens in the social context of research cannot be seen as fixed and quantified; rather, knowledge created in it is diverse, changing, and socially constructed. Thus, instead of pursuing objective facts via testing and confirming or disconfirming a priori hypotheses, qualitative researchers, using a range of tools to collect data from multiple sources (which is called *triangulation*), offer descriptions and interpretations of the behavior of participants in the naturalistic social context of the research site, the classroom. Unlike quantitative research that controls variables that are set at the onset of the study, qualitative research looks for unseen, unexpected variables that may operate in the research context. As a result, research questions are open-ended and may change during a study if the circumstances warrant them. Also, procedures may alter to collect different data, whereas quantitative approaches tend to follow predetermined research procedures. Finally, the goal of qualitative research is to construct local knowledge, providing extensive explanations and details of outcomes regarding the context and the behavior of the participants. In contrast, the purpose of quantitative research is to outline the outcomes that are seen as general knowledge. Table 1.1 provides the major comparisons of the two research approaches (Burns, 1999; Johnson, 2008; Parsons & Brown, 2002; Schwalbach, 2003). In the next section, we describe other characteristics of the two research modes, ones that are related to those noted in Table 1.1, that aid understandings of what teacher research consists of.

Table 1.1 Comparisons of qualitative and quantitative research

Qualitative research	Quantitative research
Assumes that knowledge is changing, depending upon the people and setting involved	Assumes that knowledge is fixed
Values subjectivity and the relative interpretation of phenomena	Values objectivity, the discovery of facts or truths
Sees knowledge as complex and holistic, drawing on ongoing data to develop, refine, and modify hypotheses	Tests a priori, pre-established discrete hypotheses or isolated variables in data collection
Explores naturalistic settings without controlling variables	Intervenes in the research context by controlling variables
Asks open-ended questions with data that describe and may change during a study	Asks narrowly defined questions with data that measure and do not change during a study
Collects "rich" data and analyzes and interprets them via description of patterns and themes	Reduces data that can be measured and quantified
Relies on participants' perspectives on behavior and phenomena	Ascertains cause and effect relationships
Focuses on both process and outcomes of research	Focuses on findings or outcomes to confirm or disconfirm hypotheses
Emphasizes collection of multiple sources in methods	Emphasizes consistency and replicability of methods
Has the goal of creating local knowledge	Has the goal of finding global, general knowledge

FURTHER DISTINGUISHING CHARACTERISTICS OF TEACHER RESEARCH

There are other characteristics of qualitative research (as opposed to quantitative research) that further explain the nature of teacher research. These have to do with the concepts of validity and reliability. Because the central purpose of the educational research process in teacher research is to empower the voice of the teacher, traditional concepts of validity and reliability have to be reconceptualized (Gitlin et al., 1992; Mills, 2007).

Validity has to do with how we know what we have collected is accurately representing what we think it is. How do we show that any conclusions we can come to are accurate? In quantitative terms, are we capturing what we purport to measure? Traditionally, it has been believed that validity or "truthfulness" of the data can be guaranteed only by the quantitative researcher who has followed a set of consistent, controlled set of research procedures. However, because teacher research recognizes the systematic inquiry of practical knowledge, where data collection and methods emerge in the naturalistic research site of the classroom, other ways of looking at validity, informed by qualitative research, have been developed (Altrichter, 1993). Table 1.2 summarizes some of the major ones for validity (Anderson, Herr, & Nihlen, 2007; Guba, 1981; Lather, 1986; Maxwell, 1992; Mills, 2007; Whitehead & McNiff, 2006; Wolcott, 1982, 1994).

Catalytic validity has to do with the ongoing impetus of teacher researchers to study what is really happening in their classrooms—to be persistent in their actions as they gain insights into their underlying assumptions of their practice and better understand complex teacher–student and student–student interactions (Lather, 1986). It also means that, on the basis of what they learn in their research, teachers transform their practice. They change what they do not find useful in their teaching, and further practice what does work. A study has catalytic validity to the extent that it caused a teacher to take action.

Table 1.2 Constructs of validity in teacher research

Catalytic validity: the capacity of the research process to foster participants' knowing of their reality and urge them towards self-determined action.

Process validity: the dependability and the correctness of the ways in which an inquiry is undertaken.

Descriptive validity: the factual accuracy and authenticity of the accounts offered by participants or behaviors described in the study.

Interpretive validity: the ways in which meanings attributed to participants—their perspectives—are reflective of what they actually said or did.

Outcome validity: the successful resolution of, or explanations of, the problems or research questions addressed.

Theoretical validity: the appropriateness of concepts and ideas to explain phenomena or findings.

Trustworthiness: the ability to take account of the complexities of a study and explain the patterns that have been found so that the investigation is credible, has transferability to contexts that may have similar characteristics, and includes dependable, stable data that are confirmable (via triangulation of multiple sources).

Process validity, then, has to do with the suitability of data that are collected—whether they reflect the questions of the research that is being undertaken (Anderson et al., 2007). This means that it is important that the teacher researcher is consistent in gathering *all* data that are relevant, whether they are good or bad (Mills, 2007). It means not working to avoid discrepant or "uncomfortable" events but, rather, embracing them as learning opportunities (Wolcott, 1994).

Closely related to process validity is *descriptive validity*, which underscores the authenticity of the data (Maxwell, 1992; Mills, 2007). It emphasizes that the descriptions of what actually occurs in the classroom should be detailed and factually accurate, making sure that readers "see" for themselves what happened or what was said (Wolcott, 1994).

Interpretive validity is how teacher researchers ensure that their interpretations or claims are based on the descriptions they have collected in their inquiries—that they rely on the actual wordings and doings of participants and do not gloss over the perspectives of participants (Maxwell, 1992; Mills, 2007). In addition to remaining close to the actual words spoken or actions taken, interpretive validity can be achieved through sharing data with a critical friend, or even the students or teachers who are being studied. That is, after deciding what they think is happening, others can be consulted to see whether they come to similar conclusions or not. This can be another way to involve the people you are studying in your research.

Outcome validity addresses specifically how observations and interpretations in one cycle of action research lead to useful insights for the actions of the subsequent cycle of research; it generally deals with the ways in which the findings "fit" the questions of the study (Anderson et al., 2007; Mills, 2007).

Theoretical validity requires that relevant theoretical ideas and concepts are used to explain the classroom events that were studied (Maxwell, 1992; Mills, 2007). It insists that the researcher do some "book research" to find out what other people who have studied and thought about similar topics have found.

Finally, an encompassing construct that captures many of the above aspects of validity is *trustworthiness* (Guba, 1981). It is all of the actions that teacher researchers employ to take stock of the complexities of the problems or issues they address in their studies. They conduct their inquiries so that they are credible to readers. Readers, especially other teachers, know that teaching is never perfectly smooth all of the time. When teachers are honest, forthright, and explicit with themselves in conducting research, it shows. Additionally, when communicating research, readers should be able to "visualize" what happened, so that they can consider its relevance in similar educational contexts.

As was indicated earlier, the notion of *reliability* in teacher research has also been seen in a new light. In quantitative terms, reliability is how consistently a test measures whatever it measures (in contrast to validity, which has to do with measuring what it is supposed to measure). Naturally occurring situations, such as those found in classrooms, are very changeable. Moreover, the aim of teacher research is to disrupt the status quo by developing and putting into practice certain action strategies in the hope of changing and improving it. Consequently, the traditional idea of reliability as a kind of "repeating the research"—that is, the ability of different independent, outside researchers being able to come up with the same conclusions by using the same procedures—is clearly problematic in teacher research (Altrichter, Posch, & Somekh, 1993; Gitlin et al., 1992). Procedures have to be developed in particular inquiries: as Gitlin et al. (1992) argue, "Reliability . . . cannot be based on duplicating procedures, but rather must center on attempts to satisfy the underlying principle of voice and its relation to a particular type of school change" (p. 28). In this case, voice is related to teachers' ability to articulate their needs, concerns, and desires and the ways in which others take up those articulations. Here, reliability involves the dependability of gathering observations and data that are relevant to the ongoing interpretations of the classroom events that are the topic of inquiry. That is, are teachers able to collect and interpret data in ways that not only reflect their inquiry question but also reflect the ways in which *they want* to collect and interpret data? Thus, because particular procedures cannot be applied unchanged from context to context, each teacher inquiry project attempts to develop its specific *reliability of voice* (Pappas, 2008), the voices of teacher researchers as they pursue the answers to their own questions about teaching and learning.

SUMMARY

Teacher research is intentional, systematic inquiry that highlights teachers' voices in studying their own teaching and student learning. It is an enterprise of mindfulness, an "inside" inquiry stance that involves explicit attention to re-visioning and re-questioning underlying assumptions about classroom practice. As a result, there are many benefits for engaging in teacher research. In inquiry, teachers undertake cycles of action research—observing, interpreting, planning change, and enacting these changes—to address questions about their practice. In doing so, they are also immersed in creating a living theory that informs, and is informed by, these recurring spirals of study.

Teacher research is a type of qualitative research and, as such, shares characteristics of this approach. It employs multiple data sources to address teacher-initiated, open-ended questions about practice. As a perspective through which to understand the social context of classroom events, it endeavors to describe, interpret, and explain unsuspected or unexpected factors operating regarding teaching and learning.

Because a major goal of teacher research is to empower teachers' voices, traditional notions of validity and reliability have been reconsidered. The concept of validity concerns the need to gather relevant and authentic data, interpret them in ways that are true to the perspectives of the participants and to events that occurred in the classroom, and offer detailed explanations of what and how these educational interactions were enacted. Efforts are made to provide credible, trustworthy accounts of what happened in these teacher-directed inquiries. Reliability is not "repeating procedures" but instead has to with teachers using dependable ways to gather data related to the recurring cycles of action research they are engaged in during their inquiries.

The next chapter covers the first important step of teacher research: creating your own inquiry question. This research question is the impetus of your inquiry; it launches your study. Other chapters in this first part of the book, then, extend this beginning by discussing how to plan your study and find and organize preliminary theoretical ideas that relate to the question and topic of your inquiry.

NOTE

1   This does not mean that there cannot be quantitative aspects to teacher research. See Schwalbach (2003) and Lankshear and Knobel (2004) on this point.

REFERENCES

Altrichter, H. (1993). The concept of quality in action research: Giving practitioners a voice in educational research. In M. Schratz (Ed.), *Qualitative voices in educational research* (pp. 40–55). London: Falmer Press.

Altrichter, H., Posch, O., & Somekh, B. (1993). *Teachers investigate their work: An introduction to the methods of action research*. London: Routledge.

Anderson, G. L., Herr, K., & Nihlen, A. (2007). *Studying your own school: An educator's guide to qualitative practitioner research*. Thousand Oaks, CA: Corwin.

Burns, A. (1999). *Collaborative action research for English language teachers*. Cambridge: Cambridge University Press.

Cochran-Smith, M., & Lytle, S. L. (1993). *Inside/outside: Teacher research and knowledge*. New York: Teachers College Press.

Cochran-Smith, M., & Lytle, S. L. (2009). *Inquiry as stance: Practitioner research for new generation*. New York: Teachers College Press.

Gitlin, A., Bringhurst, K., Burns, M., Cooley, V., Myers, B., Price, K., Russell, R., & Tiess, P. (1992). *Teachers' voices for school change: An introduction to educative research*. New York: Teachers College Press.

Guba, E. G. (1981). Criteria for assessing the trustworthiness of naturalistic inquiries. *Educational Communication and Technology, 29*, 75–91.

Johnson, A. P. (2008). *A short guide to action research*. Boston: Pearson Education.

Langer, E. (1989). *Mindfulness*. Reading, MA: Addison-Wesley.

Lankshear, C., & Knobel, M. (Eds.). *A handbook for teacher research: From design to implementation*. Maidenhead, UK: Open University Press.

Lather, P. (1986). Research as praxis. *Harvard Educational Review, 56*, 257–277.

Maxwell, J. A. (1992). Understanding the validity in qualitative research. *Harvard Educational Review, 62*, 279–300.

Mills, G. E. (2007). *Action research: A guide for the teacher researcher*. Upper Saddle River, NJ: Pearson Education.

Pappas, C. C. (2008). Making "collaboration" problematic in collaborative school–university action research: Studying with teacher researchers to transform literacy practices. In J. Flood, S. B. Heath, & D. Lapp (Eds.), *Handbook of research on teaching literacy through the visual and communicative arts* (2nd edition) (pp. 129–142). Mahwah, NJ: Lawrence Erlbaum.

Parsons, R. D., & Brown, K. S. (2002). *Teacher as reflective practitioner and action researcher*. Belmont, CA: Wadsworth/Thomson Learning.

Schwalbach, E. M. (2003). *Value and validity in action research: A guidebook for reflective practitioners*. Lanham, MD: Scarecrow Press.

Wells, G. (1994). *Changing schools from within: Creating communities of inquiry*. Portsmouth, NH: Heinemann.

Whitehead, J., & McNiff, J. (2006). *Action research living theory*. Thousand Oaks, CA: Sage.

Wolcott, H. F. (1982). Differing styles of on-site research, or "If it isn't ethnography, what is it?" *Review Journal of Philosophy and Social Science, 7*, 154–169.

Wolcott, H. F. (1994). *Transforming qualitative data: Description, analysis, and interpretation*. Thousand Oaks, CA: Sage.

Zeni, J. (2001). Introduction. In J. Zeni (Ed.), *Ethical issues in practitioner research*. New York: Teachers College Press.

Chapter 2

Creating Your Research Questions: The First Step in Inquiry

- How do I find and frame good inquiry questions?
- How can I use early fieldnotes of classroom observation to help reveal or clarify my inquiry questions?

CREATING YOUR OWN INQUIRY QUESTIONS ABOUT LITERACY TEACHING–LEARNING

Strategies for Finding Your Own Questions

The beginning of every inquiry is finding a good question to study (Hubbard & Power, 2003; Pappas, Kiefer, & Levstik, 2006). This feature of research—teachers exerting their own voices and agendas about what is to be explored and examined in their classrooms—is one of the defining characteristics of teacher research. However, it is also true that many teachers, especially novice teacher researchers, are unsure what their questions might be, or even what a good question is.

Some teachers start out with a general question about some classroom literacy activity or routine that they find unsettling or want to know more about: "What is going on here?" "What's the problem here?" Some begin with clear, formulated questions. Other teachers are not sure about their inquiry question at all. They may have a vague interest or curiosity about trying out something new regarding some aspect of their literacy curriculum, such as read-alouds or writing conferences that might lead to better student learning outcomes, but find that the particular focus of the inquiry question still seems elusive. Maybe students do not seem to be very engaged in some part of the literacy curriculum, or perhaps certain particular incidents may have occurred that warrant an investigation. Sometimes taking a "what if . . ." approach can help target an area or question for inquiry (Fischer, 2001). Here, you use your imagination to pose possibilities: What if multicultural children's literature was used in all areas of the curriculum? What if fifth graders created PowerPoint presentations to share their inquiry projects each term? What if students were encouraged to include illustrations in all of their writing? However, frequently it is only through careful observations in the classroom that the specific questions evolve. Your questions will arise practically—from what you deem to be important, what you are puzzled about, or what you want to improve in the teaching and learning that happens in your classroom. See what follows on how to use early fieldnotes to help you identify good questions by observing your own classroom.

Teaching–learning is a relationship—a reciprocal, dynamic connection that cannot be separated into two isolated actions. Nevertheless, we have found that a useful way to think about inquiry questions is to consider whether they focus mostly on the "teaching" side of the relationship or whether they are directed more toward students' learning. So, another strategy for clarifying your inquiry question or focus might be to ask yourself whether you might be more interested in one of the two sides of the relationship. For example, if you want to implement literature circles for the first time, where students choose their own books to read and discuss with their peers in small groups, your questions would be concerned with questions about teaching. What books should I select for them? How do I set up a system for student choice and group membership? How do I support students as they take on the roles and responsibilities in conducting their own discussions? But, it is important to notice that although you have posed questions about teaching, you cannot avoid issues of student learning. Indeed, students' reactions or learning outcomes to what you implement will be your data to help you decide on the next steps you will take or what teaching strategies you might need to change or revise during the recurring cycles of research.

Or, maybe your question is really about students' learning: How can I facilitate their authentic responses to texts? That is, perhaps this is the underlying impetus of your inquiry in the first place. However, if you had foregrounded this question, then you would have generated different questions, ones that were more clearly related to the "side" of student learning: What kinds of responses do students develop in small-group literature discussions? In what ways does the genre of the book affect their response? How do the peer discussions provide opportunities for evoking both personal and critical responses to texts? And once again, although these are student learning questions, the teaching influence in the process cannot be denied. Perhaps, because they have mostly experienced giving "correct" answers to questions about text, students may begin by just retelling parts of a book instead of offering their *response* to it. Or, maybe students' responses are mostly personal, and you were hoping that they would consider critical remarks as well. Thus, in this case you would need to address these concerns by creating a series of focus lessons to help students be aware of the range of responses that may be possible. Or, you might model ways of evoking critical responses during teacher-led read-alouds.

Thus, it is impossible to separate teaching from learning; teaching affects learning and learning affects teaching. In fact, it is the goal of teacher research that you are able to explore and understand that relationship more explicitly. But, in terms of finding your inquiry questions, it usually helps to be aware of *where* the underlying intent of your inquiry lies. Making this distinction—see Table 2.1—helps you to be clearer as to what questions you are generating, especially at the beginning of an inquiry. Do your questions reflect one side or both? Such a consideration enables you to be more conscious of their source, which helps you create an initial framework or plan for research (even though your questions are likely to become modified, or even be replaced with new ones during your inquiry process).

Table 2.1 *Potential inquiry questions about teaching and learning*

THE RELATIONSHIP BETWEEN TEACHING AND LEARNING

Questions about teaching	Questions about learning
What content should I use when I teach literacy understandings?	What content are my students learning in literacy activities?
What teaching literacy strategies should I use?	What strategies or styles are my students using in learning literacy?
How should I contextualize literacy learning experiences for my students?	In what ways is students' literacy learning being influenced by the contexts I am providing?
How do I see myself and my role in students' literacy learning?	How do students see themselves as literacy learners?
And so forth . . .	And so forth . . .

Framing and Wording Your Inquiry Questions

As indicated in Chapter 1, questions of teacher inquiry are open-ended. They are different from quantitative research that uses narrow questions in an attempt to capture cause–effect findings. This means that you want to avoid questions such as: Does teaching reading strategy X cause students' better comprehension of texts? Do young children learn to read best by emphasizing X? These questions are ones that result in a "yes" or "no" answer. They do not allow for finding rich descriptions and explanations about how or why (or why not) children in these studies learned better comprehension strategies or how to read. Being able to answer the how and why of classroom events and behavior is one of the major benefits of teacher research.

Thus, how you frame or word your inquiry questions matters. You want to have a question that is "meaty," one that encourages you to be able to fully describe and explain what happens in the classroom on a particular topic. Suitable questions are queries about the wonderings or problems you have about your literacy teaching and student learning. Below are some of the questions that collaborating teacher researchers posed at the beginning of their studies:

- How can I foster first graders' strategies in identifying unknown words while reading? What strategies do they use? [Cindy Pauletti]
- How can I increase my students' accountability during independent learning activities or centers? [Kristen Terstriep]
- What strategies help [sixth-grade] students comprehend text independently? How can I encourage, monitor, and adjust the use of these strategies? How will students' reading process change? [Tara Braverman]
- In what ways does reading workshop aid or improve [eighth-grade] students' comprehension? [Meg Goethals]
- How can I make peer writing conferences more effective for all writers in my [freshman] classroom? [Courtney Wellner]
- In what ways do my modeling and coaching support teachers? What is the effectiveness of coach–teacher collaboration in the order to support instruction? [Nicole Perez]

So, you want to create questions that start with "How . . .," "What . . .," or "In what ways . . ."—ones that help you address some kind of tension you feel about your teaching. Note that most of the teacher researchers whose questions have just been set down asked questions regarding both sides of the teaching–learning relationship: they asked how they might change their practice and also explored their students' strategies, and, in the case of literacy coach Nicole Perez, her teacher colleagues' instruction. It is important to emphasize that although your questions might involve implementing a new way to conduct your reading workshop or to foster children's writing revision, these questions are about more than just *methods* of instruction. Instead, they initiate an enterprise that captures changes in your *theories* about teaching and learning that enable you to reconsider your attitudes or views about your students as learners.

USING EARLY FIELDNOTES TO REVEAL AND CLARIFY YOUR INQUIRY QUESTIONS

It is common for teachers to have in mind only a vague tension about an area of their practice. Even after thinking about tensions in their practice, they are unsure what specific focus to explore in an inquiry. Thus, another strategy for identifying your inquiry questions is to begin classroom observations and document them via the taking of *fieldnotes*. Fieldnotes are one of the mainstay modes of data collection for teacher researchers. They consist of two kinds of writing: descriptive writing and interpretive or reflective writing (Hobson, 2001; Hubbard & Power, 2003; Pappas et al., 2006). *Descriptive writing* is the reporting of your observation component of the action research that was described in Chapter 1 (that is, the acts of observing, interpreting, planning change, acting change). You want details here because you want them to be useful at the time you write them, as well as later when you review, reread, and reexamine them. *Interpretive writing* is part of the second component of the action research cycle; this type of writing has you standing back, mulling over, and searching for connections and possible meanings.

We have found that novice teacher researchers are confronted with several challenges in writing up fieldnotes. First, it is hard to figure out how to do them *during* teaching. So, it is important to find strategies to accomplish this, especially for descriptive writing. What you decide to observe will affect whether you will take *in-the-midst notes* or *after-the-fact notes* (Power, 1996, 1999). If you plan to sit back but near small-group literature circle discussions or peer writing conferencing, then in-the-midst notes can be undertaken. However, if you want to see what happens during teacher-led read-alouds or focus lessons, then only after-the-fact notes are possible. In this case, all you can do is to quickly jot down brief wordings while you are interacting with students and flesh them out later on.

Second, learning to be truly descriptive in recording what you have observed is hard to do at first (but it gets easier and faster with practice). For example, just writing down "Tinaya and Wayne disagreed on ideas during their literature circle discussion" does not provide much information: What did each actually say? How did they respond to each other? How did they back up their claims? Did they follow the class rules about disagreeing in group talk? Thus, it is important to provide details, details, details!

Third, making the distinction between description and interpretation in taking fieldnotes is often challenging. Description is a record of observation that has to do with using our senses to obtain information—our data—about objects and events. In contrast, interpretation is the inferences we make based on this information or data. Interpretations are our conclusions or possible hypotheses about what we have observed (and described). Too often, as teachers we "leap" too soon to our interpretations. This is probably because in teaching, what is happening (the details of our observations) is occurring quickly, making our memories of our observations almost unconscious. We then tend to make fast judgments (interpretations) so we can act. However, the main purpose of teacher research is to try to be explicit about the habitual routines of classroom practice, and being clear about what we describe (observe) versus what we interpret (infer) is a critical aspect of the inquiry process. Thus, in teacher research we want to "activate our tacit knowledge" (Altrichter, Posch, & Somekh, 1993), and the use of fieldnotes is an important means to accomplish this. Teachers can use several strategies to help in this area. They can use double-entry notebooks, with two columns—"Observation/Description" on one side and "Inferences/Interpretation" on the other—to remind themselves of this distinction while writing up their fieldnotes. Or, they can create a T-chart with one column of "Things Noted" and another labeled "My Analysis" (Johnson, 2008), or two columns labeled "Facts" and "Opinions" (Macintyre, 2000). Or, if they decide to keep their notes using sticky notes, large address labels, etc., which will then be transferred to a research notebook, they can distinguish between descriptive and interpretive writing by putting one of them (e.g., interpretive writing) in brackets or enclosing them with double slashes. In any case, it is important for teachers to find their own ways to help make this difference between description and interpretation more viable for them.

Thus, taking fieldnotes early on in your study serves two major purposes: It helps you to reveal or better clarify your inquiry question, *and* it gives you an opportunity to develop skills in producing useful, detailed notes that will support the inquiry process. The use of fieldnotes is only one mode to gather data about teaching and learning; others are discussed in Chapter 5.

SUMMARY

This chapter concerns the important beginning step of your inquiry: identifying your research question. Teacher researchers do not always know exactly what they want to pursue, so several strategies have been covered to try out in this important aspect of your study. Taking early fieldnotes—using both descriptive and interpretive writing—is recommended, for they can help clarify inquiry questions. In addition, once a question is settled on, you should not feel that you are "stuck" with it, for it is quite likely that it will be modified during the cycles of action research. Nevertheless, it is important to decide on a particular research topic or question because it will guide your plans and ways to proceed.

Using fieldnotes, even in the beginning of your inquiry, is advantageous in getting you started and identifying your inquiry question. However, as noted, there are challenges in creating useful notes for novice teacher researchers, so effort and practice are required to be successful. As indicated in the Preface, collaboration with others about your inquiry is extremely beneficial (Burns, 1999; Cochran-Smith & Lytle, 2009). The Suggested Activities below offer this kind of "inquiry community" to help you frame your inquiry questions and learn how to take fieldnotes. If you are on a college or university course, your fellow students can serve as collaborators; if you are not, find colleagues (even one is OK) in your school (or in some kind of teacher network—there are many that you can find in person and online) to share ideas and gain feedback.

SUGGESTED ACTIVITIES

1 Brainstorm possible questions, similar to creating potential leads in writing, and share them with a colleague (or small group) for feedback. Are your questions open-ended and "meaty" ones (not ones that lead to a yes or no answer)? Which "side" of the teaching–learning relationships are they capturing? Try to revise and refine them.

2 Share fieldnotes with a colleague (or small group) for feedback. Can your colleague "visualize" what happened in the classroom via your descriptive writing? That is, are there enough details? Underline what you think is description and circle what you think is interpretation. Have you made leaps to claims or conclusions, without providing ample description? On the basis of the feedback, how will you approach the taking of fieldnotes the next time?

REFERENCES

Altrichter, H., Posch, P., & Somekh, B. (1993). *Teachers investigate their work: An introduction to the methods of action research.* London: Routledge.

Burns, A. (1999). *Collaborative action research for English language teachers.* Cambridge: Cambridge University Press.

Cochran-Smith, M., & Lytle, S. L. (2009). *Inquiry as stance: Practitioner research for new generation.* New York: Teachers College Press.

Fischer, J. C. (2001). Action research rationale and planning: Developing a framework for teaching inquiry. In G. Burnaford, J. Fischer, & D. Hobson (Eds.), *Teachers doing research: The power of action through inquiry* (pp. 29–48). Mahwah, NJ: Lawrence Erlbaum.

Hobson, D. (2001). Action and reflection: Narrative and journaling in teacher research. In G. Burnaford, J. Fischer, & D. Hobson (Eds.), *Teachers doing research: The power of action through inquiry* (pp. 7–27). Mahwah, NJ: Lawrence Erlbaum.

Hubbard, R. S., & Power, B. M. (2003). *The art of classroom inquiry: A handbook for teacher-researchers.* Portsmouth, NH: Heinemann.

Johnson, A. P. (2008). *A short guide to action research.* Boston: Pearson Education.

Macintyre, C. (2000). *The art of action research in the classroom.* London: David Fulton.

Pappas, C. C., Kiefer, B. Z., & Levstik, L. S. (2006). *An integrated language perspective in the elementary school: An action approach.* Boston: Pearson Education.

Power, B. M. (1996). *Taking note: Improving your observational notetaking.* York, ME: Stenhouse.

Power, B. M. (1999). When to write: Strategies to find time for notetaking. In R. S. Hubbard & B. M. Power, *Living the questions: A guide for teacher researchers* (pp. 105–109). York, ME: Stenhouse.

Chapter 3

Planning Your Inquiry

- Now that I have identified my research questions, how do I plan my study?
- How do I address the ethical issues in my proposed study?
- How do I create permission or consent forms for my study?

DESIGNING YOUR INQUIRY STUDY ABOUT LITERACY TEACHING–LEARNING

Now that you have identified your inquiry focus and questions, the next step in the process is to figure out how to design your literacy study. You want to develop a viable plan for gathering data—*relevant* data that will be *manageable in scope* (you won't have a gaggle of research assistants, as university-based researchers might have, to collect data). If you are conducting your inquiry as part of a college or university course, there will also likely be some time constraints in doing your study.

This plan will be tentative but should have enough details to ensure success in the next steps in your inquiry. That is, you want to be able to specify a particular course of action. The following five questions may help you in this effort (Pappas, Kiefer, & Levstik, 2006). Note that "observe" in these questions is being used broadly to cover a range of ways of collecting data.

- *Who* are you going to observe and study? Are you going to observe all students (for short times) during particular literacy activities or routines? Or, will you concentrate on several students or groups?
- *What* are you going to observe? Are you going to observe particular classroom events or routines, student behavior, or a certain aspect of your own behavior?
- *When* are you going to observe? And, how long is it likely to take? Deciding beforehand on the times when you will collect your data enables you to devote your energies to them and

makes the inquiry manageable. Will it be during a particular time of the classroom day when a certain activity or routine occurs, such as during writing workshop, teacher-led read-alouds, or buddy reading? Or, perhaps the focus might be on a particular child or children, or a group that requires that you gather data several times a day, or even for specific intervals each day? How long will you observe—for a curricular unit or project, a grading term, or the whole year?

- *How* are you going to observe? Besides the fieldnotes on your observations, this involves seeking out other data resources using other data collection techniques. Will you use audio or video recorders to capture classroom activity? Will you gather student work as data artifacts, and so forth? As was noted in Chapter 1, collecting different types of data enables you to triangulate your data and ensures the validity of your study.
- *Why* are you making the observations? This is the rationale of your study, which you might have captured through your inquiry questions. But, it also considers what assumptions or expectations you may be bringing to these data collection events. You want to strive for objectivity in your observations, but your prejudgments cannot be avoided. Thus, if you clarify ahead of time what your theories or preconceived ideas are about the context in which you are about to observe, you can more easily deal with them when you do your interpretive writing and other analysis.

Creating a *research proposal*, then, to document your ideas on plans for data collection is an important phase of your inquiry. Table 3.1 is a useful outline for such a proposal. A research proposal helps you spell out what you may have been thinking about your inquiry and also provides a means to get feedback and support. As you can see, this proposal covers many of the points listed above: it includes a rationale and your inquiry questions; it spells out the context and data collection techniques you may employ; it asks for early theories you might have on the topic and any initial references you may have already come across for your study.

Table 3.1 Proposal for teacher researcher inquiry

Focus and rationale	What is the major question(s) of your inquiry? What is the main purpose of your study?
Context and data collection procedures	Besides your fieldnotes, in what ways are you planning to collect relevant data for answering your question(s)? Try to be as specific as you can: (a) the context (the activities/routines); (b) the participants involved (including any focal students or groups and why you have chosen them); (c) the procedures you think you will use to collect data, including what the data will consist of (audio- and/or videotaping, interviews and surveys, artifacts, etc.); (d) how often data will be collected, including a tentative timeline for the study.
Interpretive frame and references	What are your early, initial ideas on the theoretical framework—or interpretive frame—that will inform your inquiry? That is, do you know some specific work that has been done on the topic that you would want to pursue? Do you need help in identifying articles and books on the topic to support your inquiry? What words do you think might serve as "keywords" as you search for resources?

Chapter 5, in Part Two of the book, provides more details on various data collection possibilities, and you may want to read it through before you finalize your research design. Below are excerpts from three collaborating teacher researchers' proposals regarding their data collection plans.

Recall that Tara Braverman's inquiry questions were: "What strategies help [sixth-grade] students comprehend text independently? How can I encourage, monitor, and adjust the use of these strategies? How will students' reading process change?" Tara thought of a range of multiple sources to gather data to address her questions—see Excerpt 3.1.

Excerpt 3.1: Tara Braverman's Research Proposal

Whole-class modeling and one-on-one reading conferences. Teacher notes and audiotape notes and transcriptions.

Semantic maps. Collect from students (model with whole-class novel); notes on students presenting maps to their groups on assigned novel.

Outside connections. Pictures of "word" bulletin board; students bring in words from outside the classroom, posting them, making connections.

Reference corner. Monitor student use of reference materials (dictionaries, thesaurus, etc.) during silent reading.

Reader response journal. Student log of questions, new words, connections to text.

Tara planned to use teacher–student interactions (in her whole-class teacher modeling and individual conferences), several student artifacts (the semantic maps, bulletin postings, and reader response journals), as well as how students used the reference corner. Thus, she had a range of ways to explore what she had proposed.

In Courtney Wellner's study—"How can I make peer writing conferences more effective for all writers in my [freshman] classroom?"—she also developed different ways to collect data (see Excerpt 3.2).

Excerpt 3.2: Courtney Wellner's Research Proposal

I am planning to study 2 of my freshman English I classes, 4th and 9th periods. Each class has about 30 students, and I will use the entire class for some parts of the inquiry, and specific focus groups from each class for other, more specific portions of the inquiry. The focus groups will consist of 4 students from each class, randomly chosen by me.

Peer writing conferences will be held once or twice per week. Through whole class and individual surveys and interviews, taped recordings of peer conferences, samples of student work, and my observational and reflective journals of conferences, I plan to study how different methods and strategies of peer writing conferences improve (or not) my students' writing. There will be a particular focus on questioning prompts, grouping strategies, and verbal skills among students. All students will be asked to complete surveys and take part in whole class discussions after each conferencing session to evaluate the usefulness of the strategies and the focus students will take part in audiotaped interviews on their opinions of the day's work. I also plan to take pictures of students at various steps of the process to complement the interview transcripts, student work, and surveys.

Like Tara, Courtney considered a range of data collection techniques: student artifacts, audiotaping of peer conferences and interviews, and ongoing surveys. Several different modes (from Tara's plans) are incorporated here, namely the use of focus students, ongoing surveys, and pictures.

Nicole Perez is a literacy coach at an elementary school, so her plans (Excerpt 3.3) were created to address her work with her teacher colleagues: "In what ways does my modeling/coaching support teachers? What is the effectiveness of coach/teacher collaboration in the order to support instruction?"

Excerpt 3.3: Nicole Perez's Research Proposal

I will take observation notes during my pre- and post-meetings with teachers. I will also audio-tape discussions we have about my modeling and observations teachers make of me. Because this study reflects my position at school, I will distribute a survey to teachers about areas in which they'd like coaching. At the end, I'll distribute a post survey to those teachers I've worked with.

Nicole chose surveys, notes, and audiotaped discussions as the major means of data collection. Not mentioned here, but also included, were peer observation forms (PEFs) that she developed. These were completed by teachers as they observed her modeling of various strategies in their classrooms. These PEFs served as a focus in discussions with teachers around lessons.

Thus, each of the teacher researchers in this book created action plans that incorporated multiple ways to collect data that corresponded to their inquiry questions. They had a way to begin, even though they might find during their inquiries that certain techniques could be more helpful than others, and their plans needed modification. Teacher researchers always have to develop practical, "doable" data collection schemes that are compatible with the demands of teaching, and the teachers referred to here believed that they had found ways to accomplish this as they launched their studies.

The proposal plan (Table 3.1) described here was developed for use in a course because it enables you to launch your inquiry before you do much reading. If you are doing a study that is not part of a course, you might include more about your interpretive frame and list references that you had already found to read to guide your study. (Writing a literature review to guide you study is discussed in the next chapter, Chapter 4.)

Once your proposal is completed, it is important to get feedback on it. Such support enables you to further clarify your ideas about your inquiry. Suggested Activity 1, at the end of the chapter, covers the kinds of response you might request. After you get this feedback, you might revise your proposal. Also, after this colleague input you might come up with a tentative title for your study. (If you are doing this study as part of a course, you might also seek feedback from your instructor.)

USING A RESEARCH JOURNAL AND DATA TRAILS

Although you may have already done some gathering of fieldnotes, you are now ready to "formally" undertake your inquiry. You will now be prepared to collect your data. For instance, you will know when to bring your audio recorder to capture your teacher–student writing conferences, or to set up the video camera for your whole-class teacher-led read-aloud session.

Another important feature of this phase of your study is setting up a *research journal*. This journal can take any format (Hobson, 2001). It may be a three-ring binder in which you can include your fieldnotes, as well as staple or tape in photographs, or other jottings or notes (sticky notes, index card, or large address labels). Or, you might use a smaller 6 × 9 notebook, which is easier to carry around. Or, you might create a computer folder that would comprise your fieldnotes, transcriptions, photographs, scans of student work, and so forth.

An essential feature to include in this research journal is documentation of your data collection—what are called *data trails*. Table 3.2 outlines how you might format this way of keeping track of your teaching and data collection practices during your inquiry. The example in Table 3.2 is a week of data collection from a collaborative action research project, participated in by Chris and Eli, that integrated science and literacy. The table shows the date of the

Table 3.2 Instructional and data trails (for an integrated literacy–science inquiry project)

Date	Instructional trail/activities	Data trail
September 15, 2004	■ Journal writing (and drawing) on what is above the ground, on the ground, and under the ground in a temperate forest science unit ■ Whole-class sharing	■ Fieldnotes (during student journaling) ■ Videotape of whole-class sharing ■ Copies of and notes on journals on 10 focal students
September 16, 2004	■ Read-aloud of *In the Forest* (First Discovery Book, 2002) ■ Whole-class semantic map	■ Fieldnotes (on comments by students after videotaping) ■ Videotape of whole-class read-aloud and semantic map
09/18/04	■ Read-aloud of *Animals under the Ground* (Fowler, 1997) ■ Journaling on prompt: "What did you find most interesting?"	■ Fieldnotes (during student journaling) ■ Videotape of read-aloud ■ Copies of and notes on journals on 10 focal students

instructional activities (the instructional trail) and the kinds of data that were collected for each day (the data trail). A space is provided under each day's entry so that other documentation can be noted. For example, transcriptions or notes on the viewing of one of the videotapes might be added (the viewing was completed at the end of the week). Or, a data summary (see Chapter 6 for details of data summaries) for the week might have been done, and noted on the data trail outline. As you can see, this research journal (with its data trails) is an important tool for use during the inquiry process.

ETHICAL ISSUES AND CREATING CONSENT FORMS

Another important planning aspect of teacher research is addressing ethical issues in teacher research. The advantage of teacher research is that it provides teachers with a potential window into critical insights about their practice. However, it also creates a context in which teachers are confronted with possible conflicts of interest regarding their students. Thus, teacher research is not just a good idea; it is also an ethical responsibility as teachers rethink and examine their teaching and how it may promote better students' learning (Parsons & Brown, 2002).

Ethical issues need to be considered in any kind of research, but teacher research—"insider," practitioner research—has its own characteristic features that must be addressed (Zeni, 2001a).[1] Although teachers are studying their own practices, they must think more explicitly about how their inquiry might affect their research participants (e.g., their students or, if they are a literacy coach, teacher colleagues). Teacher research impacts the social context of the classroom; it affects the community of learners that has been established in the classroom. Thus, you need to try to step out of your role as a teacher researcher and put yourself in the place of the children, the parents, or other teachers to appreciate any stress your research might have on them (Macintyre, 2000). For example, students may be used to acting in certain ways because of previous expectations in other classrooms, or because of earlier norms set up in your own classroom. As a result, even though you think new practices will benefit their learning, they might feel uncomfortable in new routines. Or, at first they might be uncomfortable with recording devices in the classroom. If you are unsure of the particular stresses your research might take, you can always talk to students about what their potential concerns might be.

Getting Permissions

Getting permissions—"informed consent"—from participants is a way to address ethical concerns in your study. There are mixed views about whether teacher researchers need to obtain them (Hubbard & Power, 2003; Zeni, 2001a). For example, if the audience for your data and findings is *only* the colleagues at your school, you may not need them (although there are school districts that do require them). This may also be true if you will be sharing your findings solely with your classmates in a college or university course.[2] However, if you plan to have a broader audience for your study results—for example, to present it to other teachers in the district or at a conference or publish it in a journal—then obtaining permissions is essential (for example, no journal will publish a teacher researcher study without them). Often, novice teacher researchers conducting their first inquiry cannot imagine that their study will be good enough to be worth sharing with this broader audience. However, their studies may end up being more successful or insightful than they had anticipated, so it is best to get the permissions in the first place.

We recommend that teacher researchers always create permission forms, for two reasons. First, they offer another opportunity to clarify their inquiry to themselves. Second, they prompt teachers to think explicitly about the ethical issues of their studies. Table 3.3 is a possible format that might be used. This permission form includes the major factors to consider: (1) a clear statement of the aim of the study and its major data collection sources; (2) a promise of confidentiality (stating that only fictitious or code names will be used); (3) the voluntary

Table 3.3 Sample parent permission form

[Date]

Dear Parent or Guardian,

For [give the timeline of the study], I will be conducting a research study on my teaching and students' learning in my classroom. [Briefly explain the nature of your inquiry, including why you are conducting it, when, and on what, as well as the kinds of data you will be collecting (e.g., notes, videotapes, children's work, audiotapes of interviews, etc.)].

In any reports using this research at presentations or in publications, a fictitious name, not your child's real name, will be used to protect your and your child's privacy. Although your child will be involved in the above activities as a part of his or her everyday instructional experiences, your permission for me to use your child's work in any research report is voluntary. Also, if you initially agree for your child's participation, you and your child can change your mind about it by contacting me. In addition, whether or not you provide permission for me to use your child's work in any report will not affect your child's grade in any way.

You child may feel uncomfortable under my careful observation of his or her work and the processes he or she engages in, in instructional activities. Also, there will be no direct benefits to your child as a result of my study. However, he or she may also enjoy the extra attention to his or her work and my efforts to provide better instruction for him or her. Other educators may also benefit from the findings of this study.

If you have any questions or need more information about the kinds of instructional activities described above or any possible research report that might be presented or published, please contact me [put in how to contact you, usually telephone number(s), and/or email address].

Please sign this form below if you agree that I may share your child's work with a wider audience.

Sincerely,

[your name]

_____

Print name of child (first and last name)

_____   _____

Signature of parent or guardian   Date

_____

Print name of parent or guardian

nature of students' participation, including their rights to change their mind; and (4) an explanation of risks and benefits for participants. As has been the case in other facets of developing an inquiry, getting feedback on a draft of such a permission form is useful. (See Activity 2 at the end of this chapter and also Appendix A, a general peer conferencing form, which might be used for such a sharing.) As we have said, besides providing means to further clarify your inquiry, it offers an occasion to discuss the ethical issues in your study. Additionally, the particular language that you may need to use in permissions can change from school district to school district. It is important to find out what your district's specific requirements are for permission. Many school districts have this information on a website or have a special office for research and evaluation that should have this information for you. They may also have permission examples to be followed.

One aspect of the sample form in Table 3.3 requires more discussion: the part that states, "whether or not you provide permission for me to use your child's work in any report will not affect your child's grade in any way," needs further examination. How can parents and children be assured that teacher researchers can be objective on this aspect of student participation (or not) in their inquiry? In fact, there are strategies that can be used by teacher researchers to minimize this risk (and others).[3] Such an approach will be necessary if the teacher researcher is doing a thesis or dissertation study that requires approval from an institutional review board (a group of professionals [often including some laypersons] at a college, university, or school district) that addresses the ethical issues involved in research on human subjects. In such cases, modification of the parent permission form will be necessary, including creating a separate child assent form (which sets out information about the study similar to that found on the parent form but in a way that can be understood by children), where children, if parents give permission, give their assent (or not) to participating. Again, see note 3 for details. In addition, if you think the primary language of the parents of your students is not English, a translation of the permission in that language is required.

Letting Parents and Students "In" on Your Inquiry

It is always useful to let your students know about your inquiry. Having them choose their own code names, for example, often lessens any possible disappointment they might have regarding your need to avoid using their real names. Moreover, explaining that you think they might benefit from trying out a different way of conducting their read-alouds, or doing peer writing conferences or literature circles, and so forth, foregrounds new practices. This differentiates this new approach from other classes they might have had or might have experienced during the current academic year in your classroom. In doing so, they might see it as a class "adventure," where all are on board to investigate some aspect of literacy teaching–learning. It also deflects some of the attention away from students as individual learners who might feel, and be uncomfortable, that they are being judged more closely than usual.

Sharing your inquiry ideas with parents also helps them understand what you are attempting to accomplish in your instruction for their children and lets them know that your classroom is inquiry based. Going over the permission form with them at a beginning-of-the-year parent meeting (or at other parent meetings during the year, if the inquiry is to begin later in the year) allows you to answer any questions or deal with any concerns they might have. Also, explaining that you will be sharing the data from their children's work in parent conferences during the year is usually appealing to them and makes them more comfortable about the permission forms that come home. Most parents recognize and appreciate the professional nature of teacher research (MacLean & Mohr, 1999). If fact, because they are interested in details about their children's learning that results from teacher research inquiries, they often ask that their children be placed into a teacher researcher's classroom, or ask the principal to encourage teacher researcher groups in their children's school.

SUMMARY

Once inquiry questions are settled, creating an action plan is the next step of the process. Deciding on the ways in which data will be gathered to address your inquiry questions, as well as specifying initial theoretical ideas to inform your inquiry are essential features of this proposal. Finding the kind of research journal to use and getting ready to document your data collection activities via data trails supports the upcoming venture. An integral facet of your inquiry is a consideration of the ethical issues involved in doing teacher research. Creating appropriate permission and consent forms is advised (and may be required, depending on the context in which you conduct your study). Moreover, letting your students and parents know about your inquiry is important, for it helps in gaining their cooperation. Indeed, an essential ethical aspect of teacher research is that teachers must be overt about the aims of their study and how they intend to go about it. Thus, getting permissions is not the end of your ethical concerns; you should maintain an active, self-questioning stance about ethical issues throughout your study.

SUGGESTED ACTIVITIES

1   Find a colleague to get a response on your inquiry proposal. Consider asking the following questions:

- Is my inquiry question(s) clear? Is it well worded or framed?
- What do you find interesting about my data collection design?
- Are there areas of my proposal that seem unclear or surprising?
- Are there any connections between my proposal and yours?
- Can you suggest any references for me to read that would support my theoretical framework?

In gaining feedback on the above points, you may want to revise your proposal.

2   Find a colleague to gain feedback on your parent permission (or teacher consent) form. Appendix A is a general peer conferencing form that could be employed for this collaborative response.

NOTES

1   See Zeni's book *Ethical Issues in Practitioner Research* (2001b) for a rich discussion on this topic. Her epilogue, "Guide to Ethical Decision Making for Insider Research," is especially useful for making ethical issues clearer for teacher researchers. MacLean and Mohr (1999) also provide a useful list of ethical principles to guide teacher research.

2   Some colleges and universities do not require that teachers (as students in the course) obtain permissions if the purpose of the course they are taking is to learn the skills to conduct teacher inquiries by undertaking one of their own in their own classrooms.

3   There are a range of strategies that teacher researchers can employ to address ethical issues of their studies. There follow some guidelines that Chris has developed for a school district to address these issues.

Guidelines for Teacher Research

Below is a list of guidelines for teacher research. Each item addresses a characteristic of teacher research, noting possible strategies to avoid or minimize risks that may be involved in teacher research.

1   Teacher research should be seen as an inquiry about the teaching and learning in teachers' own classrooms, collecting data on everyday curricular activities and routines. Thus, teachers should not use the classroom as a research site of convenience, studying variables that do not relate to the educational benefit of their students.

2   Teacher research should use academic time that focuses on teaching and learning issues in everyday curricular activities. Thus, teachers should not use academic time to have students engage in long surveys or interviews, or have these surveys or interviews address items that are not related to the curricular content teachers may be studying. Longer surveys or interviews may be appropriate if they are conducted before or after the school day *and* are concerned with obtaining students' perspectives on curricular issues being studied.

3   Teacher research should be done in ways that make sure that students feel comfortable in being participants (or not) in their teachers' inquiries. Because teachers evaluate students' behavior and learning, students may feel pressure to participate in their teacher's research. To minimize the risk, someone else at the school might obtain the parent permissions and student consent or assent forms, so that the teacher researcher does not learn which students are subjects in the study. Only after final grades have been given would the teacher learn who the subjects were. Furthermore, only the data collected from those who had agreed to participate would be used.

4   Teacher research should be conducted so as to ensure the confidentiality of subjects. To ensure confidentiality, teachers would use "code" names for students and make no mention of the particular school year (e.g., the 2007–2008 academic year); giving the month and day provides enough information about what occurred during the year or the period of the inquiry. Other identifying features (e.g., the name of the school, its specific location) would not be used in writing up and sharing the findings.

5   Teacher research should employ "objective" approaches. Because teachers are working closely with students in the classroom, there is concern that they might not be objective in conducting their research—that is, they might show bias in collecting the data and/or reporting them. To minimize the risk, collecting multiple sources of data to support findings—that is, triangulation of data sets— is important. It enables teachers to use independent sources to show agreement (and/or indicate any lack of contradiction) in findings. Other strategies can also help to ensure objectivity. For example, depending on the age of the students, they could be asked to respond to the teacher's categories of data. Also, students' names on their writing could be excised from the data, and transcripts of classroom talk or student interviews could be coded to protect identities. Furthermore, other colleagues could be asked to provide their interpretations of the data, which could help to identify bias. Such approaches also further the "trustworthiness" of the findings.

6   Teacher research should utilize videotaping in appropriate ways. In collecting data, teachers often use videotaping as a means of data collection. Videotaping is a valuable tool because while they are teaching, teachers cannot write down quickly or accurately enough the talk or complex student behavior that occurs. However, videotaping brings with it confidentiality risks. And, if teachers do not know who their subjects are (see (3) above), they cannot position the video cameras so as to film only the participants in the study. To minimize the risk, teachers need to delete retrospectively from tapes the students for whom consent or assent has not been obtained—those students whom teachers find afterwards were not subjects. Teachers should not videotape any child who does not want to be taped, even during the study.

7   Teacher research should be focused on academic reform and to promote student learning. It should not be seen as a means for teachers to attain commercial gain. Teachers may share their findings in a range of academic possibilities—in conference presentations and in journal article or book chapter publications (or in a thesis or dissertation)—but such research studies should not conducted as profitable, money-making enterprises.

Summary

There are many advantages to teachers conducting inquiry in their own classrooms. There are also risks that need to be identified and minimized, and these were addressed in the above guidelines. However, the best teachers see themselves as empowered professionals, always attempting to improve their practice, which entails doing teacher research. Indeed, certification by the National Board of Professional Standards requires that teachers engage in teacher research. Finally, teacher reflection is called for in many state standards for teachers.

Note that "research" is frequently said to involve generalized findings—that is, results that could be presented at conferences or published in journals or books. Where teachers intend to disseminate their findings, they need to gain approval for their studies before they conduct them. However, it is possible that teachers might collect data, not thinking at the onset about presenting or publishing, and decide later that they have useful findings to share. Forms for these two circumstances might be created so that the appropriate lists of issues can be addressed regarding inquiry with human subjects. Also, workshops covering the above guidelines may be provided for those teachers who want to do research. (Those teachers who are also students at a university and who may do their study as an MA thesis or a pilot or dissertation work may not need to attend such workshops, as they would have obtained the requisite training at their institution regarding the ethics of protecting human subjects.)

REFERENCES

Hobson, D. (2001). Action and reflection: Narrative and journaling in teacher research. In G. Burnaford, J. Fischer, & D. Hobson (Eds.), *Teachers doing research: The power of action through inquiry* (pp. 7–27). Mahwah, NJ: Lawrence Erlbaum.

Hubbard, R. S., & Power, B. M. (2003). *The art of classroom inquiry: A handbook for teacher-researchers.* Portsmouth, NH: Heinemann.

Macintyre, C. (2000). *The art of action research in the classroom.* London: David Fulton.

MacLean, M. S., & Mohr, M. M. (1999). *Teacher-researchers at work.* Berkeley, CA: National Writing Project.

Pappas, C. C., Kiefer, B. Z., & Levstik, L. S. (2006). *An integrated language perspective in the elementary school: An action approach.* Boston: Pearson Education.

Parsons, R. D., & Brown, K. S. (2002). *Teacher as reflective practitioner and action researcher.* Belmont, CA: Wadsworth/Thomson Learning.

Zeni, J. (2001a). Introduction. In J. Zeni (Ed.), *Ethical issues in practitioner research* (pp. xi–xxi). New York: Teachers College Press.

Zeni, J. (Ed.) (2001b). *Ethical issues in practitioner research.* New York: Teachers College Press.

Chapter 4

Writing a Preliminary Literature Review to Inform Your Inquiry

- How can I use others' work to inform my inquiry?
- How do I go about writing a "literature review"?
- How can I "keep" my voice in writing about the ideas of others?

MAKE A LITERATURE REVIEW AN EARLY VENTURE IN YOUR INQUIRY STUDY

Locating your research in the body of previous work on the topic is an important part of your inquiry. The task of finding relevant research and writing up a literature review might seem overwhelming, but it needn't be so if you do some planning beforehand. Moreover, producing a literature review can also be a useful, interesting, and creative experience.

In Chapter 1, we talked about the fact that a teacher's *interpretive* or *conceptual framework* is a critical aspect of teacher research. Some educators suggest that teacher researchers write a literature review at the end of data analysis (e.g., Hubbard & Power, 2003). However, we recommend that you initiate this facet of your inquiry early. As we indicated in Chapter 3, you don't have to complete this review before you can launch your inquiry; it can be simultaneously worked on during the first few cycles of action research. Developing a preliminary literature review is helpful in three major ways. First, it informs your initial theories about your study. As you enact the action research cycles of your study, these theoretical ideas from others' work are integrated with your data analyses and strengthen your interpretations. That is, although teacher research involves *grounded theory* (Glaser & Strauss, 1967; Schatzman & Strauss, 1973)—themes and patterns that emerge *from* the data—finding out what others have learned or have to say about the topic is an advantage. Second, reading about the different ways that others have approached the teaching–learning of a particular literacy topic offers new ideas for you to try out in your practice. You don't have to reinvent the wheel; these resources may suggest approaches to explore as part of your inquiry that are consistent with your developing theories. Finally, developing a literature review early on means that some of the work that is necessary in writing up your inquiry at the end of your study is already done (see Chapter 7). Thus, doing a literature review at the beginning of your inquiry enhances the mindful, reflective *living theory* of your practice (Whitehead & McNiff, 2006); it fosters a more conscious understanding of the underlying basis of your actions. A review makes you a more knowledgeable teacher researcher.

FINDING RELEVANT RESEARCH SOURCES FOR YOUR LITERATURE REVIEW

The first step of a literature review is finding the relevant sources on your research topic. We emphasize here that you need to seek *relevant* sources because we want to underline that your search need not be an exhaustive one that attempts to locate everything on the topic. Because the collaborating teacher researchers in this book did their literature reviews as part of a course, they limited theirs to around four or so resources. (As indicated in Chapter 3, if teacher researchers are not undertaking an inquiry as a course requirement, they might have more time to locate and read more resources; teachers who are doing their inquiries for their theses or dissertations will also want to explore more resources. Extending the number of resources at later stages of your research is discussed in Chapter 7.)

So what are these resources and where should you find them? There is a range of peer-reviewed[1] literacy journal articles available to explore. These are journals such as *Language Arts*, *English Journal*, *The Reading Teacher*, the *Journal of Adult and Adolescent Literacy*, *Research in the Teaching of English*, the *Reading Research Quarterly*, the *Journal of Literacy Research*, *Linguistics and Education*, and *Written Communication*. You might also find articles on literacy topics in more general educational journals, as well as in online journals.[2] There are many books on literacy topics that can be useful as well (publishers such as Heinemann, Routledge, and Stenhouse, and the professional organizations the International Reading Association [IRA] and the National Council of Teachers of English [NCTE] frequently publish books that are helpful to teacher researchers). Also, there are general action research and teacher research journals that can provide additional examples of the types of research projects that teachers undertake. These include *Educational Action Research* and *Networks: An On-line Journal for Teacher Research* (http://journals.library.wisc.edu/index.php/networks). Finding relevant articles from journals can be accomplished via a keyword search using ASK ERIC (http://www.eric.ed.gov). Many of our collaborating teacher researchers employed the search engine Google Scholar (http://www.scholar.google.com) to identify journal articles and books.[3]

READING AND ORGANIZING YOUR IDEAS FOR YOUR LITERATURE REVIEW

Once you have found your resources (journal articles and books), you want to read, take notes, and identify possible teaching strategies. This literature should not be seen as a body of "truths"; instead, it is best viewed as other sources or points of view that cannot be ignored or disregarded, but should be addressed when you think about your own study. In fact, in teacher research, what is typically considered a *review* of the literature is more a *response* to the literature, where teachers read, react, and build on what they already know and have experienced (Burnaford, 2001). Often, novice teacher researchers find it a challenge to "keep" their voices as they explore and study published work in the process of writing a literature review. Seeing the literature review as a response supports this facet of their inquiries.

To make your review a response to the literature, you might *skim* journal articles and book chapters and write down ideas that are directly related to your research questions. That is, you want to avoid creating an extensive summary that covers every idea of the resource. Creating a set of questions ahead of time as you read your sources is another approach (Burnaford, 2001), such as:

- What are the major ideas in the article or chapter that are related to your research questions?
- What teaching ideas presented in the article or chapter might be implemented in your inquiry? How would you employ them?
- What seems missing that you wished that the author would have addressed in the article or chapter?

As you read and take notes, you want to determine the major common themes or meanings from this literature as they relate to your questions, including complementary and contrasting claims that the authors might have made in their work. Creating a graphic organizer, such as a *comparison chart*, to document what you have gleaned from the literature is a useful prewriting activity. It will further help you in sustaining your voice as you write up your review. Below are some examples from the comparison charts of the collaborating teacher researchers.

Comparison charts have two requisite features: they have (1) the source articles/book chapters you have read, and (2) the major meanings or themes you have identified from them. You can organize the research source on the top of the chart with the major themes on the side, or vice versa. There is a variety of ways in which comparison charts can be completed. We have included Katie Paciga's chart—Figure 4.1—to show that a chart need not be detailed to be useful; it also illustrates how she attempted to include methodology features of the sources (for example, whether fieldnotes, videotapes, and focal children were used in the studies discussed). Katie's inquiry focused on how her literacy instruction might affect her kinder-gartners becoming authors. Although she ended up reading and citing thirteen articles in her subsequent literature review, her chart covered only four (found on the top of the chart): a research article written by a university-based researcher, a section from a textbook, a teacher researcher article, and a book. On the left side of the chart, she listed seventeen meanings. As indicated, some were methodological in nature, and the others were themes or meanings, such as "Process writing approach to instruction," "Used mini-lessons," "Emphasized that writing is around 'a big idea,'" and so forth. For sources that had something relevant to the theme, she noted an "x," and often a short comment; for those readings that did not mention the theme, she marked "NO."

Catherine Plocher's inquiry was on her role as a literacy coach in supporting teacher change in her school. Her comparison chart, Figure 4.2, also covered only four sources (out of the

Katie Paciga Comparison Chart Teacher Inquiry Project CIE 535	Author/audience interaction in the preschool… D.W. Rowe Ethnography	pp.359-368 of Pappas Text Hypothetical/ Theoretical piece	Creating a Writing Workshop… Wolfer Inquiry	Social Worlds of Children… A.H. Dyson Inquiry
Age group studied or referred to	Preschoolers at a daycare and 2 adults	K & 1st grade	1st grade	K-3
Focus children were mentioned	NO	Amber, Megan & Mike; Annie & Robbie	Alan, Julissa, Jon, Karen, & Ana	Jameel, Eugenie, Anthony, Lamar, William, & Ayesha
Process writing approach to instruction	NO – self selected time	x	x	
State that literacy learning is socially constructed	X - Cook-Gumperz & Cosaro	Integrated Language approach	X – Vygotsky & Wells	X – texts negotiate one's place in the social world
Used mini-lessons	NO	NO	X	
Conferences with students on content	This occurred incidentally. It was one of the discovered patterns in author/audience relationships-self initiated revisions in becoming your own audience	x- genre, message vocabulary, audience, and visual images	X – The teacher focused on main ideas.	
Conferences about the medium of student texts	This occurred incidentally. Example of Jared writing backwards and Kyle calling him on it. Author/audience relationships.	x- directionality, spacing, punctuation, spelling, grammar	NOT REALLY	
Used field notes	X – theoretical and methodological	NO	x	x
Used video tape	X	NO	x ˙ to	x
Analyzed student writing samples	X – author/audience relations	x /for content + medium	NOT FORMALLY	x
Emphasized that writing is around "a big idea"	NO– but they gave purposes for writing at class writing table	x as described in rec. for edit	x – completed a mini-lesson	
Text in emergent stage is orally constructed before writtesn	X	X	X – example with Julissa	
Revision and editing are encouraged and taught	NO	x-orally in K writing.	X – in conferences	
Students became readers of other's pieces	X – exchanging literacy pieces (like mail)	NO	x	x
Sharing of writing was done	X – author/audience relationships were examined	NO	x	x
Affective impact of writing	X – positive evaluative comments when adult audience	x- cautions not to be too critical	x – positive	
Problems or new quetions that emerged	NO	NO	Genre & Relationships of power	

Figure 4.1 Sample Comparison Chart (Katie Paciga)

Article	meaning/theme →	guide teachers act as mentors & assistants	Focus on primary goal coaching & modeling	Ongoing & consistent feedback
What am I do suppose to teach all day – Three big ideas for the Reading Coach – Reading Tchr – Dole	ongoing Prof Dev Provide collaborative community of teachers & learners	• orchestrate school reform, learning standards, instructional materials assessment. • assist teachers in their classrooms – it won't be as effective one shot doesn't work	teachers, reading instr., student learning.	Scheduling — be supportive they need to be able to depend on you.
Design staff development w/ Student needs in mind – Nat'l Staff dvmt Council	• What I need to learn, to improve learning of all students • end in mind • disaggregate performance & staff learning	• need to be valued, active part of learning shown respect, relevancy-oriented & staff learning	X	listen to teachers and refer to data.
A Roadmap for Reading Specialists – reading specialists in exemplary schools w/out exemplary Reading Programs – 7 guid'g visions RT	• Align function as reading specialist w/ school context • sustain momentum	You can't FORCE change – align w/ needs of teachers – or you will not get far.	• align efforts w/ needs of teachers & students. • strong conceptual base	preobservation Post observation grade level mtgs measurable goals
What is collaboration & how does it relate to other Current school practices?	• Coaching • Peer coaching • school based decision making • shared responsibility	• more opportunity to discuss areas of curriculum/ instruction w/ difficulty	X	peer collaboration mentors (same as above)

Figure 4.2 Sample Comparison Chart (Catherine Plocher)

eight references she cited in her literature review). These sources were two articles from the journal *The Reading Teacher* and two Internet articles. Unlike Katie's chart, Catherine's had only four meanings or themes (on the top of the chart): "ongoing professional development provides collaborative community of teachers as learners," "*guide* teachers . . .," "focus on primary goal . . .," and "ongoing and consistent feedback." Catherine also used an "X" when no relevant idea existed for a theme in an article (only twice), but filled most of the cells of the chart with bulleted comments.

As was noted in Chapters 2 and 3, Courtney Wellner's inquiry question was "How can I make peer writing conferences more effective for all writers in my [freshman] classroom?" Courtney's comparison chart—Figure 4.3—consisted of two pages and was therefore more elaborate. Like Katie and Catherine, she included four sources: three journal articles and a chapter from a book. Unlike the preceding charts, Courtney's chart included only three "significant meanings": "Based on Vygotsky's socio-cognitive theory of learning," "Writing as a social process," and "Motivation due to authentic, personally meaningful activity." Although there were only three theme categories, her chart cells were filled in detailed statements under each category for each source.

Sandra's Zanghi's comparison chart was even more detailed; it was five pages long, too long to include here. Sandra's inquiry focused on how her fifth graders' small-group discussions after read-alouds affected their participation and responses in these discussions. Like the teachers discussed so far, she used four sources: two journal articles and two book chapters. Like Katie, Sandra included some categories that had to do with the methodologies of the research studies that three of the sources presented—for example, "The purpose or research question," "How the study was implemented," and "The results of the study." However, she also had several other themes, namely, "Benefits of read alouds," "Best read-aloud practices," "Best practices for student response to literature," "Text selection," and "Benefits of student response." Except for the "purpose or research question" and "how the study was implemented" categories (in which brief statements were presented in the chart cells), Sandra provided lists of bulleted ideas on her chart, some of which were quite long (for example, for the "best read-aloud practices" category, twelve statements were included).

These examples illustrate the various ways that comparison charts can be orchestrated. Once you have completed your comparison chart, it is useful to have a conversation with someone (a classmate if you are taking a course; a fellow colleague at your school, and so forth) to obtain feedback on it. The general peer conference sheet in Appendix A could be used here. Just as sharing your fieldnotes (in Chapter 2) and your consent form (in Chapter 3) might have offered clarity about aspects of your inquiry, your discussion with others about the theoretical ideas and perspectives from the sources you read in your comparison chart also contributes to it by enhancing the conceptual framework that informs your study. Rather than copying what the authors you read have written, paraphrase the ideas in your own words. Bullets encourage paraphrasing, and the bullets and statements in the chart encourage you to articulate *your* sense of the ideas. As you put the readings into your own words, you become more confident about what ideas are important and relevant, and more ready to plunge into writing the literature review itself. The comparison chart supports your voice in the review, and your paraphrasing of the ideas and perspectives presented in the sources better enables you to avoid the pitfalls of plagiarism. That is, you are now more likely to be successful in saying things in your own words and voice because you are developing the ideas for your own purposes.

Graphic Organizer of Literature Review Articles
Courtney Wellner

Significant Meanings → Article Citations ↓	Based on Vygotsky's socio-cognitive theory of learning	Writing as a social process	Motivation due to authentic, personally meaningful activity
De Guerrero, M. and Villamil, O. "Social-Cognitive Dimensions of Interaction in L2 Peer Revision." *The Modern Language Journal*, Vol. 78, No.4. (1994): 484–496.	~ Learning is fostered when more skilled students assist less-skilled peers in revision process (ZPD) ~Teachers need to provide opportunities for students to interact with peers of various levels of regulation and skills	~Students need to be assessed according to their levels of regulation during the peer revision process; students need to be paired so as to make the collaborations most effective (self-regulated-self-regulated, self-regulated-object regulated) ~ Pairs should be regularly redistributed so as to encourage students to work with many different types of learners and writers	~As students are paired and are given specific, authentic roles to perform (reader/writer, expert/novice) they are more motivated to put time and energy into their peer revisions so as not to disappoint the partner who is relying on them for help ~Students are working on authentic, original pieces of writing that they have personal attachment to revising and wanting to improve
Althauser, R. and Darnall, K. "Enhancing Critical Reading and Writing through Peer Reviews: An Exploration of Assisted Performance." *Teaching Sociology*, Vol. 29, No. 1. (2001): 23-35.	~ "Assisted performance" at work as students effectively scaffold for each other in the process of on-line peer revision ~Students are always working at the edge of their "zone of proximal development" or ZPD	~Importance of participation in the group revision sessions was shows to be crucial in the final drafts of essays ~Students who actively participated in the paired/group activities produced better final drafts	~ Students get to know each other through their social pairings/groups and feel invested in helping each other to succeed in their writing ~Students are able to see immediate improvement in their drafts as the online revisions are posted and viewed

Source			
Street, C. "A reluctant writer's entry into a community of writers." *Journal of Adolescent and Adult Literacy*, 48:8 (2005): 636-641.	~Focuses on the importance of teacher scaffolding for students struggling with writing ~Novice writers require the assistance of experienced guides as they enter the academic writing community ~Teacher should also model the struggles of the writing process to show students how even "experts" must struggle within their own ZPD ~Writing teachers must provide students with just enough assistance to nudge them forward while still praising how far they've come	~There is a critical link between identity and writing, and small groups help students develop their individual identities in the context of the classroom ~Workshop approach is a means to guide novice writers as they developed their own expertise with writing and with each other ~Learning is ultimately a relationship among people—without the ability to work closely with trusted teachers and peers, reluctant writers may never develop the ability to be independent writers	~As students come to see themselves as participants, not just observers, of the construction of knowledge (i.e. the writing process) they are more motivated to participate in that process ~Student-initiated writing assignments will produce better results due to the inherent stake that students have in projects of their own choosing ~Students who develop identities as writers begin to contribute to the classroom community in productive ways, such as offering suggestions and comments during peer revision sessions
Nystrand, Martin. "What's a Teacher to Do? Dialogism in the Classroom." *Opening Dialogue*. Teachers College Press, New York, 1997.	~When a knowledgeable adult is not available, peer collaboration is just as effective in eliciting student engagement ~Reciprocal teaching occurs when students take on the role of the teacher in their peer collaborations—important type of scaffolding ~The best way of working within the ZPD is to have students collaborate with each other and then bring what they've learned to the teacher for help raising learning to the next level of critical thinking	~Students are shown to write best when they are allowed to demonstrate their skills to explain something to someone who really wants to know rather than simply for the teacher as audience ~Peer interaction promotes reasoning and cognitive reorganization when differing perspectives engender cognitive conflict ~Peer response groups contribute to increased writer self-efficacy and critical thinking as students engage in discussion with each other about themselves as writers	~Small groups are most effective when students are allowed some degree of autonomy to work out their own interpretations and responses to open-ended tasks, such as peer revision ~Students' main goal is to make their tests more functional and enjoyable for the members of their peer revision group—their revisions are therefore situationally motivated ~Peer revision asks students to perform an authentic, meaningful task that matters to the audience, instead of the superficial, procedural activities often required of students during writing process

Figure 4.3 Sample Comparison Chart (Courtney Wellner)

WRITING UP THE LITERATURE REVIEW

As we have said, reading and responding to the research sources written by different authors on the topic that relates to your action research project helps you think about how to conduct and focus your own research. The literature review, based on your readings and comparison chart, helps you communicate the major ideas from these texts and how they are connected by informing your study in several ways: by supporting your developing conceptual or interpretive frame for your study; by helping you think about the actual "doing" of your inquiry (teaching strategies to try out, or strategies that you are already implementing); by offering ways for you to reflect on the ongoing "findings" of your study (information to think about as you interpret your data in action research cycles); and by considering possible ways you might write up your inquiry (the articles or chapters offer examples for writing a review).

What should be included in a literature review? How should it be crafted? Table 4.1 represents guidelines for including some of the major components you should incorporate in your review report. These components are not isolated elements to be presented in sequence in your review text; instead, they need to be integrated in the review report. Below are excerpts from the collaborating teacher researchers' literature reviews to illustrate how they might be orchestrated in the review report. Recall that these teachers wrote their reviews during the beginnings of their inquiries. Thus, they sometimes mention what they are planning to do or are already doing regarding implementing their study.

Sandra Zanghi's review began with a brief description of her inquiry and then, as she discussed the relevant research related to her study (which she organized under five sections, all of which she identified as major themes in her comparison chart, as mentioned earlier), she referred to her inquiry focus. See Excerpt 4.1.

Table 4.1 *Guidelines for literature review report*

Your inquiry questions, the impetus of or rationale for your study
You want to include your inquiry questions or topic in your study. It is helpful to state these somewhat generally at the beginning of the literature review, and then at the end to state the specific questions, possibly worded as questions, you are asking.

Major, relevant ideas from readings that are important for informing your inquiry
You want to include only relevant ideas, not ones that authors might have discussed but are not pertinent to your study. Also, do not discuss each reading separately; instead, find the major ideas and make them the focus of your discussion—refer to your comparison chart for these major meanings and themes. Try to synthesize different viewpoints on each theme, noting where there may be contrasting or complementary views. When writing, this can be facilitated by including citations at the end of the sentence and avoiding using authors as subjects of sentences.

Connect themes by building a major thesis as it relates to the focus of your study
Decide how to sequence and orchestrate the major themes you identified in your comparison chart in your review. Try to integrate these meanings throughout your review so you can make a meaningful explanation or argument about them.

Use APA (American Psychological Association) conventions for citing your sources both in the body of the review and in the References at the end. See Appendix B for details on APA format.

Excerpt 4.1: Sandra Zanghi's Literature Review

Introduction

In my action research, I am inquiring on how small-group discussions during read-alouds affect the participation in read-alouds. I am also looking at how the quality of my fifth-grade students' reflections change as they are able to discuss more freely in small groups rather than in teacher-directed whole-group discussions.

Benefits of Read-Alouds

Rog (2001), Sipe (2000), and Fisher, Flood, Lapp, and Frey (2004) all support the benefits of read-alouds, which provide me with the rationale for implementing read-alouds in my classroom. Read-alouds help build vocabulary . . . [more benefits are discussed in several sentences].

Other benefits of read-alouds include the learning of factual information and encouragement of higher levels and thinking (Rog, 2001). Furthermore, students are enabled to express themselves as individuals (Fisher et al. 2004), as well as enhance knowledge of the conventions of print (Rog, 2001; Sipe, 2000). In addition, an emotional attachment to the adult reader forms during read-alouds (Sipe, 2000).

Best Read-Aloud Practices

It is important for me to know the best ways to implement read-alouds so that I may use certain best practices in my own read-alouds. According to Rog (2001) and Fisher et al. (2004), teachers should review and practice books before reading to students . . .

The above excerpt covers her introduction and those parts of the first two sections of her report that were related to themes of previously published research on her topic. Several things are important to note: First, she incorporated her inquiry focus at the beginning of each of her sections or themes. And, when she did so, she used personal pronouns (*I, me, my*, etc.), which is quite appropriate in this type of review and is generally acceptable in outlets that publish teacher research. Second, other parts of her review were expressed as third-person declarative statements as she discussed information about the themes—for example, "Read-alouds help build vocabulary . . ."; "Other benefits of read-alouds include . . ." Third, in the first sentence under "Benefits of Read-Alouds," the authors of three sources (i.e., Rog, Sipe, and Fisher, Flood, Lapp, and Frey) served as subjects of this sentence, but in the rest of the text the authors cited were added in parentheses at the end of sentences (or clauses). Citing is essential, for this is how you give credit to authors who have informed your study. But *how* citing is done is more significant than it seems. When authors of published work are subjects of sentences, they end up with having more voice than yours. Thus, although it is certainly OK to include such sentences in your report, you do not want most of your text to be written that way. After all, you are recontextualizing the ideas for your own purposes. You want the ideas themselves to be what the reader pays attention to, not the people who wrote them.

Finally, as Sandra discussed her themes in this way, she incorporated the ideas and built a conceptual thesis for her study.

Excerpt 4.1 also shows use of APA (American Psychological Association) conventions (see Appendix B for more details), which most educational journals and book publishers in the United States ask authors to follow. So, because you will rely on your literature review during your writing up of the final inquiry report, you should attempt to implement these APA conventions here, too. Some of these are: setting out the headings of sections and subsections in specified ways; listing all authors (three or more) of a source the first time it is cited and then using "et al." for subsequent citations (e.g., Fisher, Flood, Lapp, and Frey (2004); (Fisher et al., 2004)); and alphabetizing citations (e.g., (Rog, 2001; Sipe, 2000). Note that Sandra did not include the titles of the book chapters or journal articles in the body of the review text. Instead, she provided, at the end of the review, a section titled "References," which listed (alphabetically) the sources she cited in the review. (See Appendix B for how to construct the references list according to APA conventions, as well as the references sections at the end of each chapter of the book and the collaborating teachers' inquiry reports in Part Three of the book. See also http://www.apastyle.org/learn/tutorials/basics-tutorial.aspx.)

Courtney Wellner's literature review for her inquiry about peer writing conferences in her ninth-grade English class was similar to Sandra's in that she incorporated information about the focus of her study at the beginning of each of her three major themes—see her comparison chart in Figure 4.3. In Excerpt 4.2, parts of her review from the second and third themes illustrate how she composed these areas.

Excerpt 4.2: Courtney Wellner's Literature Review

Writing as a Social Process

In addition to the concept of a "zone of proximal development," I am also interested in examining the inherent social aspects of the writing process and in studying how classroom peer revision can promote healthy, engaging social interaction while also improving the writing skills of my students. De Guerrero and Villamil (1994) designed their study of the social dimensions of the writing process based on the idea of regulation, or the force that directs students' motivation and social interactions during the learning process. Students who are able to complete the given task (i.e., a revision of a peer's essay draft) completely on their own are labeled self-regulated, whereas students who are bound by the text and whose actions are directed only by that text are said to be object-regulated . . .

Motivation Due to Authentic, Personally Meaningful Activity

Finally, student motivation is a factor I am concerned with in any discussion of teaching and learning, and I am particularly interested in how I can use peer writing conferences to motive my students to engage in learning that is authentic and personally meaningful to each of them. De Guerrero and Villamil maintain that as students are paired and given specific, authentic roles to perform in the writing conferences, they are motivated to put time and energy into their work so as not to disappoint the partner who is relying on them for help . . .

So, Courtney employed an approach similar to Sandra's by introducing some aspect of her inquiry at the beginning of each of her themes or sections. And, because we hear her strong voice here, her perspective in subsequent text does not seem to be so diminished even though she expresses her ideas from the De Guerrero and Villamil journal article in each case, using these authors as subjects of sentences.

Nicole Perez's research inquiry was about her role as a literacy coach. Her literature review was also organized by three themes ("Stages of the Coaching Process," "Coaching and Effective Communication," "Coaching as a Collaborative Process"). However, Nicole included the components in Table 4.1 differently. She covered the relevant ideas in the major themes without reference to her inquiry and then, at the end of her report, she integrated her inquiry focus with summary points from these theme sections. Excerpt 4.3A shows some of the ways she accomplished this in the final part of her report.

Excerpt 4.3A: Nicole Perez's Literature Review

I am developing a better understanding of how a literacy coach can help teachers stay focused and improve instruction. I have begun a more organized system for teacher meetings where teachers observe me modeling specific lessons and their participation in follow-up sessions shortly after the observations. Moreover, these lessons have helped teachers see students' needs in a different manner and have helped assess what they are learning.

. . . [Effective communication is important.] Teachers are very sensitive and are put in vulnerable situations when their instruction is critiqued and analyzed . . . Beginning conversations by *telling* teachers what they need to do will never better instruction. I have learned that teachers need to see for themselves what are strengths and areas that need improvement in their teaching. A coach can help guide that person by asking questions and engaging in conversations where teachers take the time to think about their instruction and student learning. In many ways a coach is like a facilitator guiding teachers towards new discoveries and learning—the same way teachers should be with students.

Nicole included reference to her inquiry at the end. Her review represents a different approach from Sandra's and Courtney's, indicating that there is no "right" way to incorporate the Guidelines components noted in Table 4.1.

Nicole also included a feature in her review that warrants discussion, namely, incorporating quotes from the published sources. For example, earlier in the paper, towards the end of her third theme or section, "Coaching as a Collaborative Process," she quoted from a book she had read and used for her conceptual framework—see Excerpt 4.3B.

Excerpt 4.3B: Nicole Perez's Literature Review

Collaborating also helps teachers and coaches see different perspectives. "An effective coach not only understands these realities of teaching, but also is willing to accept a teacher where he or she is, build a trusting relationship, and help the teacher explore new avenues" (Vogt Shearer, 2003, p. 211). The coach helps teachers find answers to questions and provides a safe environment where teachers feel comfortable sharing concerns without being evaluated or reprimanded. A coach helps teachers find strengths and improve weaknesses of lessons and overall instruction. Collaborating also involves confidentiality . . .

In this part of her review, Nicole incorporates a quotation from a book on reading specialists. Inserting quotations is often useful and appropriate, but it should be done sparingly. Like making source authors subjects of sentences in expressing ideas, using lots of quotations from their work strengthens the voices of these other authors and diminishes your voice as the teacher researcher and expert on your study.

SUMMARY

Practice is real-life theorizing, which is enhanced by teacher research, and doing literature reviews further strengthens these living theories by engaging theories from other people's practices. These reviews enable you to link theory and practice by connecting ideas presented in the literature to what is occurring in your classroom. Understandings gleaned from the literature augments, complements, and may even challenge your present views on the literacy topic you have chosen to study. Doing a preliminary literature review helps you take advantage of these benefits early on in the inquiry process, clarifying your approach by offering insights and alternative strategies (and rationales for them) to implement. Thus, the process of creating a literature review also supports your mindfulness and reflective attention as you enact the ongoing action research cycles of your study.

However, as you relate your research topic to current information found in others' work, it is important for you to sustain your voice in this process. Viewing your review as a *response* to the literature is beneficial during your reading of sources. Using comparison charts can also be helpful in this respect because it enables you to identify relevant, pertinent major meanings or themes of ideas found in sources. These charts, then, can serve as valuable prewriting tools as you write your literature review. There is no right way to compose these reviews, but there are components to keep in mind (see Table 4.1). These elements can be integrated in a variety of ways, but as the examples provided above show, organizing the information you gained in reading your sources via the major meanings or themes you found and placed on your comparison chart helps you keep your voice strong about your inquiry and its connection to the published work of others. And, as we have said, constructing sentences so that authors are not always the subjects of them and limiting direct quotations from the literature further highlights your voice. Finally, it makes sense to follow APA guidelines in composing your literature review, as you will rely on it when you write your final report (Chapter 7) and any manuscripts you submit to journals.[4]

This chapter concludes Part One of the book, which has covered the beginning stages and activities of your teacher research project. The next chapters, Part Two of the book, focus on enacting your inquiry, analyzing your data, and writing up your findings.

SUGGESTED ACTIVITIES

1 As indicated on p. 35, share your comparison charts with a classmate or colleague, using the General Peer Conferencing Form (Appendix A). After you have discussed the ideas covered in your chart, discuss how you should sequence the themes or meanings in writing up your literature review.

2 Use the General Peer Conferencing Form to gain feedback on a draft of your literature review. Besides the content, examine how you are citing and using APA conventions.

NOTES

1   "Peer-reviewed" articles are those that have been sent out for a blind review to various experts in the field who recommended that they be accepted or rejected for publication in a journal. Books can also be considered as peer-reviewed publications because authors would have had to submit a prospectus (a plan for the book and usually a couple of the chapters) for review. Generally, such peer-reviewed sources are seen to be more credible.

2   Some general education journals are the *American Educational Research Journal, Cognition and Instruction, Curriculum Inquiry*, the *Elementary School Journal, Teachers College Record*, and *Teaching and Teacher Education*. Two online journals, one that focuses on literacy topics and one that is general, are *The Reading Matrix: An International Online Journal* (www.readingmatrix.com/journal.html) and *Academic Exchange Quarterly*, where many peer-reviewed academic journals are found (www.rapidintellect.com/AEQweb).

3   If you are a student at a college or university, you can often print out pdf copies of journal articles through the www.scholar.google.com search engine.

4   Often novice teacher researchers may also need support or reminders on various grammar issues—such as using parallel constructions, non-sexist pronouns, and noun and verb agreement. See Appendix C for details of some of the most common points to go over in editing your literature review.

REFERENCES

Burnaford, G. (2001). Teachers' work: Methods for researching teaching. In G. Burnaford, J. Fischer, & D. Hobson (Eds.). *Teachers doing research: The power of action through inquiry* (pp. 49–82). Mahwah, NJ: Lawrence Erlbaum.

Glaser, B., & Strauss, A. (1967). *Discovery of ground theory: Strategies for qualitative research*. Chicago: Aldine.

Hubbard, R. S., & Power, B. M. (2003). *The art of classroom inquiry: A handbook for teacher-researchers*. Portsmouth, NH: Heinemann.

Schatzman, L., & Strauss, A. (1973). *Field research*. Englewood Cliffs, NJ: Prentice-Hall.

Whitehead, J., & McNiff, J. (2006). *Action research living theory*. Thousand Oaks, CA: Sage.

Part Two

Enacting, Analyzing, and Writing Up Your Inquiry

Once the introductory steps of teacher inquiry have been completed, you are now ready to begin your research study. You might have already engaged in several preliminary cycles of action research, perhaps using fieldnotes to capture and document these classroom activities. But, now you are prepared to approach your study in earnest. The chapters in this part of the book provide tools for these processes of enactment.

Chapter 5 covers strategies for gathering data related to your teacher inquiry question. It describes various methods for collecting data: fieldnotes; audio- and videotaping; surveys and interviews; artifacts; and images and pictures. It also includes two approaches that could be employed in teacher research: case students and focal students (and/or groups). How to keep a research journal and create data trails for documenting and organizing data that have been collected are also outlined. Chapter 6 explains data analysis techniques, and because teacher researchers cannot wait until the end of their inquiries to analyze and interpret their data, how to generate ongoing data summaries is discussed and illustrated. This chapter also delineates the ways in which you might incorporate descriptive statistics in your analysis. Finally, Chapter 7 provides strategies for writing up a "publishable" paper for a practitioner audience. It offers tips and recommendations for formatting your inquiry report, and includes how to compose a critical beginning lead for your paper and how to express your findings.

Like Part One of the book, this part lays out the above features using examples from the work of the collaborating teacher researchers, and it describes suggested activities to gain feedback on these phases of teacher inquiry.

Chapter 5

Strategies for Data Collection

- How can I collect data to find out what I want to know in my inquiry?
- What is the role of case study and focal student approaches in teacher research?
- How do I organize my data collection activities?

Novice teacher researchers often think that action research isn't really research (perhaps because of their experience of reading quantitative research studies) unless something is "proved," tested, or compared (with different "treatments" or "control groups") (Johnson, 2008). However, good, useful inquiry projects, designed simply to understand what is going on in your classroom or school, are worthwhile ventures that also fall under the umbrella of research. And, there are many ways in which you can gather information to answer questions in teacher-researcher studies that are qualitative in nature. Data are "the rough materials researchers collect from the world they are studying" (Bogdan & Biklen, 1982, p. 73). Data provide evidence, enabling teacher researchers to make sense of their practice. As we shall see in Chapter 6, data support the claims and interpretations in analysis. Thus, data are the grist for the mindful attention of teacher interpretation and reflection. In Chapter 3, we mentioned different ways to collect data as you are planning your study and creating a proposal. In this chapter, we discuss these approaches in more detail.

FIELDNOTES

As we saw in Chapter 2, taking fieldnotes is a major way to collect data. These notes consist of two kinds of writing: *descriptive writing*, where you provide details of what you observe in the classroom; and *interpretive writing*, where you make inferences and make sense of the details of observation. We human beings, in our everyday lives, naturally tend to interpret social situations without even thinking about it. We often make judgments about what people are doing, because, on the basis of our interpretations, we decide how to act. So if someone shouts "Hey!" to us from across the street, we try to interpret the tone (angry, expectant) and look to see whether the person is smiling, scowling, or merely wants our attention. We also use our relationship (friend, enemy, stranger) to help us interpret the meaning of the shout. In writing fieldnotes, it is important that you are able to distinguish the descriptive factors (smiling, friend) from the interpretive (the person is saying "Hi!"), because often actions can have multiple interpretations. When you write fieldnotes both as descriptions and interpretations ("The children all raised their hands. //I thought they were eager to participate because they loved the subject.//), rather than just interpretations (the children were eager to participate because they loved the subject), you have left out the details. When you have some descriptive data, you can reinterpret data if you collect further data and decide to change your mind about what the data meant. Moreover, then people can judge whether they agree with your interpretations or not. For instance, you might find out later that the children are having a private contest to see who can be called on the most.

As was noted in Chapter 2, fieldnotes can be collected in a range of ways: jotted down in different kinds of notebooks, on sticky notes, large address labels, index cards, and so forth. Some teacher researchers then transfer these notes into computer files; others actually use their laptops to write their notes directly.

Fieldnotes can also be collected by developing your own charts, forms, or tables (Hubbard & Power, 2003; Pappas, Kiefer, & Levstik, 2006). For example, you could create a target-child observation form for one or multiple children (Sylva, Roy, & Painter, 1980) to record notes about certain children you are interested in helping or whom you have particular questions about. This scheme involves target children on whom to do repeated ten-minute observations; see Table 5.1 for such an observation sheet. The procedure consists of making a series of ten-minute observations during a literacy activity that is the focus of your inquiry. For each minute, you use the first half-minute to observe the actions and interactions of a target child, and you use the rest of the half-minute to document the child's nonverbal communication and language (jotted down under the "Activity Record" and "Language Record" columns). As Table 5.1 shows, information about the context or task and other participants involved can also be included. At the bottom of the form, interpretations (and possible instructional ideas, based on these interpretations) can be listed. Thus, descriptive and interpretive writing are both included here, but they are recorded in a different way. Although the descriptive writing is a "summary" of what you observe, you can often incorporate many details in these summaries.

This form could be used daily during a particular activity, each day focusing on two individual children, so that after a couple of weeks you would have data on all of the students in your class. Or, you might use this form for case studies, or for focal students (see p. 54 for details) on whom you have decided to place particular emphasis in your study. The form can also be used for small-group activities, such as literature circle groups, where you take turns collecting data on one of the groups each day or just follow one group in particular.

Other forms can be developed during your inquiry. For example, maybe your inquiry involves how children write up and illustrate their hands-on science explorations. As part of your study, you want to capture particular actions and language use as they engage in these experiences that precede the writing or drawing work. You might create a form that includes the major aspects of the activity so that you can take notes as you move from each group. In this case,

Table 5.1 Target child(ren) observation sheet

Name(s): .... Date/Time:

ACTIVITY RECORD	LANGUAGE RECORD	CONTEXT/TASK	OTHER PARTICIPANTS
1			
2			
3			
4			
5			
. . .			
10			
Interpretations: Instructional Ideas:			

your categories of interest would be listed on the left, with big blocks of space on the right to jot down your ideas. Possible categories might be (with short abbreviations to place in the left-hand column) as follows:

- What are some of the hypotheses (or questions) children construct about the topic? (Hypoth/Qs)
- What conclusions (or answers) do children come up about the topic? (Concl/Ans)
- What are examples of children's own language used during the activity? (Child Lang)
- What are examples of scientific language used during the inquiry? (Scien Lang)
- How does their language use reflect their feelings about the topic? (Feel Lang)
- What are examples of joint action and cooperation during the activity? (JntAct/Coop)
- What frustrations, tensions, or problems occurred during the activity? (Probs)
- What notes or drawings did children create during the activity? (Notes/Draw)

As the other forms show, you would add a space at the bottom to jot down your interpretations of (and instructional ideas on) these notes.

Other forms could be created, based on your inquiry. That is, these forms offer a focused way to take fieldnotes that are more directly related to your inquiry. They are especially helpful after you have completed a few of the action research cycles and have identified particular areas of interest: types of student responses used in literature circles, revising strategies employed by students, ideas that children initiate during read-alouds, and so forth. You can provide a form that includes these already-found categories and then a "Miscellaneous" one for new ones that emerge during your inquiry.

AUDIO- AND VIDEOTAPING OF CLASSROOM DISCOURSE

Often you want to make sure of the accuracy of what students and you are saying in the classroom. By this, we mean how students (and you) might bring up ways to talk about a book in read-alouds or peer-led literature groups—how they actually "think" as they talk, bring up an idea and reword it, overlapping talk of participants, and so forth. Because of the fast pace of classroom interaction, such talk just cannot be captured in fieldnotes, even after you have had lots of practice in doing them. Audio recorders and video cameras are now quite reasonably priced, so are used a lot in teacher research. Digital audio recorders are small now and can be easily brought along when you have conversations with students over their written texts, or can be placed on a table without much trouble in small-group work. Some teacher researchers set up a video camera (digital ones are also quite small nowadays) on a more or less permanent basis so that students get used to its presence and it is easily available when they want it for taping an activity.

Thinking about where you place the camera or audio recorder is important. Do you want it to capture a small group? The whole class? Some students in particular? In regard to video cameras, if you point the camera at you from behind the students, you may miss what students are doing and it will be harder to hear their contributions. If you place the camera where you are, you will miss recording your actions. It all depends on the data you want to collect. New recorders and cameras[1] have pretty good internal microphones to capture talk, but you may want to check how well these are capturing the discourse, especially in whole-class activities such as read-alouds or focus lessons (where you might also use external microphones). However, only some cameras have jacks for external microphones, so make sure you know what you want and the technical specifications of the audio recorder or video camera you are purchasing or borrowing. Also, if you are using a digital audio recorder, make sure it is compatible with your operating system (Mac or Windows). Most recorders are compatible with Windows-based computers but only a few are compatible with Mac. Cell phones, especially smart phones, can also make for audio recorders at a pinch. Creating transcriptions of these recordings[2] is discussed in Chapter 6.

SURVEYS

Surveys are often useful to gain students' ideas on curricular routines before (and after) teacher researchers launch their inquiry. Gathering information about what students think about the topic—their perspectives—often guides the first steps in the inquiry. They serve as "baseline data." They also "mark" for students the fact that new ways of doing literacy activities are to occur in the future (ones different from those they might have experienced in other classes or with different teachers, or ones they have encountered during the current academic year if the inquiry begins later in the year). Usually it is recommended that students do not put their names on these surveys, for you are likely to obtain more candid information if they are anonymous. However, if you are focusing on particular students, then you would want students to put their names on the survey. If this is the case, though, you may just want to find a time to interview the student, as discussed later. Consider the following in creating your surveys (Fink, 1995):

- Always include the purpose of the survey on the form or in your oral directions to them.
- You might have some "forced"-choice items—ones that require a yes or no answer, or what are called Likert-scale questions (where participants answer by circling a number between 1 and 4 or 1 and 5 [e.g., *1* indicating "always" and *4* or *5* indicating "never," with "often" and "sometimes" in between]). This type of survey response is easily quantified.
- Create some open-ended questions. You might phrase your questions similarly to your inquiry questions (see Chapter 2)—for example, "What kinds of experiences in class help you revise your writing?"; "In what ways do our literature discussions help (or not) your understanding of books?"; "What suggestions do you have regarding our class projects?" You might add a very open-ended question at the end of the survey: "Anything else?" A content analysis would be necessary to identify major themes in these responses. (We discuss analysis in Chapter 6.)
- You might select a focus group (a group of students who are likely to have different perspectives on the topic of inquiry) to help you design your survey questions (Burnaford, 2001). That is, they might come up with ideas you wouldn't have considered, making the survey more relevant and pertinent for them, and therefore ultimately more beneficial for you. For this type of survey design, you might ask volunteers and/or choose students who represent the class as a whole.

Surveys can be used to obtain information from teacher colleagues and parents as well. Also, these could serve as preliminary surveys that help and guide a survey you might design for students. Creating a post survey to understand how students see how literacy activities have affected their learning in an area is also a good idea. To complement the pre survey, some of the same questions can be used in the post survey, which would allow for documenting any changes as a result of new practices you are choosing to implement and study, as well new questions that cover new facets of literacy learning that emerged during the inquiry.

INTERVIEWS

There are two major types of interviews that you might consider in collecting data (both of which would be audiotaped). The first type is similar to a survey, except that rather than having students write down their responses, you have a conversation with them face to face. Because of this feature, you can follow up with questions about what interviewees might say. For instance, their responses might require you to ask a clarifying question, or you might want to ask a new question about a response that surprises you.

Here are some ideas to consider in conducting interviews (Holstein & Gubrium, 1995; Mishler, 1986):

- As with a survey, begin the interview by explaining the purpose of the interview, namely, that you want to get students' ideas on an area or topic.
- Design your questions ahead of time, so that you have a guide for the conversation.
- Treat the interview as a conversation, with most of the questions being open-ended ones (using forms such as "What do you think about . . .?" or "Tell me about . . .").
- As students provide responses, suggest connections that seem to be related to what they say.
- Follow up any signs of confusion or ambiguity by asking for clarification.
- Be alert for possible areas that you may not have anticipated so you can pursue these new lines of thought.
- At the end, add "Anything else?" It can be useful to ask this question at the end of some or all of the questions, too, as doing so might elicit more information.

In general, although you are asking questions in the interviews, you want to pose them and follow up on their answers in such a way that students have an opportunity to create a narrative on the topic you are interested in. Thus, although this kind of interview is considered "formal," the aim is to try to make the interview focused but also improvisational (Burnaford, 2001). It is a guided conversation (Stringer, 2004). Usually, this type of interview is conducted with only a small group of students, individually or as a group. Perhaps you are really unsure about the behavior of students in certain literacy activities (maybe they don't seem very engaged, or there appears to be a lot of whispering and uncertainty every time a routine occurs). Having an interview with them either at the beginning or during the inquiry provides a means to gain some insights to the problem you are encountering in the classroom. Like surveys, interviews can also be done with parents and teacher colleagues. In addition, post interviews might also be employed, again using some of the same questions, as well as new ones that might have surfaced during the inquiry.

The second type of interview is more informal and ongoing, usually centered on student work. For example, you might have interviews with students over their writing drafts (perhaps after they have had a peer conference and have revised their texts). Or, perhaps as students write and draw in their science journals, you might have roving interviews with them (especially for emergent writers who are using developmental spellings) to gain insights into what their illustrations might depict and what their intentions are regarding the ideas they express in both text and pictures. These types of interviews can be short. For instance, you might ask, "Can you tell me what you are writing about?" and then ask a couple of follow-up questions based on the response and your research goals, moving on quickly to another student. Thus, this second type of interviews is directly related to your practice and student learning. It is often also part of your ongoing assessment strategies. It is one way to create synergy between your research and your teaching, and can be important in not adding more to your plate in your busy life as an educator.

ARTIFACTS

Artifacts consist of the range of student work that can be collected in a study. This includes all drafts of students' written work (and illustrations); journal response entries; graphic organizers such as comparison charts, semantic maps, and K-W-L charts; notes they have taken in student-directed inquiries; and so forth. Final posters, PowerPoint reports, or other completed projects are also artifacts, as well as class charts and teacher-made materials for use in the classroom.

IMAGES AND PICTURES

As teacher researchers become interested in multimodal inquiries, images and pictures can also serve as a means of data collection.[3] Thus, the images that students include in their various texts are also important data. In addition, taking pictures during the various steps of the process in small-group projects that students make offers useful complementary data to students' written work. Pictures can be helpful in finding out how students use spatial relations or body language and/or gestures they employ when engaged in literacy activities on their own, with others, or in presenting their work, and so forth. Students may also take pictures in the community as part of their investigations. Finally, student-created videos, based on classroom projects, are image-like artifacts. Another way to collect data, and to understand activities from students' perspectives, is to give them a camera to take pictures of their literacy activities.

OTHER DATA COLLECTION TECHNIQUES

There are other aspects to data collection to consider, namely, whether and, if so, how you will concentrate on particular students in your inquiry. There are two approaches to studying certain students: using case studies and focal students.

Case Studies

Case studies are employed when you want to give attention to particular students (one or a few) in your class (Merriam, 1998). The rationale for the case study approach is that you want to find out how certain students are faring in your practice—including, say, special needs students, English language learners (ELLs), three boys who seem to be reluctant to participate in class discussions, two girls who seem to dominate peer discussions around books and writing, and so forth. The point is that you are interested in only these students (and, of course, how they might interact with others, or you, in the class). You want to gather a complete, detailed account of the experiences of these case-study students. You might also seek other sources of data regarding them—for example, interviews with their parents, or other teachers who have these students. Overall, however, you concentrate and collect data on only these students.

53

FOCAL STUDENTS

Unlike with case studies, in most inquiries teacher researchers plan to study the behavior of all their students because they are responsible for teaching all of them. Their research questions involve attention to how their various literacy practices are working for *all* students. However, it is also possible to select focal students to focus on during such studies. This approach is a version of a technique called *purposeful sampling* (Cresswell, 2002), in which certain participants are chosen for the gathering of data. Most of the time, these focal students represent the class as a whole, so that they are "typical" of the class and at the same time are likely to also reflect "diverse perspectives." So, teacher researchers would consider the following categories of difference when choosing these focal students (usually four to six students [or more if a class is very large]): gender, ability or achievement, ethnolinguistic or racial background, literacy interests, and so forth. Collecting data on all students is a challenge in an inquiry, so the reason for choosing focal students is that doing so enables teacher researchers to try to make sure that they collect the data regarding these students first, as they represent the class, and then attempt to obtain the data regarding other students in the class as much as they can. In other words, using focal students helps ease the burden of pressure of data collection, especially if a class is large.

It can also be desirable to have focal groups, perhaps two or three peer literature response groups, or small groups engaging in various inquiry projects. As in the focal student technique, teacher researchers would collect data on all groups but would make sure that they gather the data regarding these focal groups first. And, again, teacher researchers would choose students along certain characteristics of these groups so that they represent the class as a whole.

RESEARCH JOURNAL AND DATA TRAILS REVISITED

In Chapter 3, we discussed using a research journal and data trails in your inquiry. It is important to refresh your memory about their utility during the course of your study, now that you are more aware of the variety of data sources that it is possible to employ. Your research journal is the place where you include your fieldnotes, as well as the other types of data you will be gathering: transcriptions, copies of student work and other artifacts, photographs, and so forth. An essential part of this journal is your data trails—see Table 3.2—which are logs or documentation of when, what, and how you collected data. Thus, the research journal and your data trails help you organize your data collection activities. As you do more and more analysis, which is the topic of the next chapter, Chapter 6, these analyses will also be included in your research journal.

SUMMARY

Taking fieldnotes (documenting observations via descriptive and interpretive writing) is a mainstay mode of data collection for teacher researchers. However, teachers also need other, multiple sources of data for triangulation—that is, intersecting ways to gather data that can be compared (McMillan, 2000). Different data collection techniques, as described in this chapter, offer different lenses to the topic of the inquiry, thereby fostering more validity and trustworthiness in studies.

Deciding whether and, if so, how particular students (or teachers, if the teacher researcher is a literacy coach) are to be considered is also part of data collection. Two approaches are possible: case studies, where only one or a few may be the center of attention during an inquiry; and focal students, where there is an emphasis on certain students who represent the class as a whole, but all students are studied.

Finally, it is critical to find ways to organize the variety of data collected during an inquiry. Having a research journal and creating data trails help in this effort.

NOTES

1   Data captured via digital tape recorders and cameras can be downloaded on your computer, allowing for easier transcribing.
2   Two books are useful to support classroom discourse studies: *Classroom discourse: The language of teaching and learning* (Cazden, 2001) and *Using discourse analysis to improve classroom interaction* (Rex & Schiller, 2009).
3   Taking pictures of student multimodal texts via digital cameras (and then downloading them to your computer) is a great way to keep the details of illustrations (e.g., colors). This also enables you to return the drafts of these multimodal drafts to the authors in a timely manner.

REFERENCES

Bogdan, R. C., & Biklen, S. K. (1982). *Qualitative research for education: An introduction to methods and models.* Boston: Allyn & Bacon.

Burnaford, G. (2001). Teachers' work: Methods for researching teaching. In G. Burnaford, J. Fischer, & D. Hobson (Eds.). *Teachers doing research: The power of action through inquiry* (pp. 49–82). Mahwah, NJ: Lawrence Erlbaum.

Cazden, C. B. (2001). *Classroom discourse: The language of teaching and learning.* Portsmouth, NH: Heinemann.

Cresswell, J. (2002). *Educational research: Planning, conducting and evaluating quantitative and qualitative research.* Upper Saddle River, NJ: Pearson.

Fink, A. (1995). *The survey handbook.* Thousand Oaks, CA: Sage.

Holstein, J. A., & Gubrium, J. F. (1995). *The active interview.* Thousand Oaks, CA: Sage.

Hubbard, R. S., & Power, B. M. (2003). *The art of classroom inquiry: A handbook for teacher-researchers.* Portsmouth, NH: Heinemann.

Johnson, A. P. (2008). *A short guide to action research.* Boston: Pearson Education.

McMillan, J. H. (2000). *Educational research: Fundamentals for the consumer.* New York: Longman.

Merriam, S. B. (1998). *Qualitative research and case study applications in education.* San Francisco, CA: Jossey-Bass.

Mishler, E. G. (1986). *Research interviewing: Context and narrative.* Cambridge, MA: Harvard University Press.

Pappas, C. C., Kiefer, B. Z., & Levstik, L. S. (2006). *An integrated language perspective in the elementary school: An action approach.* Boston: Pearson Education.

Rex, L. A., & Schiller, L. (2009). *Using discourse analysis to improve classroom interaction.* New York: Routledge.

Stringer, E. (2004). *Action research in education.* Upper Saddle River, NJ: Pearson.

Sylva, K., Roy, C., & Painter, M. (1980). *Childwatching at playgroup and nursery school.* Ypsilanti, MI: The High/Scope Press.

Chapter 6

Analysis: What Do the Data Mean?

- What does analysis of data consist of in teacher research?
- How can I use ongoing data summaries to support my analysis?
- How can descriptive statistics be employed in analysis?

ANALYSIS WITHIN RECURRING CYCLES OF ACTION RESEARCH

Having to sift through a study's worth of data can seem like a lot. But remember, teacher inquiry consists of cycles of action research, as indicated in Chapter 1 (and referred to elsewhere in the book). Teacher researchers analyze data as they go along in their study through a cycle of observing, interpreting, planning, and enacting. Teachers don't wait until the "end" of their study to examine and interpret the information they have gathered, for they have to use their analysis of data to plan and act out changes in their practice. The immediate feedback on practice is one of the major benefits of teacher research. This chapter focuses on how to make sense of the data that have been gathered—namely, interpreting or analyzing those data in this recurring process of action. As you engage in these ongoing analysis experiences, you reaffirm or reframe your research question, sometimes changing the kinds of data to gather. To use the metaphor of a funnel (Bogdan & Biklen, 1998), you may start with a wide spectrum of what to collect, and then, as you see more clearly the topic of your inquiry and that certain data sources may not be as relevant or useful, you narrow the focus by selecting only data collection techniques that seem to be more pertinent. Another reason for analyzing *during* your inquiry is that you avoid having to wade through a mountain of data at the end of the study. Moreover, your ongoing interpretations and reflections help the process of inquiry become more satisfying, fostering your confidence in your research and its potential usefulness in transforming your practice. In a later part of this chapter, we discuss and illustrate the use of data summaries as a way of documenting your analysis during an inquiry.

ANALYSIS AS IDENTIFYING AND INTERPRETING PATTERNS

Analysis is a complex enterprise, for it involves synthesizing data, identifying significant patterns in the data, and constructing a framework for interpreting what those patterns might reveal about the data. Because data analysis is complicated, it is hard to explain and is often a scary part of teacher research. Data analysis is where the claims or statements about what the inquiry shows are generated. It consists of providing descriptions about the "what" of a study and explaining the "why" of the research (Burns, 1999). Unlike quantitative research that has a priori categories to confirm or disconfirm, data analysis in qualitative action research deals with *emerging* patterns or themes. Thus, the challenge, here, is to find ways to reveal these emerging meanings and make sense of them. By identifying patterns, the major characteristics and features across the events studied in the classroom that are related to your question, you are able to create your interpretations and theories about them. That is, your own theories *in action* are generated, which, in turn, feeds into new approaches in your practice. If you see data analysis as a messy, problem-solving adventure, it will make the process an interesting and exciting enterprise.

USING A CONSTANT COMPARISON ANALYSIS APPROACH

Organizing and Preparing Your Data for Analysis

A first step of analysis is to organize or assemble the kinds of data you have. It is useful to keep your research questions in mind as you scan through these different data sources in a general way. In doing so, you can jot down some broad impressions or ideas that can serve as possible potential areas to explore in more detail. Also, this initial review enables you to spot tentative areas where ideas from different data might be similar or complementary, or might offer a different, or even a contradictory, perspective.

Some data, such as transcriptions of audio or video recordings, need to be prepared before they can be examined in detail. Transcribing is a time-consuming activity because you may want to include all false starts, hesitations, and reconstructions that speakers use. If you are using audio and video recordings as a data source, you need to listen to and view them as you collect these data, otherwise they will not be able to inform your interpretations and decisions regarding your practice.

But how can you create such transcriptions that take so much time *during* your inquiry? We suggest that you transcribe one or two early classroom episodes or events to get a "feel" for the classroom activity. Transcriptions, more than other data, allow teacher researchers to make the familiar strange. "They allow us to freeze-frame a moment, replay and reconstruct it, and in the process of doing so, open up previously invisible choices of actions" (Rex & Schiller, 2009, p. 10). (Table 6.1 offers some possible transcription conventions you can start with; you could add to or modify these as appropriate for your data.) In transcribing videotapes, it is often useful to first transcribe the audio part, then go back to the tape to add relevant contextual, visual information (in "[]" brackets—see Table 6.1) that would be necessary to understand the discourse (for example, pointing to objects or persons, referring to texts nearby, and so forth).

Table 6.1 Conventions of transcription for classroom discourse examples

Unit:	Usually corresponds to an independent clause with all dependent clauses related to it (complex clause). Sometimes includes another independent clause if there is no drop of tone and the clause was added without any pausing. Units here are punctuated as sentences.
Turn:	Includes all of a speaker's utterances/units.
Key for speakers:	Use "Teacher" or your first name (or what students call you). Use the child's first name (which will need to be changed to a code name in any presentation or publication). If a child is cannot be identified by name, then C, C1, C2, and so forth are noted for individual children (with "m" or "f" to refer to the gender of a child): C is used if a child's voice cannot be identified at all; Cn is used to identify particular children (but not by name) in a particular section of the transcript (so that C1 or C2, etc., is not necessarily the same child throughout the whole transcript). Cs represents many children speaking simultaneously.
//	Repetitions or false starts or abandoned language replaced by new language structures.
~	Small/short pause within unit.
~ ~	Longer pause within unit.
|	Breaking off or interruption of the speaker's turn by the next speaker's turn.
==	A speaker's pause at the end of an uncompleted utterance, seemingly to encourage another speaker to talk.
< >	Uncertain words.
(***)	One word that is inaudible or impossible to transcribe.
(*** ***)	Longer stretches of language that is inaudible and impossible to transcribe.
Underscore:	Emphasis.
# #	Overlapping language spoken by two or more speakers at a time.
CAPS	Actual reading of a book or someone's writing (in a text, on the board, etc.).
[ ]	Identifies what is being referred to or gestured and other nonverbal contextual information.
. . . .	Part of a transcript has been omitted.
[m . . . .]	Part of transcript has been omitted that involved classroom management, if this is not relevant to an inquiry.

Once your transcription is completed, you should scan through it to look for anything that stands out or to generate any ideas about it. Afterwards, you can scrutinize it more deliberately. This latter process would reveal some beginning patterns, categories, or themes, which can then be followed up as you listen to or view your ongoing tapes during your inquiry. We discuss this in the next section, "Coding the Data." You do not have to further transcribe every section of every tape. At this time, you create a table of these early categories, and as you examine these newer tapes you jot down places in the tapes where you find similar categories, as well as new categories that may emerge. This method allows you to gather and analyze the data in an ongoing way so that you can make interpretive and pedagogical decisions, and at the same time identify the places that you can transcribe later on.

Other data might also need to be prepared for analysis. For example, you might make copies of student work (writings and illustrations), copying it (perhaps on legal-size paper) so that you have a large margin in which to write down codes or ideas. Children's surveys might be copied in a similar way. In other words, preparing and assembling data from your data sources would be an initial important step of data analysis.

Coding the data

After this overall examination of the data, you are ready to wade into the data more specifically by coding. Coding is an attempt to reduce the mass of data you might have gathered to more manageable categories of concepts, themes, or patterns. But how do you actually "code"? What does this involve? To identify emerging categories from the data, qualitative researchers rely on what is called a *constant comparison method of analysis* (Glaser & Strauss, 1967). The process is one that is also often termed a *grounded* theory, because it is one that is constructed inductively from your data (Schatzman & Strauss, 1973).

As you begin to do more detailed coding,[1] you should again keep in mind your inquiry questions, coding those events or behaviors that seem pertinent. Coding involves reading (and/or viewing, if you have visual data such as pictures) through your data to identify categories or themes. There are lots of ways to accomplish this, so find a way that seems useful to you. For example, you might jot down a note on the margin of a transcription whenever you find a particular tentative category, using a short phrase or a letter (e.g. "A") to mark it. As you do so, you should develop a definition for this category or theme. Then you continue reading the transcript to see whether you can find other instances of the same category or theme and new ones, for which you would enter new phrases or letter ("B," etc.), and also add new definitions for these new categories. As the method suggests, you *constantly* go over your data, *comparing* different meanings and ideas (categories or themes) that emerge. As you identify possible codes for your categories or themes, sometimes you collapse categories into one new category; sometimes a category gets broken down into new, more specific categories. As you become more certain during your analysis about tentative categories or themes, you can then assign each theme a color, and color-code (with magic markers or the different colors available from your word processing software). Color-coding helps related sections stand out when you reread them.

As you analyze the content of your data and develop coding categories, you might consider ways to view codes (Burns, 1999). These are often overlapping codes, but keeping them in mind can guide your analysis. *Participant codes* capture students' perspectives or ways of thinking or feeling about a topic. They can depict what your students are learning or their feelings about rules or norms on how literacy routines are to be run. This would also include their views about objects (e.g. texts used in class) or people (e.g. classmates in peer-group work). *Process codes* deal with sequences or stages of events, noting changes that may occur in student–student or teacher–student relations or certain students' progress over the course of a study. This code captures words and phrases indicating changes; it has to do with distinct transitions or phases. *Activity codes* focus on what happens in particular literacy activities—for example, the kinds of behavior that happen during literature discussion, read-alouds, or student writing conferences. Activity codes are very similar to process codes, but they are more about specific routines. *Strategy codes* center on strategies, techniques, and methods that students or teachers may use as they enact various literacy activities. Finally, *relationship codes* or *social structure codes* note the patterns of behavior that class members (and teacher) might engage in. How certain students act as rivals or mentors to other children, how friendships or cliques operate, how different students seem to have different status in a class can be examined. These various types of codes offer a set of possibilities as you approach coding; others may emerge as you analyze your data. As we have said, these different sets of codes are likely to overlap, so that certain sections of your data may be coded with more than one code. Other categories not listed above may also emerge during your analysis. Classroom life is a complex enterprise, so don't be surprised if your analysis is also complex.

Once you finish analyzing one type of data source, you proceed to do an analysis for all of your data sources. Transcripts of interviews might be done in the same way as transcriptions of classroom discourse in various literacy routines, as well as your fieldnotes and the open-ended questions in surveys. The closed, Likert-like questions involve calculating frequencies, means, and/or percentages (see the section on descriptive statistics [p. 69]). Student work (their writing drafts and illustrations, response logs, comparison charts, etc.) is approached by determining categories that are related to your inquiry questions. You might also think about the codes you used for other data sources and how they might be applied or adapted to your analysis of student work.

Once the various data sources have been categorized in some way, comparisons can be made. Are there similar themes or patterns across these data sources? Are there differences? What kinds of connections can you find between different sources? You also might start to note frequency counts or percentages (again, see the section on descriptive statistics). It is through this process of constantly comparing different data sources and your codes from different data sources that you begin to make sense of your data. You might also look more specifically at what does not fit into the categories or themes that you created. What is missing—what are called *outlier* instances—can sometimes be more beneficial in your interpretations than what you have determined. It is this triangulation of the analysis of a variety of data sources that enhances the validity and trustworthiness of your study. At any rate, it is at this stage that you develop descriptions and explanations of what your data mean. Often, this requires you to go back to your data, revisiting connections or relations between data sources. In addition, as you begin to generate claims about what you have found, you should review your data to identify good examples to illustrate these outcome statements.

USING DATA SUMMARIES FOR ONGOING ANALYSIS

As was indicated above, because teacher inquiry consists of ongoing cycles of action research, it is important to carry out ongoing analyses to know what your next steps might be. Thus, it is not a good idea to wait till the end of a study to start to analyze your data. Instead, it is critical that it be done in a periodic way (e.g., once a week). Data summaries provide a means to accomplish this continuing facet of research. Table 6.2 is an outline of what your data summaries might include (Altrichter, Posch, & Somekh, 1993; Pappas, Kiefer, & Levstik, 2006). And, you will note that the four questions on this form relate to the four activities of action research described in Chapter 1 (and elsewhere in the book): observing (Question 1 on Table 6.2,

Table 6.2 Data summary for ongoing analysis

Date: _____

1. What are the contexts (schools, classrooms, students, grade levels, classroom activities, etc.) in which the data were collected? What methods of data collection (and why?) were used?

2. What are the most important, surprising, and informative "facts" in the data?

3. In what ways do the data give rise to new questions, points of view, ideas, or suggestions?

4. In what ways do the data suggest your next steps, in terms of further data collection, analysis, or action?

(These data summaries can be limited to two single-spaced pages long.)

collecting data); interpreting (Questions 2 and 3, analyzing data), planning and acting out changes (Question 4).

There follow examples from the collaborating teacher researchers' data summaries. These teachers completed six summaries during the course of their inquiries—one each week. As we have already noted, these teachers' work was done during a course, so if your inquiry is not tied to a course and is conducted over a longer period (even an academic year), you are likely to generate many more of these data summaries. Also, data summaries provide opportunities to gain feedback from others—classmates and instructors if you are in a class, or colleagues at your school or if you are a member of teacher research group if you are not (see Appendix A, the general peer conferencing form).

Below we provide some examples from our collaborating teacher researchers' data summaries (DSs), including excerpts from each data summary question noted in Table 6.2, so that you get a sense of what these ongoing analyses can offer. Note that teachers conducted their inquiries during a spring semester course, so their studies began after January.

Question 1: Context and Information about Data Collection

Chris and Eli, the instructors of the course, gave feedback to the teachers on their data summaries. Because it would be very difficult to keep in mind the details of all of the teachers' inquiries, we asked that they include more contextual information than you might need to incorporate if you were sharing these with colleagues who would know the school, students, and other particulars of where you were conducting your study. Libby Tuerk's inquiry was about independent reading—see Excerpt 6.1.

Excerpt 6.1: Libby Tuerk's DS#1

The data for my inquiry project were collected in a seventh grade Reading class in a small suburban school west of Chicago. There are nineteen students in the class (5 Hispanic, 10 African-American, 2 Asian-Indian, 1 Filipino, and 1 Caucasian), and approximately 60% of them qualify for free or reduced lunch.

I observed and kept a journal of field notes during Independent Reading time, which is on Mondays and Fridays, for the first 20–25 minutes of the period. During my observations, I paid close attention to students' engagement in their reading. I also conducted a survey of student's attitudes toward Independent Reading on Thursday, February 9th. The survey asked four questions:

1 What do you like about Independent Reading?
2 What do you not like about Independent Reading?
3 What suggestions do you have for improving how Independent Reading works?
4 Approximately how much time do you spend reading your Independent Reading book outside of class?

My final source of data came from the student's Independent Reading Logs, which were collected on Friday, February 3rd and Friday, February 10th.

In her first DS, Libby told about her school and her students. She also described when independent reading occurred in her curriculum. Three kinds of data sources are noted: her fieldnotes, a survey, and students' logs. Thus, Libby provided helpful information about her inquiry and its methods that we could use in responding to the rest of her summary. In subsequent DSs, she told us that she abandoned students' logs (as both a teaching tool and research tool), but added student-generated rubrics instead, as well as taped small-group book talks as an additional source of data.

The next example, Excerpt 6.2, is from Cindy Pauletti's DS#5, whose inquiry focused on her students becoming "word detectives" as they attempted to identify unknown words. Her DS illustrates data collected from two reading activities.

Excerpt 6.2: Cindy Pauletti's DS#5

The next set of data was also collected at School X, a primary Chicago Public School where I am a first grade reading pullout teacher. It was collected in my small first grade reading group (8 students). The data I have collected this time include transcriptions from both a Star Reader activity and a paired reading activity, which I recorded. I also used my reflective field notes to aid me in this summary. It is still my goal to discover what strategies my students use to identify an unknown word in a text and to expand their use of strategies while they are reading a text and come to a word they cannot identify.

I chose to use our Star Reader activity to identify the strategies one child is using when they come to an unknown word and to see if the other children can identify the strategies the Star Reader is using while he/she is reading. I chose to use the excerpt from a paired reading activity to see what strategies the children are using without my guidance and to see if they are assisting their partner in the use of reading strategies to identify unknown words in the text.

During Star Reader a child reads a book to the class and me that they have chosen with my help and have practiced at home. All students have a turn and one child reads to us every day. Before the Star Reader reads to us I ask students to review the list of strategies we use to identify any unknown words in a text. We composed this list together on chart paper and hung it on the wall. Once all the strategies are fresh in their head, I ask them to try and notice if the Star Reader uses any of these strategies when he/she reads. I also ask the Star Reader to see if they can identify any strategies they use while reading . . .

I also collected data from a paired-reading session. This is when two students read the same new book together, each taking a turn to read a page. They read a book at, or slightly above, their reading level. I told them that I want to see them helping their reading buddy use reading strategies while they are reading, not just telling them a word they can't identify.

Like Libby, Cindy, who is a pull-out reading teacher, provided the context of the study (we used "School X" for her school to assure confidentiality), listed the ways in which she collected data, and explained two major activities—Star Reader and paired reading—she engages her students in (and collected data on).

In sum, Question 1 of the data summary consists of providing important contextual information and indicates the data source that is analyzed and discussed in other parts of the summary.

Question 2: Data Details

The second question asks for some details about what has been found in the analysis that is interesting, surprising, and so forth, and as a result is usually the longest section of a data summary. Excerpt 6.3 is from Meg Goethals's DS#5. Meg is a former teacher who took off for a couple of years to get her Master's. Because she was not presently teaching, she collaborated with her roommate, who was an eighth-grade teacher (at an inner-city school with a predominantly African American population). Both Meg and her roommate, Sally, had heard about Reading Workshop and were interested in implementing it in Sally's classroom. Several kinds of data collection sources were used in the study, but this particular DS covered journal responses (which began with prompts, but are now open-ended) and book talks. Excerpt 6.3 includes some of what Meg wrote on the journal entries.

Excerpt 6.3: Meg Goethals's DS#5

Their journals are ways in which I can hear about their reading every day since we don't have time to conference with every student each day. They write things they wonder about, connections they make, or things they wonder about. Here are some examples of their responses. One student, who my roommate has said hates school and doesn't try hard, wrote about *I Am the Cheese*, by Robert Cormier, "The boy in the story is traveling by bike (which I think is crazy!). I just read chapters three, four, and five, and I found out that his father is in a hospital. I don't know what for but I'll find the reason . . . This book is really interesting which is what really makes me want to continue to read." Another student finished *Speak* by Laurie Halse Anderson and summarized the story in her journal. At the end of her entry she wrote, "By the way I love this book." Another student I noticed reading *Monster* when we first started Reading Workshop, but didn't read the whole time and in her journal wrote that she had already read it and didn't really like it. She tried another book, but gave up on that one too. I gave her *The First Part Last* by Angela Johnson and in the journal I asked her if she liked it. She responded, "Yes, I do like my book. It's really good. It can and do give good information on teen pregnancy. It influenced me not to have a baby at a young age." My roommate also says she asks to read her book during free time. Another boy, who my roommate says she has trouble with often in not doing his work, wrote about his book *Forged by Fire* in his journal, "This book relates to me because it was a time I had not seen my dad for a long time then he just popped up like Gerald's mom." Another girl who my roommate says hates school writes often in her journal and at least half a page each time. She wrote in her journal about a character in *The Phantom Toll Booth*, Milo, who she said she connected to because "Milo waste time by watching television. I connected to this because I waste a lot of time by watching t.v. and sleeping." So I asked her if this helps her understand the story better and she replied, "My connection to Milo does help me understand the story better because I know some of the reasons why he waste so much time. He feels like there is nothing worth using time, but wasting it." Another student I noticed in the beginning not reading the entire time and instead, stopping to draw. He participates in minilessons and is very insightful when we have discussions however. This week I noticed him reading the entire time, even after my roommate said it was time to stop. This is what he wrote in his journal this week. "I can't even guess what will happen because there is so many people that could have done it . . . The book is getting even better. I can't wait to find out what happens at the end, but they are only giving little pieces at a time which makes it impossible to figure out what will happen." . . .

More was said about journal entries, but Excerpt 6.3 shows the flavor of Meg's journal data. She incorporated actual quotations from the journals, noted what they had written when she had asked questions about an earlier entry, and provided information from her colleague about the students, some of whom at the beginning of the inquiry hated to read and didn't read. She also sometimes referred to how these readers participated in other activities during Reading Workshop, for example during mini-lessons. Thus, in her analysis she is already making connections among her multiple data sources.

Shannon Dozoryst's DS#5 is another example of data details. Shannon's inquiry was on the influence of peer conferencing on students' revisions in a high school creative writing class. She had developed a peer conferencing form (similar to the one in Appendix A), and in the summary given as Excerpt 6.4 she describes what she found out regarding the relationship between what some of the students wrote about what they plan to do as a result of their peer conference and their revised draft.

Excerpt 6.4: Shannon Dozoryst's DS#5

Student #1 wrote, "I plan to work on the expression when I read and make my characters come to life and elaborate more on the actions." I noticed that she did add a considerable amount of dialogue to her revision which did help to make the characters come to life. On the conferencing sheet, one of her peer reviewers suggested that she should "make the dialogue more clear." I think that this reviewer meant that the writer should use quotation marks and structure the dialogue in paragraphs correctly, because it was mixed into the rest of the story's prose. However, I did not see that the writer changed this in the revision. Maybe she was unclear about what the reviewer was telling her to do, or maybe she does not understand how to structure dialogue.

Student #2 wrote, ". . . the resolution of my story, to extend it to make more sense— elaborate with detail on the whole story, expand it—give the story more background and more meaning so that the story doesn't become confusing." I did see a dramatic difference in the amount of detail used in the revision in comparison to the original. In the original version, she wrote that her main character was "raised by her grandmother when an unfortunate accident led to the death of both of her parents." In the revised version, she wrote, "As a child, Nia went through some difficult times. One night, at the age of 9, she was at home alone sleeping while her parents were out on their occasional dates to spice up their marriage. It had been a bad storm and the weather was just getting worse. On their way home, Nia's parents went over a pothole and skidded into a nearby lake where they drowned. Their bodies were found the next morning. Nia then had to go through three years of a custody battle between her maternal and paternal grandparents, who lived on either sides of the country. She ended up going to live with her favorite grandmother by the name of Nana Jane." As you can see, the student truly worked on incorporating more detail in her revision . . .

You can see from the above that this second question has to do with the details of analysis— examples that reflect how students are responding in the their journals (Meg's DS) and how students in a writing course are taking up (or not) peer feedback, and, more specifically, how they follow up their own plans noted on the peer conferencing form in their revisions (Shannon's DS). These teacher researchers are beginning to make some inferences and claims about their data, and, more importantly, they are offering details and examples to support them.

Question 3: What Do the Data Mean?

The third question of the data summary gets at what the data mean—what do the data suggest regarding new questions or points of view? In her DS3, Libby Tuerk, whose inquiry was on independent reading (see Excerpt 6.1), had analyzed data on her students' use of student-generated rubrics for book talks. In Excerpt 6.5 of this summary, she reflects on what those data described under Question 2 (not included here) meant.

Excerpt 6.5: Libby Tuerk's DS#3

As I watched my student using the rubric they created and thought about some of the ideas presented in Wilhelm's book, *You Gotta Be the Book*, my students set up a rubric that does not measure engagement in reading. Much of the rubric is more like a test of students' memory—how many details they can recall. This made me question if my students are focusing on these aspects because this is what I focus on. On days when we are not doing independent reading, I realize I focus a lot on comprehension and a more efferent reading of text, especially now that we are preparing for ISATs [Illinois Standards Achievement Tests]. Are my students carrying this over to their independent reading instead of recognizing the experience in reading a book for enjoyment? What can I do to change this? Obviously, I don't want my students to lose track of comprehension—you need to understand a book to enjoy it—but I need to look at how we can do both.

As she examined her data regarding students' use of rubrics, Libby begins to worry that the nature of these rubrics and the emphasis on recall information from books, as a part of preparing students for standardized tests, might conflict with students' enjoyment of books, which is what she was attempting to foster in her inquiry. As she notes in Excerpt 6.5, she wants both, so she decides (as stated in her Question 4 on plans of action [not included here]) to broaden book talks to include ideas from the Wilhelm book that she mentioned above to resolve this dilemma; she plans to have students bring props or cutouts that represent characters or something to represent themselves as readers. Note also that Libby used her readings into theory and practice to inform her analysis as well. The term "efferent" comes from Louise Rosenblatt's (1978) transactional theory of literature.

Cindy Pauletti's DS#5 also illustrates decisions made based on the data, in case details she noted while students used word identification strategies during the Star Reader activity and pair reading—see the description of this routine in Excerpt 6.2. In Excerpt 6.6, which is from the same DS, she poses new questions for herself about these two activities.

Excerpt 6.6: Cindy Pauletti's DS#5

Some more new questions and ideas arose from all this data. I wonder if I should have the Star Reader read a book that they didn't practice to see if the students and reader could use strategies to identify any unknown words. This way, he/she will be reading it for the first time and may use more strategies than if he/she practiced the book at home. I am excited to see what strategies they will use when I give them the next modified miscue. Also, for the next paired reading I think I need to pair Delia with Juan or Sonia so that she does not get discouraged by reading with Maria every time. I also think it is a good idea to switch the other partners too. In this way students can be exposed to the strategies other children are using too.

So, here Cindy thinks about seeing how children would fare in using strategies if they are reading a book they hadn't read before in the Star Reader activity and she considers a different reading buddy for Delia in the pair-reading one.

Question 4: Plans for Action

The last question on the data summary consists of teacher researchers' plans of action based on their analysis of data. The first example is from Dawn Siska's DS4. Dawn's inquiry focused on literature circles (or book clubs) for high school freshmen. It was a large class, which she team-taught with a math teacher and a physical education teacher. This particular summary dealt with how students employed what she called a "trifold" sheet that she created. The trifold consisted of three sections: discussion questions (e.g., "What do you notice?", "What do you wonder?", "What do you think?", and so forth, which they completed ahead of time); a peer evaluation; and a self-evaluation that asked students to reflect on their own participation in discussion. She collected data on two groups for this summary and her analysis indicated that one group had a lively discussion, whereas the other group only talked when she was nearby. Excerpt 6.7 covers her next steps, based on this analysis.

Excerpt 6.7: Dawn Siska's DS#4

I need to figure out how to get the students more involved in their discussion groups! I knew at the get go that I would have a difficult time getting them started and into the process but I never thought that some of the groups would be so unresponsive. I'm concerned about the majority of the students' lack of interest in everything. And I thought self-selected reading was supposed to increase student motivation. I'm going to have students generate their own group questions for discussion for the next literature circle meeting and don't want to have to resort to giving them the literature circle roles just for the sake of giving them worksheet questions to respond to.

Before Dawn began her inquiry, all of the students read the same book and answered study questions or recorded responses in a reader response log. Most students were interested in reading, so Dawn's hope that literature circles, where students get to choose their books, would motivate their reading and discussions. She tried different approaches, including the trifold described above. Because she still has groups not participating in discussions, she now plans to have students generate their own questions.

As indicated in Chapter 4 (see Excerpt 4.1), Sandra Zanghi's inquiry question focused on how small-group discussions during read-alouds might affect the participation in read-alouds. Her DS#5 covered her analysis of one of her data-collection sources: students' written responses. Thus, the last question of her summary listed what she planned to do the next week—Excerpt 6.8.

Excerpt 6.8: Sandra Zanghi's DS#5

I need to work on the following for next week:

- Talk to students about their written responses. Discuss how I don't want them to write a list of what they talk about, but write their own thoughts, opinions, and connections to the literature. I should give an example of a good response.
- I need to collect their journals after they write in them. A lot of students were writing their responses in random notebooks and I only got the written response the day I collected.
- I need to keep the video camera on one group during the whole discussion time. That way I can see how the discussion helps their written responses.
- I am interested in focusing more on students who have difficulty responding to literature. I think small group discussions on read-aloud books will help them the most.
- Give them more time to write.

Sandra's plans of action covered several areas based on her analysis of one set of their written responses. Her steps included both pedagogical and methodological ones, namely, showing students what a good response looks like and giving more time to write, as well as focusing on certain students in data collection, making sure she could always find their written responses in the same place, and positioning her video camera for a whole discussion.

Summary on Data Summaries

Ongoing data summaries are critical in teacher research. They provide an important tool for documenting the recurring cycles of action research. Novice teacher researchers are sometimes challenged in completing them, especially in answering the second and third questions, where they have to articulate their interpretations based on their analysis *and* provide examples or evidence for these claims. Obtaining feedback from others helps in the same way that getting others' ideas did when you learned to write fieldnotes. These summaries do not have to be long (most can be single-spaced, two pages long or less), and the time you spend in creating them is worth it, for they aid your next steps and enable you to accomplish the data analysis process more gradually, spreading the work, and the thinking, out.

USING DESCRIPTIVE STATISTICS: THE POSSIBILITIES FOR "COUNTING" PATTERNS

Quantitative research relies a lot on counting cases covered by dependent variables, often using various statistical procedures (ANOVAs, regression analysis, etc., which are called inferential statistics) to determine the "truth" of researchers' hypotheses. However, as seen above, qualitative researchers attempt to define classroom events holistically, focusing on identifying emerging patterns and themes, and the above statistical methods are not appropriate for their data. However, *descriptive statistics*, a method of "counting" of codes, for example, may be useful to employ in teacher inquiries. As the term suggests, descriptive statistics *describes* an existing set of data; they are values that represent overall characteristics of such a set. If used, the report of such counting is only a small part of the detailed account of how certain behaviors happened and how they were related to other behaviors within the setting. The following are some of the most common types of descriptive statistics[2] that can be utilized in teacher research:

- **Frequencies/range/percentages**. These tell how many codes, themes, patterns occur. *Frequencies* can be used to report the number of survey responses, or how many children used intertextual responses (referring to other texts) while discussing literature, or how many books children read during independent reading during a term, and so forth. Sometimes a *range*, which is simply the highest and lowest number of a particular action (that is, offering a certain survey or literature response, or reading books ["individual students read anywhere from 4 to 14 books over the course of the quarter"]), is included. *Percentages* can also be calculated, rather than just the number of behavior. For example, instead of just telling how many times students responded to particular survey response, such as "What do you like about independent reading?", you explain that 10 students out of 20, or 50 percent, did so.
- **Modes/medians/means**. Modes, medians, and means are considered to be measures of central tendency. The *mode* is simply a measure of the behavior, event, or response that occurred most frequently. The *median* is the middle score of a set of scores. For example, perhaps a teacher researcher might be interested in the genres that his or her students read out of class. Students might respond with a list of different types (e.g., realistic fiction, fantasy, historical fiction, biography, science non-fiction). As the teacher researcher calculates the total number (frequencies) for each genre all students checked, the number in the middle, with exactly half the genres occurring with more frequency and half with less, would be the median. The *mean*, which is the most common measure of central tendency, is the average of each genre.

These descriptive statistics can be reported in the body of the text in teacher researcher reports or articles. They may also be displayed in tables or in different graphs, for example in line or bar graphs, pie charts, and so forth. See note 2 for more references on such displays.

SUMMARY

Analysis involves identifying codes, themes, and patterns in your data. Because in teacher research, findings *emerge* from analysis, a qualitative, constant comparison approach is employed. And, since teacher research consists of recurring cycles of action research, your analysis cannot be left for the end of your inquiry, but must be done in an ongoing way. As a result, creating data summaries—which provide information about context and data collection sources, details about the data analysis, your interpretations or viewpoints based on your analysis, and, finally, ideas on new plans of actions that are warranted on such analysis—are a critically important aspect of inquiry. Depending on the kinds of data you have, you can also consider using descriptive statistics to make sense of codes or responses.

NOTES

1   There are also qualitative data analysis software programs that can be used for coding: ATLAS-ti (www.atlasti.com) and Nud*ist (www.scolari.com). Microsoft Excel spreadsheets can also be a tool for analysis, providing counts of categories.
2   More details and examples of descriptive statistics can be found in the following books on action research: *A Short Guide to Action Research* (Johnson, 2008); *Teacher as Reflective Practitioner and Action Researcher* (Parsons & Brown, 2002); and *Action Research for Educators* (Tomal, 2003).

REFERENCES

Altrichter, H., Posch, O., & Somekh, B. (1993). *Teachers investigate their work: An introduction to the methods of action research*. London: Routledge.

Bogdan, R. C., & Biklen, S. K. (1998). *Qualitative research in education: An introduction to theory and methods*. Boston: Allyn & Bacon.

Burns, A. (1999). *Collaborative action research for English language teachers*. Cambridge: Cambridge University Press.

Glaser, B., & Strauss, A. (1967). *Discovery of ground theory: Strategies for qualitative research*. Chicago: Aldine Publishing.

Johnson, A. P. (2008). *A short guide to action research*. Boston: Pearson Education.

Pappas, C. C., Kiefer, B. Z., & Levstik, L. S. (2006). *An integrated language perspective in the elementary school: An action approach*. Boston: Pearson Education.

Parsons, R. D., & Brown, K. S. (2002). *Teacher as reflective practitioner and action researcher*. Belmont, CA: Wadsworth/Thomson Learning.

Rex, L. A., & Schiller, L. (2009). *Using discourse analysis to improve classroom interaction*. New York: Routledge.

Rosenblatt, L. (1978). *The reader, the text, the poem*. Carbondale, IL: Southern Illinois University Press.

Schatzman, L., & Strauss, A. (1973). *Field research*. Englewood Cliffs, NJ: Prentice-Hall.

Tomal, D. R. (2003). *Action research for educators*. Lanham, MD: Scarecrow Press.

Chapter 7

Writing Up Your Inquiry as an Evocative Account

- How do I write up my inquiry as an evocative, publishable account?
- How can I use beginning leads to launch my inquiry paper?
- How should I report my findings?
- How do I put it all together to write up my inquiry for a wider audience?

THE CHALLENGE OF WRITING UP YOUR INQUIRY

Once all of your analyses have been completed, you are confronted with the decision of how and with whom to share your inquiry. Written reports, in the form of publishable articles or chapters, or orally shared conference presentations, come from the products of data analyses. We noted earlier in the book that not every research study needs to be written up. However, we do think that the expertise and experiences of teacher researchers can contribute greatly to a range of audiences. That is, written reports can be a means to document the problems and dilemmas that teacher researchers as individuals have addressed and solved, which may also contribute to the understandings of the culture and practices of their school and/or district. But their reports may also offer relevant information for the educational community at large. Thus, learning how to compose texts that can be published and/or presented to a wider audience is important.

Yet, it is a challenge to write for a wider audience about the personal, contextual knowledge that characterizes teacher research. Action research itself is seen as *writerly text* (Sumara & Luce-Kapler, 1993): "[I]t expects research to be like our reading of [a novel]: unpredictable, often uncomfortable, challenging, yet infused with the possibility of what the next page will bring" (p. 394). Thus, readers of teacher research are not looking for a definitive or objective account, but instead are expecting an *evocative text*—one that offers interpretations and understandings of the messiness of people's lived experience (Denzin, 1997; Stringer, 2004). In articulating the story of their inquiry, teacher researchers attempt to communicate insights into classroom events and activities.

The purpose of this chapter is to help you write a "publishable" text for a wider audience. Our collaborating teacher researchers wrote their reports as part of a spring semester course. Thus, they had a limited time period to carry out their inquiry and write up their findings. Many of them continued their inquiries to the end of the academic year, but for their final report they wrote up what they had completed up to a particular point. Thus, their papers—included in Part Three of this book—must be seen from this perspective.

Also, the goal of their efforts was to write manuscripts for a practitioner journal (e.g., *Language Arts*, *The Reading Teacher*, or *Journal of Adult and Adolescent Literacy*). In the class, we explored articles from these journals, examining the format employed by the authors.[1] In the following section, we offer some overall tips for writing publishable texts for such an audience. Our collaborating teacher researchers tried out, or drafted, two parts of their inquiry report before writing a final draft: (1) an introduction or beginning of their inquiry report; and (2) one finding, or important result, from their research. The initial part of their paper represented a possible "lead," a way to begin the journey of going public. Novice teacher researchers find writing up their findings challenging, so having a go at writing up one finding and getting feedback on it is an invaluable experience. Subsequent sections of this chapter include examples from these collaborating teachers' beginnings and findings.

OVERALL TIPS FOR "PUBLISHING" TEACHER INQUIRY

There is no right or wrong way to communicate your inquiry, but there are some useful ways of reporting and representing your study. Here are some possible tips or ideas to keep in mind (Macintyre, 2000; Pappas, Kiefer, & Levstik, 2006):

- Be sure to explain the context of your inquiry: who the participants are, what was done, and why. This contextualization enables others to relate your account to their own situations or experiences.
- Be sure to use "code" or fictitious names for participants and the school. This helps keep the participants' identities confidential. (See Chapter 3 on these issues.)
- Use the first person (e.g., "My major inquiry question was to . . ." or "I chose to do . . ." or "I found that . . ."). This preserves your own voice in your text; it also makes it reader-friendly, inviting others to explore *with* you the classroom events you discuss.
- Try not to include a lot of educational jargon, terms that most educated laypersons wouldn't understand. You do want to "educate" others in your text, but you don't use words or phrases just because they may sound good. When you do include important terms or concepts, be sure to explain them.
- Use the past tense throughout when you articulate your reflections and describe classroom actions and events (except perhaps in the last section of your paper, where you might talk about future plans and explorations based on your current study).
- Tell about your own theory-in-action or interpretive framework and how it might have developed or changed over the course of your study, as well as your stance or values regarding your inquiry and your interpretations and conclusions.
- When relevant, weave in the ideas of other work you might have read that you think is related to your inquiry topic, but be sure to explicate these ideas through *your voice*. You

may rely on your preliminary literature review as you include such work, but watch out that this earlier text doesn't keep you from re-visioning your perspective. In addition, depending on what happened in your inquiry, you may seek other work to include.

- Don't feel that you have to report on every single data "fact" of your inquiry. Choose the major themes or patterns as they relate to your inquiry questions. These themes can be used to organize your written report by serving as major headings (or subheadings).
- Give examples and illustrations to support your findings. Also, in presenting your examples, be sure to help readers understand your interpretation of them or *why* you think they are significant as evidence of the themes or patterns you found. Sometimes teacher researchers think that examples can "stand on their own." However, you need to explain in the body of your report just *how* certain aspects of the examples are illustrative of your claims or points.
- Try to be accurate and honest in telling about the difficulties and vulnerabilities that arose for you in your inquiry. Include any findings that didn't seem to fit. Sometimes teacher researcher's inquiry reports sound so rosy that others reading them either do not find the account credible, so do not try out the ideas and benefit from them, or, if they do attempt them and end up with unsatisfactory results, they blame themselves—or worse, their students.
- Include implications for practice. Share new insights and/or pedagogical approaches to be enacted that are based on what you found in your study.
- Because teacher inquiry is an ongoing enterprise, mention new questions or ideas that you plan to pursue in future inquiries, and say why.

CREATE A BEGINNING LEAD TO YOUR INQUIRY REPORT

Writing up your inquiry is easier said than done. Why is writing so difficult? Teacher researchers often have writer's block, for several reasons. They are often afraid that they might not have anything worthwhile to say. However, if you think back to when you were beginning your inquiry, wouldn't you have been thrilled to find an article on the topic that you studied? So, it is quite likely that others would be interested in what you have to say as well.

Another reason writing is difficult is that teachers are likely to be out of practice. That is, teachers don't write at any length in the course of their everyday professional work, so they feel vulnerable about writing in general. So, see writing up your inquiry as the beginning of that practice, and remember that it will become easier *with* practice.

Finally, teachers often don't know how to go about writing up their inquiries; they may have read mostly traditional research reports and can't imagine how to shape a paper with a different format. We hope that this chapter (and book) helps you in this respect.

It is best to just admit that writing is difficult; even expert, professional writers think it is so. You just have to take the plunge! Don't worry ahead of time that you need to create a perfect, finished document. Face that blank page by taking the first step of your paper—creating a beginning.

The collaborating teachers approached their beginnings in different ways. Several began by discussing a tension in their teaching. This was the case for Libby Tuerk, who explored independent reading in her class—see Excerpt 7.1. (Note that because these were drafts, teachers were mostly concerned with getting content down, and not particularly grammar or such, although their feedback partners [using the Appendix A general peer conferencing form] often offered it. The examples below are as they wrote them.)

Excerpt 7.1: Libby Tuerk's Beginning

Let's Read: Motivating Junior High Students to Become Life-long Readers

Introduction

Over the past four years, I have come to recognize independent reading—time when students can read texts of their own choice and at their own reading level—as an important and valuable component of my junior high reading curriculum. I view independent reading not only as a time for students to practice and improve their reading skills, but also as an opportunity for them to develop a lifelong love of reading, to see as I do the pleasure that can come from experiencing the world through books. However, in reality, it remained a constant struggle to engage my often reluctant students in their reading. On independent reading days, I was repeatedly faced with students who had left their books at home, others whose eyes drifted off the page and stared into space, still others who tore through pages of book after book at lightning speed yet could not recall *anything* about the books, and the groups of students who viewed independent reading time as nothing more than nap time or social hour. As I was not willing to give up independent reading altogether, I decided to conduct my inquiry around the question of how to engage these reluctant readers.

> Theoretical Foundation
> Choosing Books
> Coming to Class Prepared
> No More Reading Logs
> Measuring Engagement: Enthusiasm during Book Talks
> Measuring Engagement: Dialogue with the Book
> Conclusion

So, Libby's beginning was short (not even a full page) but it is enough to let the reader know why she chose her topic of study. She sets up her paper by letting readers know that she values independent reading, but that the time that she set aside for it in her class wasn't working (and for a long time: four years). Because we also encouraged the teachers to come up with headings for the sections of the rest of their papers, Libby included those. (Many teachers didn't always end up using these initial headings to organize their papers, but it helped them to think about their formats ahead of time and get feedback on them from their peers.)

Shannon Dozoryst also started her beginning by referring to her dilemmas in developing and teaching a creative writing class for eleventh- and twelfth-graders, and relating them to the creative writing classes she had when she was in high school and at college—see Excerpt 7.2. Shannon's beginning text was much longer than Libby's, so only parts of it are included here.

Excerpt 7.2: Shannon Dozoryst's Beginning

Introduction: Starting from Scratch

In the summer of 2005 I was faced with the somewhat daunting task of developing a Creative Writing curriculum from scratch. After lobbying for four years to have this course included in the English curriculum at our school, my wish had been granted. I was both excited and overwhelmed at the same time.

Over the course of my summer vacation I thought a lot about what I wanted the students who took this class to achieve. I thought back to the Creative Writing class that I took in high school. Although we produced a huge quantity of writing and were given the opportunity to try our hands at a variety of types of writing, we rarely shared our work with others in the class and there was no revision of our work to speak of. My experiences in college-level Creative Writing classes were much more positive . . . Although each of the class members received a lot of useful feedback, it was difficult, even as a college student, to learn to give and receive constructive criticism. I knew I wanted to create a class environment that would include a combination of writing instruction and peer writing workshop. My goals were to get my students to write about a variety of topics, experiment with form, learn to give and receive constructive criticism, and learn to use peers' feedback to revise written work . . .

[Shannon describes her students and the initial experiences in her new Creative Writing course.]

Towards the end of first semester, I began to introduce students to the revision process. I asked students to review comments their peers had made about their writing and use the useful comments to guide their revisions. I found that my students needed more structure than I was providing them. I noticed that many of my students were not providing the level of criticism that I felt would be beneficial to their peers. Most of the feedback they provided was superficial, and they rarely provided suggestions for improvement. I also discovered that although they were happy to provide their peers with feedback, they were reluctant to use this criticism to make concrete changes to their work.

My inquiry questions for this study emerged as a result of this. How could I encourage my students to write more critical comments when evaluating each others' writing in the workshop setting, and in what ways was workshop helping or not helping my students revise their own work?

In a similar way to Libby's beginning, Shannon addressed the difficulties she was facing in her new class and, more specifically, how peers' feedback might influence their revisions. She used this initial discussion as the impetus for her inquiry questions for her study. Shannon also included some possible headings for other sections of her paper (for example, "Assessing What Is Working and What Is Not," "A New Strategy for Criticism," "Self-Reflection," "Is It Working?" and so forth). She also added a subtitle to her Introduction: "Starting from Scratch." We encouraged teachers to come up with interesting heading titles (we called them "sexy" ones), and Shannon tried out one in her beginning.

Sandra Zanghi began by recalling what participation was like for her when she was a student. Excerpt 7.3 includes her first short personal "remembering," and then the first paragraph of her beginning.

Excerpt 7.3: Sandra Zanghi's Beginning

Will the teacher like my answer? Will people think my thoughts are pointless? Will everyone think I am stupid? Darn it! Someone just said what I was about to say! Why can't I just sit in the back of the room and just listen?

I can remember the guts it took for me to raise my hand and speak in the front of the entire class in elementary school. Questions and thoughts would race through my head every time before I would make that brave move to participate. Math was not as severe because I could calculate and see the answers blunt and clear before me. However, in reading class, there was no formula for making inferences and connections! How would I know I was right? As an adult, I gained the confidence to work past these fears. I also understand that there is value in how everyone responds to literature. Now, as a teacher, I find the need to pass on this understanding to my students.

Sandra started her beginning in a similar way to Shannon by referring to prior experience as a student. However, she did it differently by first giving some of the "thinking aloud" that she must have done when she was a student. Her following first paragraph extended this idea and set the stage for her helping students regarding participation. Sandra continued her beginning text (not included here) by talking about how only a few of her students offered their response during read-alouds, wondering if the others "have the same fears as I did as a child," after which she posed her inquiry topic: "I studied how small-group discussions during read-alouds affect participation."

So far, the examples that have been provided have not included any citing of published work. Not citing such work is certainly OK, but another way to start your paper is to include references early on. Tara Braverman tried to do that: she began with a short paragraph that included a classroom vignette where a student comes up to her asking her, "What does this word mean?" She then offered a section she called "The plan," where she incorporated connections to other work on the topic—see Excerpt 7.4.

Excerpt 7.4: Tara Braverman's Beginning

What's This Word? Helping Students Use Reading and Vocabulary Strategies Independently

[Tara includes a classroom vignette and then mentions briefly the nature of her inquiry focus.]

The Plan

[With all of the reading strategies we have discussed and used during the year,] I needed a way for students to make these strategies tangible during their independent reading time. I decided to use "coding," a system of making marks and abbreviations on sticky notes during reading (Harvey & Goudis, 2000). This way, students could quickly record a prediction, exciting moment, connection, or confusing words or phrase and continue reading.

To help students build deeper meanings with new words, I decided to utilize the semantic map (Bromley, Irwin-De Vitis, & Modlo, 1995). Students are inundated with graphic organizers in every subject area, but I had never thought to use anything other than a horizontal chart to help record new words. With a semantic map, students were able to record more than just the definition, namely, connections they made, other forms of the word, original sentences with the word, how it added to the story, and anything else they found relevant (Blachowitcz & Obrachta, 2005). Instead of memorizing a list of teacher-selected vocabulary words, students would have the freedom to learn words they chose during their own reading. I hoped this choice would make their vocabulary development more authentic and therefore more meaningful (Harmon, Hedrick, Wood, & Gress, 2005). I wanted students to become self-motivated "Language Detectives" (Monohan, 2003), so that instead of memorization, students investigated how certain authors used words differently to create a style of writing that appeals to certain readers.

Thus, after a short initial paragraph Tara discussed what she planned to do in her inquiry, citing the work that informed these pedagogical moves.

Nicole Perez, a literacy coach, also apparently planned to incorporate citations of others' work in the onset of her paper, but at the beginning she shared that she just noted the fact, seemingly to remind herself when she returned to writing her paper. In Excerpt 7.5, she includes introductory statements to introduce the need for literacy coaches and how long she had been one, and then poses a series of questions regarding her role as a literary coach.

Excerpt 7.5: Nicole Perez's Beginning

Teachers are some of the most challenging people to work with. We work in an environment that is unique and no one knows what it's like to be a teacher unless you are one. Today public schools are under pressure to achieve high test scores. Many schools have hired literacy coaches to help teachers with their instruction. I am one of those people. I have been a literacy coach for almost two years and at the beginning of the school I asked myself several questions: What makes an effective literacy coach? How can teachers warm to the idea of having someone analyze and discuss their instruction? What do I know that others don't know? I then thought about the role of a coach and how he/she could help teachers improve their instruction. Is the model of planning, observing, follow up, and implementation beneficial to instructional improvement? Would teachers begin to trust me if they saw me as a peer rather than as an authority? **(insert ideas from lit review).**

    Cathy Toll (2005) wrote a lot about coaching

So, this was the first part of her beginning, and although she did not include citations, she noted that she anticipated to incorporate them, relying on what she had composed in her preliminary literature review (see Chapter 4 on examples of literature reviews). She also refers to a person who also has written about coaching, which she seemed to think would be important to include in this early section of the paper.

Nicole's beginning consisted of several pages, launching into sections of findings, which other teachers also did. That is, once teacher researchers find a way to begin, they seem to be spurred on to write more sections of their papers. Because writing up findings in their papers is also a challenge for teacher researchers, we also asked the collaborating teachers to try out "one finding" before they moved into writing a full draft of the paper. The next section covers examples of these findings.

REPORTING YOUR FINDINGS

Teacher researcher reports need to have lots of description to invite the reader in to the study, but as the researcher, you also need to go beyond mere description. You need to tell the reader what it all means. So what if you or your students did or said such and such? What do the details mean? What do you *know* based on your analysis?

What you know are *findings*. Teacher researchers "often describe their learning as finding or discovering something [but] . . . there is also a sense in which what you find is already there and what you are really doing is interpreting what exists" (MacLean & Mohr, 1999, p. 69). Sometimes teacher researchers call research findings "conclusions." But no matter what label is used, findings are statements—claims—you can make about your teaching or student learning *because of* your analysis. That is, it is the analysis that led you to these statements of what you know.

But what findings should you include in your inquiry paper? Start by thinking about some major ones; you won't be able to incorporate everything you found out. Consider the following three steps to identify each of the findings you might include (Hubbard & Power, 2003):

1 Think about something you are certain of.
2 Think about what data led to or support this conclusion.
3 Think about other data that might be offered *against* this conclusion.

78

This approach is considered a "critical" method toward your findings, because in step 3 you "test" your data or finding (Altrichter, Posch, & Somekh, 1993). Another way to see findings is to view them as the major themes or patterns that you identified (across all of your data sources) in your analysis.

We have acknowledged that launching or starting your inquiry paper was likely to be hard. Most teacher researchers see writing up findings as even more of a challenge. However, findings are the backbone of your report, and as such they take up the most space in your paper, so you want to face the task with confidence. But which ones should you include? We suggest that you visualize a conversation you might have with a colleague who didn't know about your study. What major findings or themes would you share, and how would you structure your paper to explain them?

Because crafting findings is so difficult, we asked our collaborating teachers to try writing up "one finding" so that they could bring up issues about their efforts and gain feedback on them before they began full drafts of their papers. Below are some examples—and as a reminder, note these are drafts where teachers attempted mostly to put down ideas (which we have not edited).

Excerpt 7.6 is from Shannon Dozoryst's one finding about an interview with a focus group (see Chapter 5) toward the end of her inquiry to see what they thought of the writing workshop she implemented in her Creative Writing class.

Excerpt 7.6: Shannon Dozoryst's One Finding

Is Writing Workshop Worth It? Students' Perspective

Following my inquiry, I decided to interview several students to find out what their perspectives on the writing workshop sessions were. I asked four students, all from different workshop groups to voluntarily participate. I conducted the interview more like a discussion. The students remained after class and sat down alone with me to answer my questions. My objective of this interview was to try to find out their general impressions of writing workshop, whether or not they felt their peers' suggestions helped them with revising with writing. To begin my interview, I asked these students if they thought the writing workshop was worthwhile.

Sally: Yes, it helped me to do my papers better. I learned, like, how to use certain techniques and what not to do.

Anne: At first yes, but then people kept doing the same thing. Like, they were writing the same comments and so it wasn't as useful.

George: No, not everyone in my group was prepared. I didn't always get quality responses.

Keisha: The same [as George]. They did it as an assignment. You know, just for a grade, just because they had to. I don't feel that I got quality feedback from them most of the time.

After talking to these students, I felt that perhaps I had made a mistake by not making them change groups at the beginning of the study. It seemed obvious after talking to George that the members in his group were not treating the workshop sessions seriously and that they might have benefited from being moved to other groups. Keisha also confirmed George's responses about group members' lack of participation and inability to provide quality feedback. I do wonder whether or not changing group dynamics would have helped shake some of these students out of the routine that they had seemingly developed with each other. After receiving this negative feedback, I was curious to hear the positive things they had to say about workshop. The next question I asked was what they liked about writing workshop . . .

The above excerpt was only the first part Shannon wrote up on the interview from a focus group (focus group interviews are discussed in Chapter 5), but you can get a sense of what this finding was about. She provided a catchy heading for this section and nicely formatted the interview responses. "Following my inquiry" is probably not the right wording to use at the beginning of her text as this interview was *part of* her inquiry. However, the important point to make note of is that she offered interpretations about her interview data and suggested implications based on her conclusions. In findings you are telling and showing.

Catherine Plocher, a literacy coach at a K-8 urban elementary school, turned in several pages for her one finding. Excerpt 7.7 is the beginning of this document and then a part she wrote under "Check list/brainstorm."

Excerpt 7.7: Catherine Plocher's One Finding

One finding in my research is that literacy coaches need to coach teachers by helping them achieve *their* goals of increased student learning. Instead of seeing themselves as the "literacy expert," they need to be a colleague, sounding board, friend, and a resource for teachers in their school. Literacy coaches must not see their job as one in which they tell teachers the "right way" to do things. Instead, they need to realize the challenges their teachers face and find ways to support them as they figure out how best to meet the needs of their students. The following examples, grouped categorically, illustrate how literacy coaches can acquire coaching areas of focus with their teachers. I have been learning to "provide" teachers with ideas in more comfortable situations for them, and different teachers address what they would like to try with me . . .

Check List/Brainstorm:

I ask them what are their frustrations and how can I support them. Lately I have been asking them to write down their frustrations and ranking them based on level of frustration. This is because many pre coaching conferences initially started out with "I want to fix everything now" and needed to prioritize. For example, Mary wants to work on reader's workshop, writer's workshop and word study at the same time. She recently went to a workshop that had clips of these models, and she came back wanting to drop everything she was doing and implement them all at the same time. After organizing and prioritizing what SHE feels is most important TO HER, we decided to start on reader's workshop (and we eventually broke that down into first: working with her on interactive read-alouds and fine-tuning minilessons, then effective independent reading and learning how to do running records, then move onto differentiated instruction/guided reading). Then add on word study after she gets that rolling, and maybe next year begin with writer's workshop. I reminded her that she is still teaching everything, just learning one at a time; if she tries to take on too much, she might become overwhelmed and frustrated. Learning to do something well takes a lot of time and reflection. She agreed, so I also have seen part of my coaching designated to help organize (or be a sounding board) for ideas and implementation.

Catherine's finding had to do with the role of literacy coach. She wanted to become more collaborative with teachers, so her finding in the above excerpt focused on one of the ways she was accomplishing it, namely, brainstorming what teachers want to concentrate on. She gave the example from her interactions with Mary to illustrate how she was learning to work with teachers "in more comfortable situations for them," ones where she served more as a sounding board.

The next two examples illustrate ways in which classroom talk can be incorporated in findings. Courtney Wellner's one finding—Excerpt 7.8—centered on peer writing conferences.

Excerpt 7.8: Courtney Wellner's One Finding

"How D'Ya Get Yours to Sound Like That?" Students Using Each Other as Writing Models during the Peer Revision Process

Whenever I attempt to use peer writing conferences with my students, one of my biggest frustrations is that even if I get students to share their writing and give constructive feedback to each other, only rarely do they actually take that feedback to heart and go back and revise their own drafts. Which, in the past, has always led me to say to myself with disappointment: So what's the point? However, when I stepped back more carefully and observed students during their writing conferences, I discovered an unexpected yet consistent occurrence: students were using each other's writing as informal models to improve their own drafts. Even if they never looked at what their partners had written as feedback on their drafts, they were taking it upon themselves to examine the form and function of another's draft and were often transferring those modeled ideas to their own writing, a skill I had never explicitly taught them but one that they chose to engage in as novice writers.

For example, when my focus group of students met for their second peer revision session about their original short stories, both Erica and Lorenzo focused on the structure and organization of Edgar's short story and took various ideas from his draft to revise their own original stories:

Edgar: Are you finished with mine yet?
Lorenzo: Yeah, almost.
Edgar: What d'ya think of it?
Lorenzo: Good . . . yeah, it's good. How did you know how to make it into chapters?

Edgar: What do you mean? I just broke it into different chapters.

Lorenzo: Did we have to do that?

Edgar: No, I just wanted to make it look like that. And did you see how I made each chapter from a different character's point of view . . . perspective? Did you get that part?

Erica: What did you do? You made different chapters?

Edgar: Yeah. I made four chapters, and all of them were from a different character's point of view. I thought of that on my own—you don't have to do it that way.

Erica: That's cool. I could do that too, maybe. Would that work for mine?

Monica: I don't know. You only have one main character. Who else would tell the story?

Lorenzo: That would work for mine. I have the one guy, the brother, the guy he kills, and that guy's dad. I could have the dad talk about how he felt after his son was killed, like in the last chapter.

Erica: Yeah, that's good.

Edgar: Erica, you could just use different chapters to show the different days in the story since it jumps around so much, but just all from that one girl's perspective.

Erica: Oh, yeah. That would be good. Yeah, I like that better than how it is right now.

According to Vygotsky, communicative collaboration with more peers helps struggling students, through dialogue, towards completion of a particular task that could not be accomplished alone—in this case, the revision of a short story draft into a more mature, well-written piece. Through the kind of social interaction described above, both Erica and Lorenzo were encouraged to challenge themselves by changing the form of their stories to include multiple perspectives from different characters. Neither Erica nor Lorenzo would have come up with this higher-level writing strategy on his/her own—these skills were within their proximal development in English writing, however, and encouraged by collaboration with Edgar, a more skilled peer.

Courtney's finding or pattern in this excerpt (also foregrounded by her heading)—"an unexpected yet consistent occurrence: students were using each other's writing as informal models to improve their own drafts"—was illustrated by a discourse example from a peer revision session. And, this was followed by a discussion of her interpretation of what the talk meant, using a Vygotskian idea to emphasize how the collaborative dialogue in the peer group facilitated Erica's and Lorenzo's development as writers.

Libby Tuerk also included classroom talk in her one finding, but she did it differently. She wrote about how students engaged with books and how that was seen in their book talks about their independent reading books—see Excerpt 7.9.

Excerpt 7.9: Libby Tuerk's One Finding

Measuring Engagement: Dialogue with the Book

One of the means through which I attempted to gauge student engagement in his/her independent reading book was student dialogue with the book. By this, I mean evidence that a student is putting him/herself into the book: conversing with a character, sharing feelings about a plot event as it would affect them, or placing him/herself into the setting. As Wilhelm (1979) noted, students' comprehension improves when they are able to see themselves as active constructors of meaning and as a part of the text. Although I did not see this very often initially in my class's book talks, as the quarter progressed, more and more students began to make comments that demonstrated their own dialogue with the book.

One poignant example of this can be seen in comments made by Marisa during a book talk mid-way through the quarter. Marisa is a thirteen year old girl who moved to the school from Mexico when she was in third grade. She spoke no English and continues to speak only Spanish at home. Despite this, her English is quite good, although there were still occasionally some language-related comprehension issues. Marisa chose Becoming Naomi Leon by Pam Muñoz Ryan as her independent reading book. During a book talk, she showed that she was putting herself in the book when she told her group that Naomi "told us, well told me about her brother's disability problem." When her group asked her more about the brother's disability, she continued to talk about it from Naomi's point of view, saying how bad she felt for her that she had to deal with her brother. These comments showed Marisa is looking at the book as a conversation between Naomi and herself and is able to empathize with Naomi.

Another example that demonstrated dialogue with the book took place . . .

One of Libby's major themes or findings was the ways in which students engaged with books. The above excerpt illustrates what Libby called "dialogue with the book," which she defined in terms of the work of Wilhelm, whose book she had read as part of her literature review. She included data from a book talk, but unlike Courtney, who set the discourse as a separate section (Excerpt 7.8), she included quotations and paraphrases from the conversation in this classroom activity within continuous prose. As can be seen by the last line in Excerpt 7.9, Libby also included another example, not included here, where she also inserted quotations and paraphrases. Thus, classroom discourse can be incorporated in various ways. This is also the case for talk from interviews. That is, instead of formatting the talk from her focus group about the working workshop as a separate section, Shannon (Excerpt 7.6) could have used quotations and paraphrases of what they said within her prose.

How to include writing is a similar decision: Do I put the excerpts of writing examples within the running prose, or show how I position them as a separate small section in the paper? The major point of reporting findings is *telling* what they are and giving examples (*showing*) to support them. But you cannot just "drop them in"; you also have to talk about them by giving readers your interpretations of them. That is, a discourse example may represent several meanings; you have to help the reader to see what is significant about it from your point of view.

SUMMARY: PUTTING IT ALL TOGETHER

We hope that the overall tips on and the examples of ways to create a beginning lead and to report findings give you confidence to put it all together and take a stab at writing the whole inquiry report.

Further ideas can be gleaned from reading and examining the collaborating teacher researchers' final reports found in Part Three of this book. Two appendices also provide information in writing up your inquiry paper: Appendix B, which covers APA (American Psychological Association) citing conventions, and Appendix C, which outlines reminders on common grammatical usage.

It is important to gain feedback on beginnings and one-findings, as well as full-paper drafts—see the "Activities" section below. We recommend that you find someone who is not very familiar with your inquiry—a naïve reader—to provide feedback on the latter text so that you have a "fresh eye" exploring it. Others who have seen parts of your inquiry may make assumptions about its content that you want this last reader not to make.

As already indicated, the aim of this chapter was to support your efforts in writing up your inquiry for a practitioner-oriented journal (or book chapter). Your write-up, or paper, should be an evocative account—that is, one that offers descriptions, explanations, and understandings of the lived classroom experiences you explored in your inquiry. We have acknowledged that writing is hard, but it can also be seen as "hard fun" (Murray, 1990) if you approach it as a problem-solving adventure where you are able to share what you have discovered about your own teaching and student learning. Know what you want to say in your paper, but don't put pressure on yourself to have it all figured out before you begin. Remember that people *are* interested in new voices and insights; your inquiry *can* contribute to others in the educational community at large. Outlets for publishing your inquiry papers can be the practitioner-oriented journals we have mentioned here and in Chapter 4 (where we covered reading others' work and writing a preliminary literature review). You can also submit your paper to online journals.[2] Be sure to check the specific publishing guidelines on journals' homepages before finalizing your papers for submission.

SUGGESTED ACTIVITIES

1 Create a lead beginning for your paper. Try also to envision how you plan to format your paper as a whole, using headings. Does your beginning launch your paper in an interesting way? Using the general peer conferencing form (Appendix A), share these with a classmate or colleague to obtain feedback.

2 Identify a major finding or theme. Tell what you know; show with examples; provide interpretations from your point of view. Get feedback by using the general peer conferencing form.

3 Take a stab at putting it all together. Consider the overall tips, beginning and one-finding examples to compose an evocative account of your inquiry. Get feedback by using the general conferencing form.

NOTES

1 These articles are rarely organized in terms of sections called "Introduction," "Theoretical Framework" (or "Review of the Literature"), "Methods," "Results," and "Discussion," which are commonly used in research-

oriented journals (e.g., *Reading Research Quarterly* or *Research in the Teaching of English*). However, if you are doing your inquiry as a Master's thesis or doctoral dissertation, your school may want you to follow such a format. See Macintyre (2000) and Johnson (2008) for more details for such a scheme. Or, if you decide to submit your manuscript to a research-oriented journal, you would likely employ such a format but you would also want to look at articles in these journals and follow how reports of studies are formatted.

2 Here are two online journals to consider: *Networks: An On-line Journal for Teacher Research* (http://journals.library.wisc.edu/index.php/networks/index) (Managing Editor, Catherine F. Compton-Lilly); and a very new one at the Center for Practitioner Research, *Inquiry in Education* (http://digitalcommons. nl.edu/ie/) (Editors, Arlene Borthwick, Wendy Gardiner, Virginia Jagla, and Linnea L. Rademaker).

REFERENCES

Altrichter, H., Posch, O., & Somekh, B. (1993). *Teachers investigate their work: An introduction to the methods of action research.* London: Routledge.

Denzin, N. K. (1997). *Interpretive ethnography.* Thousand Oaks, CA: Sage.

Hubbard, R. S., & Power, B. M. (2003). *The art of classroom inquiry: A handbook for teacher-researchers.* Portsmouth, NH: Heinemann.

Macintyre, C. (2000). *The art of action research in the classroom.* London: David Fulton.

MacLean, M. S., & Mohr, M. M. (1999). *Teacher-researchers at work.* Berkeley, CA: National Writing Project.

Murray, D. (1990). *Shoptalk: Learning to write with writers.* Portsmouth, NH: Boynton/Cook.

Pappas, C. C., Kiefer, B. Z., & Levstik, L. S. (2006). *An integrated language perspective in the elementary school: An action approach.* Boston: Pearson Education.

Stringer, E. (2004). *Action research in education.* Upper Saddle River, NJ: Pearson.

Sumara, D. J., & Luce-Kapler, R. (1993). Action research as writerly text: Locating co-labouring in collaboration. *Educational Action Research, 1,* 387–396.

Teacher Researcher Reports

Throughout the book, we have used examples from our collaborating teacher researchers' work to illustrate various strategies in the inquiry process. In this part of the book, Part Three, we include their actual final reports. Recall that these were written for a spring semester course, so teachers had to create a draft by the end of the course even though their inquiry might have continued. And, as indicated in Chapter 4, the prior published work of others that they were able to draw on was limited. Nevertheless, an aim of their projects was to create a "publishable" paper for a practitioner journal. All teachers attempted to follow APA conventions when citing within the text and in their references section (see Appendix B), which would be required if they wanted to submit their papers for publication in a journal (for purposes of this book, each of the teacher researchers signed a standard publisher's Contributor Agreement). This part of the book is organized in the following way. The twelve teacher-researcher reports (Chapters 8–19) are included according to the grade level (starting with kindergartners) that teachers investigated, with the two literacy coach studies at the end. Teachers' papers are formatted as if they had been submitted for publication. That is, we haven't inserted their tables or figures where they are mentioned in the body of the text, but instead we have placed them at the end, which is the conventional practice in submitting manuscripts. At the beginning of each teacher researcher paper, we provide a brief "Introductory Highlights" section to point out certain bulleted features of their papers that others might find useful to consider in writing up their inquiry projects. These include certain aspects the teacher researcher might have used in her inquiry (e.g., use of focal students, focus groups, descriptive statistics) and formatting techniques (e.g., use of interesting headings for sections of her paper, quotes in running text and/or separate sections, vignettes).

At the end of the book, following these teacher inquiry papers, is an Epilogue, which includes final reflections and possibilities regarding teacher research.

Chapter 8

Katie Paciga's Inquiry Paper

INTRODUCTORY HIGHLIGHTS

- Used focal students, explaining the criteria for choosing them.
- Talked *about* language.
- Included a table listing topics of mini-lessons and figures that illustrated children's writing.
- Included quotations in running text.
- Referred to her data sources as citations.

Reading, Writing, and Sharing: The Journey to Become Kindergarten Authors

Katie Paciga

I am standing by the doors on Elmwood to let my kindergarten students into school. It is a cold, windy February day—the kind of day when you cannot warm up, even if you are wearing a coat, hat, scarf and gloves. Anna comes running down the sidewalk from her mother's car, her hands full of home-made envelopes with her friends' names written across the front. She is smiling. As she enters the school, Anna grabs my hand and asks, "Are we going to have 'writing time' today?" I squeeze her hand and smile as I tell her, "Yes."

Although writing is often neglected in a jam-packed curriculum (National Commission on Writing, 2003), my goal in my inquiry was to integrate my curriculum so that I could have time for writing instruction. My focus was to examine how my literacy instruction supports kindergarten writers as they are authoring texts.

What Is Writing?

As a teacher of writing, it is important to have a clear picture of what the writing process entails. Hayes (1996) offers a cognitive process model of writing in which he describes writing as based on three components: the task environment (social factors, writing assignment, and the text produced thus far), the cognitive processes used in writing (planning, organization, text generation, rereading, revision, and editing), and the writer's long-term memory (which includes knowledge of topic, audience, and genre). This model indicates that as a student gains more information about how a specific text (genre) works, he or she will become more fluent as a writer and be able to better express him- or herself in written form. In other words, children's writing depends on their purpose for writing (assignment, topic, and genre), their intended audience, and their ability to accurately and fluently transfer their ideas onto the paper, as well as everything they know about how literacy is used and experienced in socioculturally specific situations (Barton & Hamilton, 1998; Dyson, 2003).

Writing Contexts in My Classroom

In my classroom there are several contexts for writing: there is a writing center where children can work with a variety of media (stapled 6-10 page blank books; paper of various shapes, sizes, and colors; markers, pens, pencils; envelopes; and a mailbox); an art center filled with paper, glue, markers, paint, clay, colored pencils, scissors, and paper of all sorts; and a dramatic play center, which changes from a house with phones and notepads to write phone messages, to a restaurant with paper pads to take down customers' orders, and so forth. In addition to these self-directed writing contexts, I also introduced journal writing and writer's workshop contexts for writing.

My entire writing time began as journals (consisting of stapled 20 mostly blank sheets of paper with 5–6 black lines to write on). I chose this type of journal to begin the year with because I wanted students to feel free to tell a story through pictures, as that is where the majority of my students were developmentally. About two weeks into the inquiry, I noticed that my more advanced writers were using more than one page for their texts. At that time, I decided to give children the option to compose in this journal, or to write books, which would eventually become published documents. Before I sent children off to individually write, I always read a book, and as I read it, I "thought aloud" about the genre and an aspect of the author's craft in writing the book. Following the read-aloud, I did a mini-lesson on some aspect of writing (Table 8.1 outlines some of the topics of my mini-lessons), sometimes followed by an interactive writing session, and then sent the children off to write in their journals or books. They were always free to choose their topic, and I held roving conferences with students as they were writing.

To me, this format of writing activities was very similar to a writer's workshop context for writing (Fletcher & Portalupi, 2001; Graves, 2003; Liao, Ruben, & Wolfer, 2001; Ray & Cleaveland, 2004). The writer's workshop model provides students with an evolving context for writing in which students participate in four different writing components: mini-lessons, writing, conferencing, and sharing. Students first participate in a mini-lesson where a specific skill or topic is addressed by the teacher in a whole-group format. These mini-lessons usually are 5–15 minutes in length and range in topics, including issues that might arise as the writer's workshop evolves. Such a topic is one that Pam Wolfer (in Liao et al., 2001) employed on keeping on a main topic. In her mini-lesson, she used webbing as a brainstorming activity to help generate content around one main idea.

Following the mini-lesson, children are sent off to write for an extended period of time: to plan, draft, revise, edit, or publish. During this time, Fletcher and Portalupi (2001) suggest we guide our students "to find *a* writing process that works for him or her" (p. 62). In other words, not all students will be at the same stage of the writing process on the same day. Some children may need to plan before they write, and others may not. It is the teacher's job to help children at the various stages of the writing process. This requires a continuous assessment of what each child has accomplished.

Assessing Students' Writing through Conferences

Oftentimes, in a writer's workshop context, a teacher will meet with a student in a conference to talk about issues that the teacher observes or problems that the student brings up. During this time, the teacher meets with a student to scaffold him or her through some aspect of the writing process (planning, drafting, editing, revising, or publishing).

Pappas, Kiefer, & Levstik (2006) describe two different types of conferences: content and editing conferences—content conferences that deal with message or content of text, and editing conferences that address medium issues (e.g., grammar, punctuation, spelling) after children have revised their work. In their guidelines for analyzing student work and examples of conferencing from this message/medium framework, they caution against stressing too much revision or editing for emergent writers, noting that revision in emergent writing is often done orally. I found these ideas very useful, for they helped me examine my expectations and gave me some very specific guidelines for meeting with my students in a conference.

I found other useful conferencing advice from Ray and Cleaveland (2004). They describe some typical kinds of writing conferences we have with our youngest writers. The goal is "that our conferences will leave children with energy for the work they're doing and that the teaching will also be leading children toward independence" (p. 144). Ray and Cleaveland describe the teacher's role in each kind of writing conference: helping children grab hold of ideas and grow them; helping children get words down on the page; helping children imagine new crafting possibilities; helping children with the conventions of writing; setting specific agendas for individual children; and giving children access to writer's language.

Conferences help children to become better writers. They should be predictable (Fletcher & Portalupi, 2001; Graves, 2003; Liao et al., 2001; Ray & Cleaveland, 2004). Also, teachers should spend the majority of their time listening to the child, asking open-ended questions such as "How's it going?" Conferences should also be times in which teachers listen as readers and attempt to understand the students' intentions. Conferences should build on students' strengths and cover only one thing at a time. They need to be quick and to the point (especially when you have 20-plus students to get to).

In my own inquiry, I learned about conferencing the hard way. When I began conferencing, I only would get to 4 students during a 20-minute session. That meant that each child was writing for 5–6 sessions without any teacher support. I restructured my conferences so that I could see about 10 students a day, addressing only one thing per conference. I saw the neediest children every session (as Graves recommends) and the others every other session. My students became familiar with the conference structure and knew that they would have a chance to speak with me when it was their turn.

Context of My Inquiry

For the four years prior to my inquiry, I had been employed as a kindergarten teacher in a half-day program that serves a low-income Latino community with a high mobility rate. During a typical day, children would be in class for nearly three hours. Twenty of those minutes were required for a mandatory snack time. Thirty minutes were budgeted each subject (math, science or social studies, and social development) on a daily basis. That left only an hour to complete reading and writing instruction every day. I integrated science and social studies into my reading block and restructured the rest of my day to include a writer's workshop two or three times per week.

At the time of my inquiry, I was teaching primarily Latina/o students, but some other cultures were represented in my two half-day classes. I decided to use focal students in my study. Initially I selected 3 focal students from each class, totaling six students, but ended up with 5 children as one child was absent from school for three weeks due to an emergency surgery. These decisions were made after 4 weeks of data collection.

Focal Students

I used several criteria for choosing focal students: my observations of their work for the past four weeks, their language proficiency, January DIBELS (Dynamic Indicators of Basic Early Literacy Skills) assessments (which are a series of short tests given to students in kindergarten through third grade to screen and monitor their progress in learning the necessary skills to become successful readers, one of which is a child's ability to separate a word into its individual phonemes, a skill necessary in writing), and other distinctive characteristics about individual children.

The two AM kindergarteners were Manuel and Henry. Manuel, who was Latino, received ESL classes twice per week. He was performing below average academically (as indicated by the DIBELS), but I observed him successfully telling a story by using a picture. Despite his lack of English proficiency, he showed some potential for growth through focused, individualized writing instruction. Neither of his parents spoke English. He went through the first semester of school without glasses, so he struggled in recognizing letters in books and other texts. In December, Manuel began to wear glasses. Henry was a high-achieving Latino English-only student. He demonstrated good decoding skills, phonemic awareness, and sense of story, but struggled, even orally, to tell a well-connected story.

The three PM kindergarteners were Edgar, Anna, and Claudia. Edgar spoke English with his father, siblings, and classmates, but communicated in Spanish with his mother. He was one of the highest-scoring students on the January DIBELS assessment but he appeared to be bored in school: he was often looking around the classroom, whispering with his friends during read-alouds, and making tangential comments. He regularly celebrated when I announced, "Time to clean up and put our coats on to go home," or "We do not have school tomorrow." I chose Edgar as one of my focal students because I thought that writing might spark his interest in school. Anna was Arabic, but spoke only English. She was enthusiastic about school. Like Edgar, Anna was among the highest-scoring PM students on the January DIBELS assessment. She was inquisitive about everything, and strived for perfection in all of her work. It often took Anna extra time to complete in-class assignments because she spent a lot of time erasing and rewriting. I hoped to help her become a more fluent writer. Claudia was a Latina student who also scored well on the January DIBELS. Prior to the start of this inquiry, I had observed Claudia fluently using writing to compose letters to friends in the writing station. I chose her because I was interested in comparing the thought processes of a fluent writer with those of less fluent, struggling writers.

Studying My New Writing Workshop Format

As already indicated, because of the nature of my inquiry, I was forced to reorganize my curriculum to incorporate a writer's workshop for students. Within this framework, I focused to teach writing through genre study. My writing instruction was connected to reading. Children were immersed in authentic children's literature, and I read aloud and modeled my thinking processes for the children, commenting on genre-specific conventions. I collected a range of data. I reflected upon my literacy instruction by writing for 20 minutes in a reflection journal. I wrote about a variety of topics: things that were bothering me, accomplishments, particular students, or questions that I needed to research to help me with my instruction. I wrote fieldnotes on individual writing and conferences. I looked for and noted self-directive language, enacted writing patterns, and how they interacted with their peers. In addition, I attempted to have the child explain how they knew to write the way they did.

In the fourth week of the inquiry, I began a large group share time, which I audiotaped. I modeled how to participate in this part of the writer's workshop. I always controlled who was sharing, choosing students who had accomplished something remarkable in their writing, or those who that needed help with some aspect of their writing. I also taped weekly interactive writing sessions to offer children support in genre writing. On the day we had this activity, I used individual writing time to conference with each child on what genre they were using in their writing, which is called status-of-class documentation. I wanted to see if my genre instruction was promoting students to write in a variety of genres. During this time, I would approach one student at a time and ask, "What kind of writing are you working on?" Some students had a lot of difficulty responding to this question, especially in the beginning, so I often had to ask several questions to get a good picture of what genre they were attempting to write. Finally, I collected students' written work.

From my class observations, I was able to determine that students were writing in nine distinct genres. Personal narrative was when the author related something that had really happened to them. The fiction genre was separated into two categories: fiction with themselves as a character and fiction without themselves in the story. The ABC books illustrated some sort of sound–symbol connection. The process writing genre provided the reader with directions for how to do something. Letters were correspondences to specific persons. Informational text (nonfiction) gave the reader information about a specific topic. Response to literature genre was when a child made connections, retold a story, or created questions that stemmed from literature. The final genre was their record or log of learning (these usually began "I learned . . ."). Although a typical writer's workshop model does not usually include responses to literature or records of learning, I neither encouraged my students to experiment in these genres nor discouraged them from doing so. I was happy to see them writing, so I just recorded what I observed into the status of class tables I developed.

What Did I Find?

Part of a good inquiry is engaging in reflective teaching and gathering data to create change within your classroom. Putting together the information I collected throughout the ten weeks was a difficult task. I struggled with creating categories for my findings that were clearly supported by the data I had collected. I came up with three major categories of results that are described in the following sections.

Explicit Exposure Led to Experimentation

I never expected the children to be successful authors of various genres without support. The first form of support I provided them was in our genre study. To begin, we built on what we already knew about literature: authors create literature, and no two authors write in the same way. I taught them that authors have different kinds of writing, or genres. The goal of my inquiry was to illustrate the ways my literacy instruction supported kindergarten students as they developed as authors. Over the ten weeks, I realized that explicit exposure to genres led to experimentation. Experimentation is an important step in becoming expert at anything, especially writing. I was happy to see that many children experimented with the various genres I had modeled throughout my interactive writing sessions. My status-of-the-class observations helped me illustrate this.

I first modeled writing about myself and things that really happened to me. We labeled this kind of writing "personal narrative." After witnessing my personal narrative writing three times, I asked for the class to help with some of the composition in an interactive writing time (January 25). On that day, I completed a status of the class observation during conference time to examine what genre children were writing: ten AM students and eight PM students had chosen to write in the personal narrative genre on that day. Those numbers are higher than the number of children writing in any other genre.

The next week (February 1), I taught an interactive mini-lesson on fiction. In recording children's genre efforts, I wanted to note when they used "fiction with self" as a main character. I already knew that children have a tendency to fantasize about themselves in fictitious scenarios (Dyson, 2003), but I wanted to see if any of my children could also engage in developing a character that was not familiar to them. After reading *The Three Billy Goats Gruff* (Carpenter, 1995) and *Goldilocks and the Three Bears* (Brett, 1987), I created a character named Super Dog. I told the class, "I want him to do something heroic, like save an old lady." I created the majority of the content but also requested students' help in composing the text. Compared to the increased use of personal narrative, this time only a few children from each class (four AM students, three PM students) tried to write a fictional piece, but this was more from the earlier, January session. That is, my scaffolding led to children's efforts to attempt this fictional genre.

The status-of-the-class observation of the PM class followed an interactive writing session on composing a letter to someone they knew. On that day, an evident spike appeared in the letter genre for the PM class, which was not present in the AM class, which had not received the interactive session on that day because there had been an all-school assembly that morning. Both classes had been immersed in authentic text; I brought in letters from friends of mine. I printed out email messages from colleagues. I even read literature that was based on correspondence—*Dear Daddy* (Schindel, 1996) and *Dear Mrs. LaRue* (Teague, 2002). I believe the AM class did not experiment in this genre because there was no explicit exposure or scaffolding to help the students in it work through that genre in their own writing.

95

There was a similar trend for children's writing other genres, suggesting that there was a correspondence between the genre taught in my mini-lessons or interactive sessions and an increase in the number of students writing in that genre. For example, on March 17, I intentionally chose to guide children through the genre of informational text. For the next four school days we read information books and examined the content and medium aspects. On March 23, my students and I started to work on an informational text about sea turtles, and on that day five AM students and six PM students chose to write their own informational texts. Prior to this day, none of the students had thought to write an informational text.

Kindergarten Authors' Experimentations Were Impressive

I was thoroughly impressed with student authors' experimentations across genres. Unfortunately, I cannot possibly share all of the samples I collected over the ten-week inquiry project. The following are four examples from some of the focal students in some of the genres previously described.

Anna wrote in the personal narrative genre. For Anna, and for many other students, personal narrative was the easiest genre to write. Figure 8.1 illustrates one of Anna's earlier experimentations in the personal narrative genre. This was completed in her journal, so the entire narrative is on one page. She told the reader about a trip she took to the store. In her illustration, she drew two people: herself and her mother. They are standing inside a building. Anna is holding an apple in her illustration. The text below reads, "My mom took me to the store. I got an apple." Although her story did not have a beginning, middle, and end, it did have two sentences about a single topic and she used her illustrations to help convey her message.

Anna's writing comprised a mixture of capital and lower-case letters. She used one letter to represent the words "my," "took," "me," "to," and "got" with the initial consonant sounds. Her writing followed the conventions of directionality, left to right and top to bottom, but it lacked spacing and punctuation. She correctly spelled "mom" and "the." When I pointed that out in our conference and asked how she knew to write those letters, she told me, "I chopped up 'mom' $/m/$, $/o/$, $/m/$. I know 'the' is on the train, so I copied it" (fieldnotes, January 10). (The "train" in our room is a high-frequency word wall list. At the end of the kindergarten year, there are 32 words on it. I teach students to use the train to help when they write.)

Manuel and Claudia wrote in the fiction genre. I found that more boys than girls experimented in the fiction genre, but that this genre was the most difficult for all of my students. Manuel's piece in Figure 8.2 is a typical example of this genre in kindergarten writing. He includes himself as a character in his story. His topic is centered on superheroic action. In this example, Manuel relied primarily on his pictures to tell his story. When he read it to me, he said, "The robot, it was in space and I was with the Power Ranger. We were killing the alien." He also made attempts at spelling the words "robot" and "Power Rangers" after I suggested that he try to write some words. I knew that Manuel lacked confidence, so I chose to encourage him to write some of the sounds he heard in those words. He nearly correctly spelled "robot" with some support in "chopping up" the sounds. He also used an ABC chart to help link the sounds he heard in the word to the letters to stand for them.

In her experimentation with the fiction genre, Claudia also included herself as a character in the story about a dinosaur's first day at school. She was a much more confident, proficient writer than Manuel. This book was eight pages in length and was written in the ninth week of the inquiry—see Figure 8.3 for the first two pages. Claudia's story had a coherent beginning, middle, and end. In the beginning she set up a problem: the school was too small for a big dinosaur. In the middle, she described the solution: the class was held outside. The end tells of a sequence of events that the dinosaur, Claudia, and her friends participated in: they ran and played tag, saw a rainbow, and ate a snack. She included pieces of conversation in her text, which helped to engage her audience. When Claudia shared this piece at share time, a classmate commented, "I like how you said, 'Dino said . . .'" (Share time, March 25).

On page 2, Claudia labeled the dinosaur's scales. When I questioned her purpose in including this label in a fiction story, she replied, "I want to tell that dinosaurs are real and they really had scales." Although she used a convention of informational text in a fictional piece, her rationale was appropriate, and indicated that Claudia was considering her audience while she composed her story. Another example of how Claudia considered her audience can be found on page 7: she directed a question directly toward her reader: "Wasn't that fun?"

Claudia's directionality was appropriate. Her spelling approximations were excellent. She confused the initial /d/ in "Dino" and replaced it with "B," but did so consistently throughout the entire text. Claudia utilized classroom resources to help her spell words like "school," "rainbow," and "The End." She correctly encoded simple CVC pattern words like "had" and "fun." She used spacing and was able to reread her piece to her friends at share time.

Edgar wrote an informational text. Edgar definitely understood the purpose of an informational text: to provide the reader with a lot of factual information about a single subject matter. He wrote an informational text about apples. Figure 8.4 is a copy of a draft of this piece. He was so excited about the published piece that he took it home to show his grandparents, who were visiting from Mexico, and who took the piece back with them after their visit. As a result, I was not able to copy his final draft.

In the final draft, he added the other color apples on page one and labeled them "red" and "green." His text talked about the different qualities of apples. He described apples as "hard," "really sweet," and "great." In a conference with Edgar, I asked him what he meant when he wrote, "Apples are different." He told me that "some are big or small or spotty" (fieldnotes, March 25). We decided that a picture was necessary to help his readers understand what he meant when he wrote that. His final picture had four different apples in it: a big green apple, a red and yellow apple with spots, a tiny red apple, and a medium-sized red apple with spots. I was surprised that Edgar was able to revise his text with some guidance. This piece was shared with his classmates and was well received. The consensus was that the illustration on page four was the best: as Edgar explained during share time, he drew an apple falling out of a tree and smacking his brother on the head and his brother yelled, "OW!" A roar of laughter ensued from the class.

I was impressed by Edgar's ability to encode his text. He correctly spelled "apples" on some of the pages. His directionality was correct. He generally put one word per line of text, but when there was more than one word, he correctly used spacing. His spelling was brave and did not rely solely on initial consonants to encode his words. Like Claudia, Edgar used environmental print to help him encode his piece. He correctly spelled words like "you," "can," "and" and "yellow." When I asked him how he knew to spell "yellow," he pulled out the yellow crayon from his cup and said, pointing to the crayon, "It's right here!"

Kindergarten Students Were Acting Like Authors

Being an author requires energy and dedication, courage, skill, and a positive attitude. My students demonstrated all of these traits by the end of the inquiry project. I found four major types of enthusiasm toward writing.

Dedication to writing. Many students were very dedicated to their work. They would revisit pieces they had started in the previous session. For example, Henry was very dedicated to his book, which he worked on over eight writing sessions. His enthusiasm for writing carried over into free-choice time, as he often elected to work on his piece during this period. Anna was also very dedicated to her work. Every day we had writing time, she would ask, "Can I take this home to finish?" Anna was so keen to finish her pieces that she wanted to finish and publish them right away. Manuel, who was a struggling writer, also showed signs of dedication to his writing projects. During the tenth week of the inquiry, I observed him complaining to a classmate about the amount of writing time I had given that day. He looked at his friend and said, "We don't have the time. I didn't write the words yet" (fieldnotes, March 4). After his comment to his friend, Manuel requested more writing time.

Writing for enjoyment. My classroom is no different than any other classroom. There were times when I awarded my children with free-choice time. During this time of day, students could choose from a variety of activities within our classroom: puzzles and games, blocks, dramatic play, listening to books on tape, or working on writing.

During the first week of the inquiry, there were no children in either class that chose to work on writing during free choice. Usually, the majority of students elected to engage in dramatic play (AM class) or puzzles and games (PM class). Five weeks into the inquiry, I observed 12 of the 22 students from the PM class working on writing during free choice. Like professional authors, my students were engaging in writing during their free time: they found enjoyment in writing!

Investigating literature at home. On March 23, Edgar presented his piece to me during our conference. The title page was labeled "non-fiction." I asked Edgar, "What made you write this label here?" He reached for a book, opened to the copyright and publishing information page at the beginning, pointed to the "Library of Congress Cataloging-in-Publication Data" part, and said, "My brother told me that they list what the book is about on this page." I questioned, "What made you look on this page?" Edgar answered, "I was looking for the book's birthday." Thus, he was researching books on his own time at home and asking higher-order analytic questions about text formatting. I never mentioned anything about the summary by the Library of Congress. The only references I made to that page of a book in my instruction pointed out the copyright date. In two separate mini-lessons (February 22 and March 17), I pointed out that authors tell their readers when the book was published by putting the year inside the book, drawing on an analogy between a copyright date and a book's birthday.

Desire to share their work with others. One of the most repetitive questions associated with writing time was "Can I share today?" But it did not start out that way. When I began this inquiry project, I did not include sharing as a part of writing time. Three weeks into the project, I saw that some students were losing interest in writing. At that time, I started to select 2–4 students per day to share their pieces with the class. I made this out to be a really big deal. The student author got to sit in my big chair and read to his or her classmates. We celebrated accomplishments, provided the author with feedback and compliments, and learned from one another at this time.

After three share times, I was bombarded with this question from the moment I opened the doors on Elmwood to let the class into the school. I started to feel guilty that I could not let everyone share every writing time because of time restrictions. In the seventh week, I decided to begin a sort of roundtable share format where 4 students all shared their writing in small groups. These roundtable share times followed the same format as the large-group share times: the student author held their work, read one page, showed the illustrations, and repeated the process for each page they wanted to share. The other students listened. When the student author completed reading and sharing, his or her peers could ask a question to clarify, suggest how to make the illustrations go with the words, or offer compliments to the student author. Although I was not able to monitor conversations or provide my input on all of the roundtable discussions, more students were able to share per day.

What Now?

Creating change in my classroom required planning, observation, and reflection. In ten weeks' time, my class accomplished a whole lot. The majority of my students came to school ready and eager to write and tell their personal stories to their peers. It was hard work, especially tackling the fiction genre. We studied, practiced, and provided each other with lots of support. Without that support, I don't think this inquiry would have been as successful as it was. In a very short time, we learned about several different genres, studied genre-specific conventions, and composed a lot of pieces. We laughed when someone wrote something funny and we felt sad when someone told about how their pet rabbit died. We celebrated our accomplishments together. We were kindergarten authors.

This inquiry will not end here. I plan to continue my study of genre writing in a kindergarten classroom. I hope to explore poetry and informational text in more depth in the next school year. I will also begin sooner than January. Writing is such a powerful tool, one that can be used to persuade, entertain, or to inform. It is every teacher's responsibility to ensure that we prepare our students to actively participate in society. To accomplish this end, we, as teachers, have to start early and hold our students to high expectations.

Although there are many contexts for writing, the research supports that all writing is socially situated. As Kress (2000) states, "social groups who control [society's most specific] knowledge also control the forms of literacy; and they define themselves, their identity—who they are—through this form of literacy" (p. 15). And so it must be for the children we teach in our classrooms. We need to teach them how to think critically about the world around them. Children need to see that all print is always trying to convey someone's message. If it is their own message, teachers need to teach children how to create and manipulate texts. As I have discovered, there are many contexts to accomplish this end, such as writer's workshop. In addition, children will need time to work through the process of writing, so they may become fluent writers and carry with them the power that potentially comes with literacy.

References

Barton, D., & Hamilton, M. (1998). *Local literacies: Reading and writing in one community.* New York: Routledge.

Brett, J. (1987). *Goldilocks and the three bears.* New York: Dover Publishing.

Carpenter, S. (1995). *The three billy goats gruff.* New York: HarperCollins.

Dyson, A. H. (2003). *The brothers and sisters learn to write: Popular literacy in childhood and school cultures.* New York: Teachers College Press.

Fletcher, R., & Portalupi, J. (2001). *Writing workshop: The essential guide.* Portsmouth, NH: Heinemann.

Graves, D. H. (2003). *Writing: Teachers and children at work.* Portsmouth, NH: Heinemann.

Hayes, J. R. (1996). A new framework for understanding cognition and affect in writing. In C. M. Levy & S. Ransdell (Eds.), *The science of writing* (pp. 6–44). Mahwah, NJ: Lawrence Erlbaum.

Kress, G. (2000). *Early spelling: Between convention and creativity.* New York: Routledge.

Liao, J., Ruben, D., & Wolfer, P. (2001). Creating a writing workshop in first grade: How to teach literacy "skills" and help children "come to voice." In C. C. Pappas & L. B. Zecker (Eds.), *Transforming literacy curriculum: Working with teacher researchers in urban classrooms* (pp. 35–59). Mahwah, NJ: Lawrence Erlbaum.

National Commission on Writing in America's Schools and Colleges. (2003). *The neglected "R:" The need for a writing revolution.* Retrieved March 24, 2006, from http://www.writingcommission.org/prod_downloads/writingcom/neglectedr.pdf.

Pappas, C. C., Kiefer, B. Z., & Levstik, L. S. (2006). *An integrated language perspective in the elementary school: An action approach.* Boston: Pearson Education.

Ray, K. W., & Cleaveland, L. (2004). *About the authors.* Portsmouth, NH: Heinemann.

Schindel, J. (1996). *Dear Daddy.* Morton Grove, IL: Albert Whitman.

Teague, M. (2002). *Dear Mrs. LaRue: Letters from obedience school.* New York: Scholastic Press.

101

Table 8.1 Topics for mini-lessons

- Classroom procedures—getting out journals, date-stamping, and putting away journals, conferencing, sharing
- How to get ideas for writing—we watched some interviews with real authors/illustrators
- Genre studies—personal narrative, ABC, fiction, letters, etc.
- How to make illustrations work with text
- How to use the word wall and environmental print to support our writing
- How to reread your piece to self-monitor
- Using brave spelling—"stretching" or "chopping out" the sounds, syllables, small words inside bigger words
- Walking out a sentence—kinesthetic activity to support writing, where students orally compose their sentence and then take a step for every word they say, to help them to organize their sentences
- Keeping on topic—brainstorming, graphic organizers, informal peer conferencing
- Considering your audience
- Sketch to stretch—drawing a picture first, telling your story based on what you drew
- Talk with a friend about an idea or a "how to"
- Looking at ABC chart for help with brave spelling
- Looking in real books for ideas or help
- Spacing, directionality, and punctuation—how do these conventions help a reader?

Figure 8.1
Anna, Personal Narrative.

It reads, "My mom took me to the store. I got an apple."

Figure 8.2 Manuel's Fiction Story (with Himself as a Character)

It reads: "The robot, it was in space and I was with the Power Ranger. We were killing the alien."

p. 1 – Dino said, "This school is too little," Dino said.	p. 2 – Dino had to go to school outside.
Rihoz SeD, Dio school is too LitL Binoz SeD *[child's drawing of a dinosaur]*	Binoz HaD too GO too school out SiD *[child's drawing of dinosaurs]*

Figure 8.3 First Two Pages of Claudia's Fiction Book, "Dino's First Trip of School."

p. 1- Apples are different colors. Yellow	p. 2 - You can eat apples.
APHee R DiFit Kulrz Yellow	you can et APP lez
p. 3 -And apples are hard.	**p. 4 -And some apples are really sweet.**
Ahp APPles horp	AnD Sdm APPlez Hel zwet
p. 5 Apples are different.	**p. 6 - Apples are great.**
Ahp APPle R LFnot	APPles. P GRAYt

Figure 8.4 First Draft of Edgar's Informational Text on Apples.

Chapter 9

Cindy Pauletti's Inquiry Paper

INTRODUCTORY HIGHLIGHTS

- Included initial and post assessments in inquiry and paper.
- Used italics to talk *about* language.
- Employed both quotes in running text and in separate sections.
- Described the positive and challenged in doing action research.

Word Detectives: Students Using Clues to Identify Unknown Words in Text

Cindy Pauletti

It was January already and my students were reading, but not to the best of their ability. They were ill-equipped with the strategies they could use to help them identify unknown words in a text. I realized I needed to do something more to help them to become the best readers they could be. Too often children are not equipped with the strategies they need to help them become great readers. They often rely on the same one or two strategies of word identification and find themselves at a loss when those strategies cannot help them. It was my goal in this action research and in my classroom everyday to help my students expand their knowledge and use of the various strategies to identify unknown words in a text.

I chose to use explicit instruction with my students. This means that I included demonstrations, questioning, making statements, and eliciting practice and participation (Fisher, 1995). I taught skills and strategies through practice *in context*, not through drilling skills.

What Are Some Strategies Children Use to Identify Unknown Words in a Text?

Word identification is the process of determining the pronunciation and the meaning of an unknown word. In this inquiry I refer to word identification strategies, which means that when children are reading a text and come to a word they cannot read, they have a repertoire of strategies to use to help them identify the word correctly. There are many strategies students can use to identify unknown words in a text, but I just focused on a few with my students. *Decoding by analogy* is one strategy my students learned—children use a word that they can read to identify a word that they cannot read (Goswami, 1986). For example, if they can read *night*, they should recognize the word ending that they know and be able to also read *sight*. *Context clues* (or cues) refer to when a child reads nearly all the words in the text by sight and then uses the sense of the text to guess unknown words (Gaskins, 2004). For example, to read the word *spacious* in the sentence "The house was so spacious with all those rooms," a child needs to have some background knowledge of such a setting so that he or she is able to come up with a possible word that "looks like" this word and still might make sense.

"Phonics" instruction teaches children the relationships between the letters of written language and the individual sounds of spoken language. It teaches children to use these relationships to read and write words. The goal of phonics instruction is to help children learn and use the understanding that there are systematic and predictable relationships between written letters and spoken sounds. Knowing these relationships will help children recognize familiar words accurately and automatically, and "decode" new words. Teaching phonics in the context of a text makes a bigger contribution to children's growth in reading than traditional, stand-alone phonics (Dahl, Scharer, Lawson, & Grogan, 2001). If there is a picture in the text, *exploring these images* could also be taken into consideration, making it another strategy.

Finally, *cross-checking* is a strategy that should be used in conjunction with all of the above strategies. It refers to a child cross-checking to be certain that the word identified by one or more of the above strategies makes sense both syntactically and semantically (Cunningham, 1995).

Background

All data for this inquiry were gathered through audiotaping, fieldnotes, and journaling. The data were collected over a three-month period at a Chicago public school where I teach. This school includes Head Start to third grade, with 99% of the population being Mexican and 1% African American. Nearly all the Mexican children are English language learners. The school has monolingual (English), bilingual (Spanish), and immersion classes (English with the support of a Spanish-speaking teacher). I teach a first-grade reading pull-out program. The six students that I did the action research with are in a monolingual room and come to my class at the same time for forty minutes a day. Two of the children are male and four are female. Sam, Maria, and Darlene were fairly fluent readers. They were in my highest-level guided reading group. The other three children, Cesar, Sonia, and Denise, were in my low to medium guided reading group. Cesar and Denise were starting to become fluent readers, whereas Sonia was not as yet a fluent reader, reading in a very slow and choppy way.

Initial Assessments

I began by asking the teacher what word identification strategies she had taught our students. She informed me that she had taught them to find a little word in a big word; look for a word family ending that you know; stretch out the word, ask yourself if it sounds right and if it makes sense; and to look at the picture for clues.

I also had an individual interview with the children to ask what they did when they came to a word they could not read in a text. I also used an Informal Reading Inventory (IRI) to determine the students' instructional needs in reading. A student's performance on the IRI can help determine the instructional level and the amount and kind of support the student is likely to need in the areas of word recognition, word meaning, reading strategies, and comprehension. My main purpose for administering an IRI was to see if the children were using the strategies that their teacher had taught them or other strategies that they had discovered on their own. Children read a book at their level—one I would use with their guided reading group. I made sure that the book they read was one that they had not read previously. I wanted these books to be texts they had not yet been exposed to so that they would be more likely to use their current strategies to identify any unknown words.

Sam told me that he used two strategies: "I look for a little word in a big word and I look at the picture." In the IRI, Sam employed both strategies he said he would use in the interview. He found the word *fly* in *butterfly* and the word *row* in *grown-ups*. He looked at the picture to figure out *birthday* once he saw the birthday cake in the picture. He also self-corrected when he first read "She likes happy" for "She looks happy." This means he was cross-checking to see if what he read made sense.

Maria also reported that she looked at the picture and found a little word in a big word as strategies for identifying words, and she used both in the IRI. She looked at the picture to help her read *fingernails* when she saw a picture of the troll with long fingernails: she read *f-ing-er* and then was able to correctly guess *fingernails* through observing the picture. Maria found a little word in a big word when she read *f-all* and *him-s-e-l-f*. She also reread "He washed his hands" after first reading "He wished his hands," realizing that the first try didn't make sense. This told me that she was also reading for meaning and monitoring her own comprehension.

Cesar first said, "I sound it out" as a strategy, and then, with prompting as to whether he did anything else, he stated, "Then I guess, practice, and keep trying." Cesar was also true to his replies in the interview. Unlike Sam and Maria, Cesar rarely looked at the pictures when he couldn't identify a word. He relied on sounding out words, identifying words such as *th-e-n*, *bl-e-w*, and *w-e-n-t*. However, he often guessed and did not self-correct when what he read did not make sense—for example, reading, "One up on a tame" for "Once upon a time," and "There little Pigs" for "Three little Pigs." He seemed to just guess at words, not following through to see if what he had come up with made sense. Sometimes he would reread when he did realize that what he read didn't make sense, but he was still unable to self-correct. Cesar also used a strategy that he did not mention in the interview. He found some little words in bigger words when he read *f-all* for *fall*, *up-on* for *upon* and *a-way* for *away*.

Similarly to Cesar, Darlene said, "I sound out the words I don't know," and she used that strategy when she read: for example, she sounded out *br-u-sh-d*, *s-and-w-i-ch-s*, and *sc-r-u-b-d*. I also noticed that she was finding little words in bigger words when she read *some-one*, *no-thing*, and *cry-ing*. She looked at the pictures only one time: when she was stuck on *troll*. When she finished reading, she also told me she sometimes pointed to words to figure them out. When I asked her why pointing helped her, she could only tell me that it helped her read.

Sonia told me that she both looked at pictures and sounded out words as strategies when she read. She looked at the pictures to figure out *chimney* and *bricks*. She sounded out *ch-in* and *cr-ep-t*. The only other strategy I saw her use was guessing. Oftentimes her guess made sense, but when it did not, she did not self-correct. For example, she read, "he ran was he called" for "he ran as fast as he could" without any attempts to correct.

When I asked Denise about her strategies, she said, "I sound out the word. I find a "*a, e, i, o, u* letter.'" When I asked her why she did the latter, she indicated that she didn't know. She also reported, "I take a picture walk." Denise also seemed to use the strategies that she reported on in the interview. Before she read, she took a picture walk by going through the book by looking at the pictures. She also sounded out words in the text such as *n-ah-t* for *not* and *h-ow-ss* for *house*. After reading the book, she also told me of another strategy that she used that she didn't mention in the interview—finding a little word in a big word—and she did use it while reading when she read *up-on* and *no-t*. She could recognize *not*, but read *note*. When I asked her to give me an example of when she found a little word in a big word, she pointed to the word *house*. She said, "The *ou* says *ow* and then *house*," which didn't really seem to be finding a small word within a big word. She also told me she used the strategy "turned the page and found the other same word," which she tried out, looking elsewhere for other instances of *if* in the book.

Thus, the children used the strategies during reading that they mentioned in the interviews, and what they used, they had been taught by their classroom teacher. But they did not use all of the strategies that their teacher had shared with them. Moreover, they also sometimes used other strategies that they didn't mention in their talk with me. In any case, most of them used a limited number of strategies.

Getting Started

After the individual interviews and IRIs were completed, we had a brainstorming session. We composed a list of strategies that students said they could use to identify an unknown word. I thought this would help the children understand what strategy is and to expand their knowledge of the possible types of word identification strategies that are available. The following is what they came up with:

1 Sound/stretch out the word.
2 Look at the picture for clues.
3 Find a little word in a big word.
4 Point to the word and sound it out; it will help you not lose your place.
5 Guess and see if it makes sense.
6 Skip the word, read on, go back and see if you know it now.

I especially emphasized the fact that it was always important that whatever they came up with make sense, and if not, they should go back and try again. I also wrote down three questions on chart paper and put them up on the wall: *Does it look right? Does it sound right? Does it make sense?* I discussed what each question meant and encouraged them to use the three questions when they were reading.

The following activities reflect how we focused on our chart of strategies and three questions when a student got stuck. As you will see, they tried out every strategy for figuring out unknown words.

Star Readers Shine

One routine that children engaged in regarding learning to identify unknown words was called the Star Reader activity. The aim of the activity is to identify the strategies one child—the Star Reader—is using when he or she comes to an unknown word and to see if the other children can identify the strategies. The Star Reader reads to the class a book chosen by the child (with my help), after having practiced at home. All students have a turn and one child reads to us every day. Before the Star Reader read to us, I asked students to review the list of strategies that we composed together on chart paper and hung on the wall. We also went over the three questions they needed to be thinking about when reading. Once all the strategies were fresh in their head, I asked them to try to notice if the Star Reader used any of these strategies when he or she read. There follow some examples from these Star Reader sessions.

Sonia as Star Reader of *The Lost Mother*

Sonia was the Star Reader reading the first part of *The Lost Mother* (Prince, 1999), which was an early session of the activity. After she had finished, I first asked Sonia about what strategies she thought she had used, and then asked other children about what they noticed:

Teacher:	What strategies did you use to identify any words you did not know in the text?
Sonia:	I sounded out the words and I looked at the pictures.
Teacher:	What words did you sound out?
Sonia:	Umm, *butter* and *shopping* . . . I saw *b-ut* and the *t-er* . . . I remembered that *o-p* says *op* like *hop* and *i-n-g* says *ing*, so *shh-op-ing*.
Teacher:	When did you use the picture for a clue?
Sonia:	I looked at the picture for *grapes* . . . [There were other strategies that Sonia used as well, but did not tell us about. Therefore, I asked the other students if they had noticed her using any other strategies.]
Sam:	She was pointing at the words all the time.
Teacher:	Why is that a strategy?
Sam:	'Cause it helps you not lose your place when you look at the pictures, and when you sound out the word, you kinda move your finger when you make the sounds.
Denise:	Sonia looked at the picture when she was reading *cheese*. She didn't know it, then she saw the picture of the cheese and figured it out.
. . .	
Darlene:	I think Sonia found [the word] *out* in *checkout*.
Teacher:	So you're saying she found a little word in a big word, then?
Darlene:	Yes.

Sonia, as noted above, was not a very fluent reader, yet she could talk about two strategies that she used (and others she used that she didn't mention). I was very surprised at the way the children were able to note so many of the strategies we came up with so soon. Between Sonia and the other students, they were able to identify every strategy that she used and that was on the list. Pointing to the words, which Sam brought up, was one of the strategies from the chart that the students came up with. He explained that it helps to keep a reader's place if he or she is going back and forth between pictures and text. Dahl et al. (2001) offer another rationale: they argue that pointing is a useful strategy for getting some children to look more closely at miscues and recheck their reading. Often, I will just point to a word when a child makes a miscue, and most of the time he or she catches it and then rereads with the correction. I noticed that children were becoming more comfortable with identifying the strategies and more aware of the strategies the Star Reader used. I found this to be a great way to really focus my students on use of word identification strategies within a text.

Cesar as Star Reader of *Good Sports*

As indicated above, Cesar relied on sounding out words and rarely referred to pictures. However, after about a week and a half of doing the Star Reader activity, it was clear that he had already expanded his repertoire when he read *Good Sports* (Eschenbach, 2004):

1. *Teacher:* What strategies did you use when you were reading?
2. *Cesar:* I practiced, pointed sometimes, looked at the pictures, sounded out the words, and I saw a word family we learned.
3. *Teacher:* When did you use those strategies?
4. *Cesar:* I sounded out [the words] *player* and *winners*.
5. *Teacher:* When did you use the picture for a clue?
6. *Cesar:* I looked at the picture to figure out the word *goal* and *soccer*.
7. *Teacher:* When did you see a word family we learned that helped you read a word?
8. *Cesar:* When I read *kick* I saw *ick* and then I knew it was *kick* and I did that for *ball* too.
9. *Teacher:* What did you do for *ball*?
10. *Cesar:* Like I know *all*, so then I can read *ball*.
11. *Darlene:* Oh, like if we can read *he*, we can read *be* and *we* and *me*.

I was amazed that Carlos was able to identify and use so many strategies. In his initial IRI, he offered that he sounded out the words, guessed, practiced, and kept trying. Although these are strategies, they are very basic. He was now using more strategies and was recognizing the strategies he was using. The strategies that the other children identified were very observant as well. Darlene's reference to decoding by analogy was right on. She reinforced the idea that you can think of a word you know that has the same ending as the word you do not know and that will help read you read the word (unit 11). The session continued as follows:

12. *Teacher:* So did anybody else notice any more strategies that Cesar used while he was reading?
13. *Maria:* I think he saw *or* in *scores*, but he read it *sc-or-ez* and then he knew it was just *scores*.

. . .

14. *Teacher:*   Did you do that any other time, Cesar?

15. *Cesar:*   [fishing through the book] *The-* I read *uh-the-err*.

. . .

16. *Teacher:*   But *uh-the-err* isn't a word, so how did you figure out it said *other* instead of *uh-the-err*?

17. *Cesar:*   I just knew then.

. . .

18. *Denise:*   He pointed, but not every time.

19. *Teacher:*   Should he have pointed all the time?

20. *Denise:*   Yes, because he lost where he was when he looked at the picture on that one page.

21. *Teacher:*   Pointing to the words helps us keep our place, but pointing also helps us for another reason: when we sound out a word we can move our finger across it when we say the sounds.

Maria brought up the finding a small word in a big word strategy that she thought Cesar used, and then I asked whether he used it any other time. He came up with the *the* in *other*, which ended up not being a very successful strategy because he ended up with nonsense word. Nevertheless, he argued that ultimately it helped him identify the word. Darlene also suggested pointing as a strategy, and argued that it was a good one for him because he lost his place when he looked at pictures. I wanted the students to realize that pointing to a word doesn't actually help us identify an unknown word, but can help them sound it out and keep their place.

Sam as Star Reader of *Last One Picked*

After students had been doing this activity daily for nearly three weeks, Sam became Star Reader, reading *Last One Picked* (Feely, 2000). Afterwards, I asked him what strategies he used when reading.

1. *Sam:*   I sounded out words, looked at the pictures, and self-corrected.

2. *Teacher:*   When did you use those strategies?

3. *Sam:*   I sounded out the words *always*, *whoosh*, *swished*, and *through*.

4. *Teacher:*   When did you use the picture for a clue?

5. *Sam:*   I looked at the picture to figure out the word *basketball* and *stood*.

6. *Teacher:*   When did you self-correct?

7. *Sam:*   Yesterday, when I read the book with my mom. Yesterday I read *everybody* instead of *everyone*.

8. *Teacher:*   How did you realize you read the wrong word, because *everybody* also makes sense in that sentence?

9. *Sam:*   Because the word don't got a *b*.

. . .

10. *Teacher:*   Did anybody notice Sam using any other word identification strategies?

11. *Cesar:*   He sounded out *scored* because he said *ssskk-or-dd*.
12. *Sam:*   No, that's a little word inside the big word . . . but I kinda sounded it out too.
13. *Teacher:*   What little word was in the big word?
14. *Cesar:*   *Or.*

By now, students were quite adept at talking about strategies. In unit 1, Sam noted three strategies he used: sounding it out, looking at the picture, and self-correcting, and in subsequent units he offered examples for the first two when he read in class. However, when I asked about the third one, self-correction, he gave an example of when he had ready *everybody* for *everyone* while he read with his mom at home (unit 7). I thought that it was impressive that he could recall what he done earlier at home and that he was thinking about strategies whenever he read. And he could answer my question about how he realized his self-correction because substituting *everybody* for *everyone* is semantically and syntactically appropriate by noticing the *b* in everybody. In unit 3, Sam tried to sound out *through*, but could not. We have not discussed the point that *ough* can stand for the sound *eww*. Subsequently, I told the group that *through* was a "weirdo word," but didn't make a big deal about it. In the last unit, all showed that they knew that *or* was the small word in *scored*.

When I asked if anyone noticed anything else, Darlene offered that she knew that Sam practiced. I asked Sam how many times he had practiced the book and he said, "About four times." I reminded them that we reread books for fluency so we can commit these new words to memory. Sam interrupted, "Yeah, 'cause, like when I kept reading the book to my mom I kept saying *al-ways* instead of *all-ways*, but know I know that word already."

Partner Reading Means Succeeding

Another activity students engaged in to foster their word identification strategies was partner reading. This routine involves two students reading the same new book together, each reading a page in turn. They read a book at, or slightly above, their reading level. This routine allowed me to see what they did without my guidance—how they might assist their partner in the use of reading strategies. I told them that I wanted to see them helping their reading buddy use these reading strategies while they were reading, and not just tell them a word they cannot identify. The excerpts below show the ways in which different partners used strategies.

Darlene and Sam

Darlene: [Reading the text] HE IS THE TALLER IN THE CLASS.
Sam: *Tallest.* He can't be the *taller* in the class.

It was very enlightening to see Sam not only correct Darlene's *taller* but provide her with a reason as to *why* it was not correct. This was something I also modeled and stressed in class. Children should constantly be making sure that what they are reading makes sense.

Sonia and Cesar

Sonia: MAYBE I'LL BE A B . . . [She was unable to read *builder*.]
Cesar: Think about what it could be. Look at the picture. What does that boy look like? [In it, a boy has on a hard hat and is at a construction site.]
Sonia: A builder guy.
Cesar: Right. So then read it again.

This was a great moment for me. Cesar, who rarely uses picture clues himself, was able to take ownership of this strategy and pass it on to Sonia, who also isn't in the habit of using picture clues. Listening to Cesar speak to Sonia was like listening to myself with the students. He had taken what I had modeled and become Sonia's teacher.

Denise and Maria

Denise: FIRST, HE PUT ON HIS S . . . [She was unable to read *scarf*.]
Maria: [Pointing to the picture of the scarf.] What is that?
Denise: FIRST, HE PUT ON HIS SCARF.

Here is another example of referring to the pictures as a strategy, and one that was very successful for Denise. However, looking at the picture doesn't always work so well; see another excerpt from Denise's reading, with Maria as partner.

Denise and Maria

Denise: SAM WENT JOE-GING.
Maria: No, *joe-ging* doesn't make sense.
Denise: I don't know then.
Maria: Look at the picture.
Denise: Running . . . it isn't *running* because it don't start with a *r* and I don't know.
Maria: *Jogging*.

At first, Denise put in a nonsense word for the word *jogging* in the text. Maria noted that that didn't make sense, and Denise was "stuck" and was about to give up. However, Maria suggested that she refer to the pictures for some ideas. She came up with a good idea—*running*, which ends with -*ing*, as does the text word—but she realized that that couldn't be right because "it don't start with a *r*." At this point, Maria, the more fluent reader partner, gives her the word so they could continue reading.

Although the partners often relied on the pictures as a clue for word identification, they did use other strategies. Denise in the preceding excerpt, for example, also explored the spelling details of the word she was having trouble with. Also, they used cross-checking to see if the words they came up when referring to pictures made sense. They were using the strategies that we had talked about in class, and it was clear that they were also reading for meaning because they were correcting themselves or their partner when something did not make sense. I think that modeling the strategies when I read to them and discussing the strategies during the Star Reader activity helped them to expand their use of strategies and to work harder at identifying the words they didn't know.

Final Assessment

Towards the end of my inquiry, I asked the students' classroom teacher if she had noticed their use of strategies to identify unknown words. Her response indicated that the students had been increasingly using the strategies when they were reading. She said they no longer first asked what a word was, but were inclined to try out a strategy or two instead. Moreover, they were also starting to sound out silently and not out aloud, which showed some confidence in reading. Children were tackling a range of strategies: besides sounding out, they explored finding a little word in a big word, looking at pictures, asking themselves if it sounded right, and reading it again.

Each child was interviewed individually again to find out what reading strategies they used when they came to a word they didn't know in a text. I also used an IRI to assess their reading. All six showed an increased use of strategies, but below I provide information about the assessments of five of the six children (Denise was absent when I did the post assessment): Sam, Maria, Cesar, Darlene, and Sonia.

In his interview, Sam reported: "Well, sometimes I look for a little word in a big word and if it doesn't work or sound right then I just try again. I skip the word. I think if it rhymes with another word that I like know. I look at the ending to find a word family like -ug, -ill, -ack."

Sam read *The Lonely Troll* (Jones, 2000) for the IRI. Here are examples of what he did during this reading. He found two little words in a big word when he read *himself*. He tried to sound out *scrubbed* and when he couldn't, he looked at the picture and was able to read it correctly. He used his knowledge of word families to read *clip, clop*, saying *c-l-ip, c-l-op*. Then he said, "I knew those were the word family." He tried to read *smiled* and then he asked me, "Does the *i* say its name?" I replied, "Look at the v-c-v [vowel–consonant–vowel] pattern and you tell me." He offered *sadly* and then said, "No, it can't be *sadly* because there's no *m*." At this point, I think he also realized *sadly* didn't make sense in the sentence, which read *He smiled* . . . He tried again and was then able to read *smiled*. He also corrected himself when he read *can* for *could* in the sentence *Then he ran as fast as he could, over the bridge* . . . Sam used all the strategies that he said he used. He had expanded his use of strategies since the first IRI. Before, he didn't skip words and go back to read them, nor did he say that he looked for a word family of endings that he knew. Lastly, Sam did not think of rhyming words to help him read unknown words (decoding by analogy). This time he didn't mention that he also used picture clues and checked to see if the word he read looked right and made sense in the text, but he did employ these latter strategies when reading. He knew how to use every strategy we had covered.

In the interview, Maria stated, "I sound it out, stretch, look at the picture, find a little word in a big word, look for word families, see if there's a vowel." When I asked her for an explanation or an example for the last comment regarding a vowel, she responded,

"Like if there's *i-e* I say *i*, which meant that she was aware of vowel digraphs and was trying to come up with a strategy around this feature of English.

During her IRI, she found a little word in a big word when she read *whoever*, *upset*, and *necklace*. When she read *necklace* she pronounced it *lace* and then realized it didn't make sense and corrected herself to read the word correctly. She noticed the *-est* word family when she identified and read *-est* for *highest*, but didn't know to read the first part of the word, *high*. Maria sounded out various words, and she recognized the *-unch* word family because she could read *l-unch*. Maria also had expanded her use of strategies since the first assessment. Now, she self-monitored to see if what she read made sense, looked right, and sounded right. Maria also continued to sound out or stretch out a word, looked for a little word in a big word, and referred at the picture for ideas. She, too, was using all of the strategies we have studied.

In his initial interview, Cesar could offer two strategies when he was faced with a word he didn't know—sounding it out and trying it again. Now he had many things to say: "I like to skip it, go back, and read it again, if I know it then. I ask people what's the word. I point. I look at the pictures and then I make an inference, like a guess that the book doesn't tell you." During his reading, he employed the above strategies, and in addition he recognized a word family, e.g., *-ick* when he read *p-ick-ed* and *-al* and *-ay* for *al-w-ay-s*. He found a little word in a big word when he read *captain*, where he could read *cap* but not *tain*. Cesar sounded out some words as well.

Like Sam and Maria, Cesar had broadened his knowledge and use of strategies. He even remembered the word *inference* and its meaning. Cesar was also beginning to grasp self-correction. Yet although his repertoire of reading strategies has expanded, he still doesn't seem to use context as much as he could.

In the first interview, Darlene reported only one strategy—sounding it out. Here, she added two others: "I sound it out, point, and look at the picture." During her reading, she employed the first and third strategies. For example, she sounded out minimal words and looked at the picture for a clue to figure out *jewels*. She also used the "find a little word in a big word" strategy when she read *t-or-n*, *to-morrow*, and *who* for *who-ever*. Thus, Darlene had slightly expanded her repertoire of reading strategies. In the first interview, she only knew to sound out the word if she could not identify it.

Sonia noted four strategies in her second interview—"I look at the pictures, sound out the words, find a little word in a big word, and ask a friend what the word is"—whereas she had mentioned only two (looking at pictures and sounding it out) in the earlier interview. Three of these (the exception being asking a friend) were also shown in her IRI reading. She looked at the picture to figure out *bridge*, *scrape*, *knee*, and *teeter totter*. She also sounded out some words, and she found a little word in a big word when she read *com-fort* and *walk-ed*. In addition, in one instance she employed three strategies: Sonia recognized a word family and sounded out *op-en* as *ahhp-en* but then changed it to *open* when she realized that *ahhp-en* is not a word. So, just like the students mentioned, Sonia used more strategies at the end.

Learning to Be Word Detectives

It has been very insightful to see young first-grade children becoming able to name word identification strategies. It is even better to see the students *using* the strategies. Every student showed growth in both areas. I have witnessed them taking ownership of their own learning and being able to support their peers. Their classroom teacher also noticed their use as well. Moreover, the children do not need to refer to our classroom list of strategies anymore because they have become natural. I think this is because they weren't learned through rote memorization, but through valuable learning activities.

I feel that my explicit instruction and use of authentic texts were critical in helping students grasp the strategies. I will continue to teach in this way. I also think that students liked listening to their peers tell them what strategies they saw others use. I wasn't the only teacher in the class, and I liked the sense of communal learning that this project helped to foster.

My students are no longer at a loss when they come to a word they do not know. I accomplished my initial goal of helping my students expand their knowledge and use of the various strategies to identify unknown words in a text. I plan to continue to foster my students' abilities by teaching them to help themselves.

Challenges in My Inquiries

I would love to say that everybody and anybody can do this and that this action research has been a piece of cake. However, it is the most time-consuming and challenging thing I have ever done. Don't get me wrong, the rewards outweigh the labor and the insight gained is astonishing. I can now tell the action research critics that there is nothing "willy-nilly" about teachers doing research with their students. It is real and it is valid!

Data collection was a challenge. I had tapes, Post-it notes, and journal entries that were very hard to stay on top of and keep organized. It was difficult to determine what I should include in my inquiry and what to put aside. I felt that everything was important. Every time a child demonstrated a new insight, I wanted to include it. Transcribing our conversations was also very time-consuming and stressful. I had to sift through many conversations to recognize the children's voices in the two major activities.

I also encountered other difficulties. For starters, I was unable to conduct a final assessment from Denise. She was absent when I was doing the assessments, and then, when she finally returned, I was pulled out of my program to sub for a teacher on maternity leave, which led me to another problem. I was pulled to sub frequently, which interrupted the instruction and coherence of my reading program. I had seen great progress with Denise and was looking forward to seeing her final assessment. I am still planning on doing so when I finish subbing. I feel strongly that my students would have benefited even more from daily instruction.

The Star Reader activity was beneficial, but I also saw a possible flaw with it. I wonder if I should have had the Star Reader read a book that he or she had not practiced reading, to see how the strategy use played out. In this way, they would be reading it for the first time and might have used more strategies than when they had also practiced reading the book at home. Sam's reading was a perfect example of this. He practiced so much at home that he was able to read it without a hitch, leaving minimal strategies for the other students to identify. I would like to try to set up the Star Reader activity with this in mind next year.

The paired reading activity reminded me to be extra-cautious when pairing the children up. Denise sometimes became extremely annoyed and probably somewhat discouraged when reading with Maria. I need to remember to switch partners more often as well so that students can be exposed to the strategies that other children used.

Lastly, my initial plan was to keep expanding the list of strategies. However, we only added on one or two more strategies. I hope to add more as I continue to work with the students. I think they have a firm enough grasp of the strategies on our list for us to move on to others, keeping what we know at hand.

It is safe to say that all my work paid off. I am very happy with the success of my students and my very first inquiry. I think my action research has definitely improved my instruction. I look more critically at what I am teaching my students and ask myself what I want them to accomplish, and why. I am constantly asking myself these two questions. I don't stop once the lesson plans are written or the lesson is taught. I have become much more reflective with my instruction and I am a better teacher because of it.

References

Cunningham, P. M. (1995). *Phonics they use: Words for reading and writing.* New York: HarperCollins.

Dahl, K. L., Scharer, P. L., Lawson, L. L., & Grogan, P. R. (2001). *Rethinking phonics: Making the best teaching decisions.* Portsmouth, NH: Heinemann.

Fisher, B. (1995). *Thinking and learning together: Curriculum and community in a primary classroom.* Portsmouth, NH : Heinemann.

Gaskins, I. W. (2004). Word detectives. *Educational Leadership, 61,* 70–73.

Goswami, U. (1986). Children's use of analogy in learning to read: A developmental study. *Journal of Child Experimental Psychology, 42,* 73–83.

Children's Books

Eschenbach, B. (2004). *Good sports.* Chicago: Wright Group/McGraw-Hill.

Feely, J. (2000). *Last one picked.* Marlborough, MA: Sundance Publishing.

Jones, S. (2000). *The lonely troll.* Marlborough, MA: Sundance Publishing.

Prince, S. (1999). *The lost mother.* Marlborough, MA: Sundance Publishing.

Chapter 10

Kristen Terstriep's Inquiry Paper

INTRODUCTORY HIGHLIGHTS

- Provided a useful format to cover major themes of research she cited, which were then used as steps of practice that were implemented.
- Used italics to talk *about* language.
- Used quotations in running text and in separate sections.
- Used interesting headings.

Toss Out Your Dictionaries: A Look at More Effective Vocabulary Instruction

Kristen Terstriep

Why Vocabulary?

The link between vocabulary and comprehension is well documented. Creating meaning from a text is difficult if you lack the necessary vocabulary knowledge. In fact, vocabulary difficulty strongly influences the readability of text (Klare, 1984). Just try picking up a text on an unfamiliar subject and you can empathize with students as they struggle to read unknown words and make meaning with them. As a skilled reader, you could probably accomplish this task by using word strategies and prior knowledge. But our students do not have the strategy toolbox of a skilled reader, and if you have observed a student wrestle with a text, you have witnessed this firsthand. Novice readers skip unknown words, replace them with incorrect words, or spend so much time decoding that the context is completely lost.

Vocabulary instruction, then, is a very important aspect of a balanced literacy program, and even more so with disadvantaged children. Children who grow up in poverty have substantially lower vocabularies than their more advantaged peers (White, Graves, & Slater, 1990). Further, Hart and Risley (1995) show that growing up in poverty can seriously restrict the vocabulary children learn before beginning school and make attaining an adequate vocabulary a challenging task. Becker (1977) extends this situation to illustrate that lack of vocabulary can be a crucial factor underlying the school failure of disadvantaged children. If we consider this relationship between word knowledge, comprehension, and the likelihood of school success or failure, it becomes obvious that for children to succeed in literacy, they need a sufficient vocabulary.

Why Me?

As a third grade teacher in an inner-city school in a large urban district, this situation is particularly important to me. Ninety-eight percent of my students live below the poverty line. They come to school behind and the gap widens as they move upwards through the grades. Because third grade is a benchmark grade, only those students with a serious and obvious deficiency are retained before they reach me. Students are then promoted or retained based on their scores from the Illinois Standards Achievement Test (ISAT), which they take in the spring. I have taught third grade for four years and vocabulary is always an issue with my students and their performance on the ISAT. Even confident readers are challenged by the words they find in the passages.

Why Now?

This year is no different and, in fact, has proven even more trying because of how many students were behind when school started. Based on ISEL (Illinois Snapshot Early Literacy) scores from the previous year and my classroom assessments, most of my current students are reading below grade level. Of my twenty-one students, three are non-readers, six are reading at first grade and seven at a second-grade level. Only five students are reading on level. Contributing to this situation is the fact that five students performing below grade level have already been retained once in the K-3 cycle, and so must be promoted to fourth grade at the end of this year regardless of ability. I worried about these students continuing to drown in the system. I knew they would need a major boost if they were to become competent, make it through the ISAT, and, most importantly, become better readers. To accomplish this, I decided to focus on vocabulary. But where should I start? How could I be the most valuable to my students? Basically, what does effective vocabulary instruction look like?

Step One: Admitting There Is a Problem

I began by reflecting on my current vocabulary program and observing students' responses. I use the word "program" loosely because what I found was that despite my attempts to keep instruction differentiated and engaging, I was not being effective. There was no cohesiveness in what I was doing—I was picking and choosing "activities," from Word Maps to Word Walls. I thought I was successful because students were actively participating. They completed their work and were engaged. However, I discovered through my reflections that what I truly wanted to see—students using new words in their writing and speech—was not present. Students continued to write and respond about being "mad" or "sad" even though "furious" and "depressed" were on the Word Wall. Students were not showing the improvement I hoped for in assessments, either. Mid-year classroom assessments administered in January showed little improvement over the same assessments given in September. Scores on the San Diego Quick Assessment, running records, and comprehension tests, used to assess word recognition, fluency, and comprehension, respectively, demonstrated some growth. However, 85 percent of students were still "working on" these standards (scoring below 80 percent). Obviously, changes were needed, but what to change and what to change it to?

Again with the Dictionaries?

To answer these questions, I looked to the research for direction. There I found many ideas about how to alter my instruction—and how not to. Many of the traditional models of teaching vocabulary, where definitions for words from the basal are copied and memorized for a weekly test, are ineffective (Richek, 2005). First of all, vocabulary words that correspond to stories in basal reading books are often insignificant and irrelevant to students. Students are not invested in them and therefore do not retain or integrate them into their speech or writing (Graves & Watts-Taffe, 2002). And just watching a student laboriously look up and copy definitions from a dictionary demonstrates this activity's uselessness. Students are often unable to read the words in the definition themselves, much less distinguish between multiple definitions or explain the definition in their own words.

Five Themes of Effective Instruction

Why Do I Have to Learn This?

The old-school models of learning word meanings lack the necessary components of what current research has found to be effective in teaching vocabulary. What is effective incorporates five themes. First, vocabulary instruction needs to be purposeful, authentic, and meaningful. The new words should be important for making meaning, and students should learn them by interacting with them in authentic ways. For example, the teacher should choose words that are central to the plot in a novel study or key to conducting an experiment in science (Pardo, 2004). To make instruction more meaningful, students can also choose their own words to learn. When students choose their own words, they learn the meanings more successfully and retain them longer (Blachowicz & Fisher, 2003). Further, self-selection of vocabulary words fosters word consciousness, creating an awareness of, and interest in, the words students hear, read, speak and write (Graves & Watts-Taffe, 2002). Regardless of who chooses the words, both teacher and student need to be aware of the importance and necessity of the words for making meaning.

This Can't Be Learning—It's Fun!

The next theme of effective vocabulary instruction is that it allows for practice and play. Students need practice using a word for it to become a part of their functional vocabulary. They should actively and frequently engage with words in writing and discussion (Pardo, 2004). With guided practice in the classroom, students will become comfortable using new words and more likely to use them outside of the classroom. Games and word play are highly effective instructional strategies that provide this guided practice. Games support flexible and metacognitive thinking as students manipulate meanings and see words in new contexts (Blachowicz & Fisher, 2003). Graves and Watts-Taffe (2002) describe numerous games that involve word play, such as Homonym Bingo and Homophone Concentration. The multiple meanings of words can also be used to create games. Activities such as these provide students with opportunities to play with words, making learning fun as students practice.

That's a Math Word, Not a Reading Word!

Instruction that reaches across settings is the third theme of effective vocabulary instruction. New words and strategies for understanding words need to be encountered in multiple settings. Simply teaching vocabulary words and strategies during literacy lessons is not sufficient for increasing word knowledge (Graves & Watts-Taffe, 2002). Familiarity with a word or word-learning strategy in only one setting may not translate to other settings without explicit instruction. Word consciousness in all settings is necessary since students often encounter new words incidentally (Graves & Watts-Taffe, 2002). Teachers should model, recognize and encourage word-learning strategies so that when students meet an unknown word in any given setting, they are able and motivated to investigate it (Graves & Watts-Taffe, 2002). Teachers can model good word-learning behaviors by seeking out new words and being excited about words. They can recognize students for their use of language and encourage them to experiment with new words. Doing these things across the curriculum in all the content areas will help students transfer word knowledge and strategies across settings.

I Know More Than You Think! Use It!

Effective vocabulary instruction must connect and integrate new words to students' existing knowledge. Students profit from definitional information, contextual information, and usage examples that connect to prior information (Blachowicz & Fisher, 2003). To connect new words to existing vocabulary, students learn definitions, contexts and examples by engaging in meaning making activities. Richek (2005) describes an activity in which students work in small groups to explore and create relationships between seemingly random pairs or groups of words. Blachowicz and Fisher (2003), Pardo (2004), and Graves and Watts-Taffe (2002) all explain and advocate the many uses of graphic organizers to illustrate word relationships. Word webs, semantic maps, arrays, and matrices visually depict a word's connection to students' prior knowledge. Students may brainstorm words relating to a topic, such as arctic animals or types of machines, and then use the words to create or complete a graphic organizer. As students make connections between new and old, new words are assimilated and integrated, ready to be used as future building blocks.

Last, But Not Least . . .

When each of the previously described themes is put into practice, deep processing is fostered, and this is the final theme I found in the research. Effective vocabulary instruction allows for deep processing of new words. Purposeful, authentic instruction that facilitates connection making through practice and play allows for deep processing (Graves

125

and Watts-Taffe, 2002). By exploring and discovering word meanings in many contexts through authentic activities, students see the many dimensions of words, and those words become a part of their personal vocabularies (Blachowicz & Fisher, 2003). An example of an optimal situation for learning vocabulary that involves each theme would be learning new words as they relate to a skill, such as sewing or boating (Blachowicz & Fisher, 2003). However, while first-hand learning might be most efficient, it isn't always possible. Just as I probably won't be able to go to Spain to learn Spanish, I probably won't be able to ensure students encounter all the words I want them to learn incidentally. What I learned from the research, though, is what I could do—create as many meaningful opportunities as possible for students to encounter, make connections to, use, and explore new words.

So Now What?

After the review of the literature, I knew what I needed to change in my vocabulary instruction and I had a general idea of how I could make the changes. First, my teaching needed more purpose and authenticity. I could accomplish this by ensuring vocabulary words were necessary for making meaning and by allowing students to choose their own words to learn. Second, my instruction needed to incorporate more practice and word play. I could do this by scaffolding students' use of words in their writing and conversations, and integrating games and fun activities into lessons. The next thing I needed to change was my tendency to teach vocabulary in isolation instead of across settings. I could do this and increase students' word awareness by involving word study in all areas of the curriculum. Next on the list was activating prior knowledge by making connections to words. This I would do by modeling how to connect words visually through graphic organizers. Finally, I needed to support deep processing by changing my "pick and choose" tendency towards vocabulary instruction and develop a sustainable, cohesive program that incorporated the themes for effective instruction.

Three R's

What It Is and How It Came to Be

To implement and monitor these changes, I decided to focus specifically on two daily routines to teach and observe vocabulary usage. One was morning literacy block and the other was Three R's. Both are times when students tended to discover new vocabulary words, or "spicy words," as we call them in our classroom. These are also times when literacy strategies are modeled and practiced. Three R's routine, which stands for *Read, Relax, and Refresh*, grew out of the fact that students are not allowed to have a recess at my school and so were in desperate need of a calming activity after lunch. It has evolved into a wonderful ritual that students and I both value and look forward to each day. Three R's begins as soon as we return to the classroom after the lunch period. To begin, I turn down the lights and I light a candle. Children recite "Listen to the Mustn'ts," an inspirational poem by Shel Silverstein (1974), and then I read aloud from a chapter book. The book is always above my students' reading level, something they could not read on their own but that is age-appropriate. This year, we have read *Catwings* (Le Guin, 1988), *James and the Giant Peach* (Dahl, 1996), *The Mouse and the Motorcycle* (Cleary, 1965), and *Because of Winn-Dixie* (DiCamillo, 2000), and during my research, we were in the process of reading *The Tale of Despereaux* (DiCamillo, 2003). The duration of Three R's varies from day to day, depending on the length of chapter and the richness of the discussion around it, but I allow Three R's time to last as long as we need it to.

We Love Spicy Words!

Three R's has always been an important part of my vocabulary instruction. This is the one time of the day that I can ensure all students encounter new and interesting words. With so many students reading below grade level, they are not often presented with words that challenge and extend their word knowledge. By reading aloud a more difficult text, I expose students to new words and show how words can be used in speech and writing. At the beginning of the year in our first Three R's story, I explained the difference between a regular word, like *happy*, and a spicy word, like *delighted*. I modeled how to choose spicy words as I read aloud. Now, as I read a chapter, students listen and choose words they feel are spicy. Students agree upon spicy words and then determine the meaning of these unfamiliar words from the context of the story. We discuss the meanings and add the words to our spicy word wall. Spicy words are words students feel are important. They tend to be words students relate to, such as *scurry* or *trotted*, which they connect as a spicier version of *run*. However, students have also selected more difficult words like *perfidy* and *melancholy* as spicy words. I agree with Blachowicz and Fisher (2003) that permitting students to choose words to learn does lead to an increase in ownership. However, as I explain below, without the presence of the other themes, deep processing does not occur.

Three R's is important to my vocabulary instruction beyond simply the acknowledgement of spicy words. The discussion concerning spicy word selection is rich with insights into students' current vocabulary knowledge and how they are assimilating this new word into that knowledge. I am as interested in why students choose a particular word as I am in the word itself. After students have chosen a spicy word and we have discussed the meaning, it is written on chart paper labeled with the story title. I also make a laminated color copy of the book cover and paste it on the poster. This spicy word poster hangs on a small bulletin board, which constitutes the spicy word wall, until we finish the book. Spicy word posters from each of Three R's books serve as an artifact and remain hanging somewhere in the classroom for the duration of the school year.

Although students had been exposed to wonderfully rich vocabulary through Three R's, as I mentioned before, it was not evident in their writing or spoken language. Before I began my research, I had yet to see most of the words used outside of that specific Three R's time. Even though students could explain the meanings of spicy words when asked, they were not connecting them to their lives. Instruction was not reaching across settings, for obvious reasons. I needed to do more than simply add words to a word wall, despite the fact that students themselves chose the words. I had to bring in the other themes as well.

When I looked at my second daily routine, morning literacy block, I discovered another gap in instruction. The two routines, morning literacy block and Three R's, were operating independently when they could have been enhancing each other. In my own head, I had thought of them as separate entities—one was work (literacy block) and the other was fun (Three R's). I realized I was missing an opportunity to capitalize on the enthusiasm students and I both have for Three R's. I decided to shift my own thinking and inspire a change in my students as well by bringing Three R's into morning literacy block, thereby creating the optimal situation for inclusion of the five themes.

Morning Literacy Block

The logistics of the routine remained the same before and after I began my research. Morning literacy block, from 9:30 to 11:15, begins with a read-aloud that is connected to a following short, whole-group strategy lesson, lasting about 20 minutes. We meet for the lesson on the large carpet in the back of the classroom. The focus of the lesson may be a comprehension strategy like visualization using a wordless picture book as the read-aloud, or I may read aloud a non-fiction book to model how to determine importance from a text. An artifact is created from the lesson and displayed for future reference. Artifacts include student-created posters of T-charts, KWL charts, poems, pictures, and anything else that connects to an important concept. Every available inch in the classroom is covered with these reminders of previous lessons, surrounding students with a visual representation of what they have learned. Posters and pictures hang on the wall, file cabinets, window shades, even from the ceiling!

After the strategy lesson, students rotate between small-group or independent center activities and guided reading groups. This portion of the literacy block lasts for one hour, from 9:50 until 10:50. Center activities focus on that morning's strategy lesson and allow students to practice using the strategy in context. Activities vary but have included using sticky notes to practice self-monitoring, reading with a buddy to practice fluency, or journal writing to practice responding to literature. More intense practice happens during guided reading groups. I meet with 3 to 4 students at the same reading level for 15 to 20 minutes of individual reading practice to scaffold their strategy use and monitor their progress.

The final portion of the literacy block runs from 10:50 until 11:15. The students meet back on the carpet to review the whole group lesson and to complete their independent learning logs. In these logs, they reflect on what they did that morning, what they learned, and how they will use the new information. I respond to them at least twice a week and collect them at the end of the week.

Three R's Meets Morning Literacy!

For the duration of my research, from mid-January through April, I modified the content of morning literacy block to focus on vocabulary and, more specifically, vocabulary gained from Three R's time. Mini-lessons provided the perfect opportunity for introducing, modeling, and reviewing vocabulary strategies. Each day, the focus of the mini-lesson was some form of word study. During the mini-lesson each morning, I connected the chapter from previous days' Three R's reading to the focus strategy. Following the mini-lesson, small-group or independent activities offered students time to practice using the vocabulary strategy. I designed activities that supplemented the morning's lesson by extending and incorporating strategies and spicy words. Finally, students also practiced the strategy with me during guided reading groups. I encouraged students to use vocabulary strategies and spicy words to increase their fluency, comprehension, and word knowledge.

The Five Themes, My Way

Making Spicy Connections

Throughout my research, we were reading *The Tale of Despereaux* (DiCamillo, 2003) for Three R's. This is the story of a mouse, Despereaux, who is sent to certain death by his father for the crime of falling in love and speaking to a human princess. During one reading, students chose *miserable* as a spicy word. From the context, in which Despereaux is sitting alone, waiting to be taken to the dungeon, they concluded that miserable meant *very sad* or *upset*. I wrote *miserable* on the Despereaux poster and added it to the spicy word wall. The following day, I read *The Blue Day Book* (Greive, 2000) for the mini-lesson read-aloud. This is short book that personifies photographs of animals as having bad days; the text under a very pathetic-looking bulldog reads "everyone has blue days" (p. 2). After reading the book, students brainstormed words that meant *blue*. The following is an excerpt from the discussion:

Teacher: So we should have lots of ideas for blue words after that book. Does anyone have a suggestion for our poster?
Trenton: *Unhappy* is a good one.
Mariah: *Depressed* is like unhappy and blue.
Teacher: You're both right. Depressed is like very, very sad or unhappy.
Crystal: [Excited] It's like that word from *Despereaux*!
George: [Looking around to the word wall] Yeah, yeah. Very sad or upset!
Carolina: [Waving hand in the air] *Miserable*! *Blue* is like *miserable*!

Students made the connection between the new word—*miserable*—and their prior knowledge—words that meant blue. They continued to brainstorm words and add them to the poster. After the brainstorming session, I drew their attention to the connections they had made between words. I told them that making connections between words would help them in their reading and writing by giving them a larger bank of words to draw from.

Center activities for that day continued the exploration of *blue* words and allowed for more connection making. Students created sensory webs (Graves & Watts-Taffe, 2002) in which they wrote what the word *miserable* looked, sounded, tasted, felt, and smelled like to them. George wrote that *miserable* "tasted like tears" and Donny wrote that it "felt like your dog running away." Jamara wrote that *miserable* smelled like "dirt and smoke."

129

Bianca wrote that it sounded like your friends teasing you, and Michael said *miserable* was your mom yelling at you.

In the following Three R's reading, students chose *melancholy* as a spicy word. They immediately connected it to *miserable* and we added it to the *Blue Day* poster, as well as the spicy word wall. The next day, I read the picture book *Jennifer Jones Won't Leave Me Alone* (Wishinsky, 2003). This is the story of a boy who dislikes Jennifer Jones until she moves away and he misses her. Students used both words, *miserable* and *melancholy*, in our discussion after the reading. Below is an excerpt:

Teacher: How did the boy feel when Jennifer Jones moved away?
Trenton: Sad.
Carolina: He was really sad, he was miserable. Like Despereaux.
Donny: He was melancholy like Despereaux, too.
Trevon: Miserable, melancholy, depressed—he was blue!

Students connected *miserable* and *melancholy* in their writing in the sensory webs and in their speech in whole-group discussions. I also found these and other blue words in students' Learning Logs. Trenton wrote that he had learned that *miserable* means very sad, a synonym for it is *melancholy*, and that he could use it to describe his feelings on blue days. Alice wrote that *miserable* comes from the word *misery* and she could use the word to describe how she feels when her dad leaves.

I continued lessons on connection making with spicy words in this same format throughout my research. Students chose the words *fortunate*, *daft*, and *naughty* from Three R's readings. After students chose a spicy word, I found a read-aloud for the mini-lesson that lent itself to a connection with it. We created artifacts like the *Blue Day* (Greive, 2000) poster of our brainstorming for related words for each spicy word. Students then made connections and created sensory webs for them in center activities. I continued to find spicy words in students' Learning Logs as well. Although I definitely stacked the deck in students' favor in my selection of books, I still feel that their use of spicy words in our discussions and in their writing was authentic.

Blue *Day, Not* Blew *Day!*

To take advantage of the connections students made with *The Blue Day Book* (Greive, 2000), I used the opportunity to introduce word play with homonyms and homophones. I began by explaining that some words sound exactly the same but are spelled differently and have different meanings. I wrote *blue* and *blew* on a sheet of chart paper and asked students to tell me what the words meant. Students were eager to share words from our brainstorming poster for *blue* and to explain that *blew* meant to blow something out, as in "he blew out the candle," or to do badly, as in "you blew it." I titled the chart paper with *Homonym* and asked students if they could think of any other words like *blue* and *blew*. They generated a short list, including *male/mail*, *scent/sent*, and *new/knew*. After we had discussed the different word meanings, I read aloud *A Little Pigeon Toad* (Gwynne, 1988). From the book, we were able to add many more word pairs to the chart: *toad/towed*, *road/rowed*, and *plane/plain*, for example. I explained that students would use the words from the chart to create a Homonym Book during center activities. First, students chose a homonym word pair and labeled each half of a piece of construction paper with one of the words. Then, they wrote a sentence for each word and illustrated it.

The pages students created were very imaginative and demonstrated their developing word awareness. Mariah created a page for *piece* with a drawing of a pizza and a corresponding sentence, and *peace* with a drawing of a white flag and a sentence about stopping violence. Students constantly added to the poster, too. Donny found the homonym pair *great/grate* in his sister's poetry book and wrote it on the poster. We played Homonym Bingo and added those word pairs as well. Again, I noted that students wrote about homonyms in the learning logs. For example, Mitch wrote that he learned that you could spell some words differently but they still sounded the same. He wrote that this is important "because you don't want people to think you don't know what you're talking about."

Students continued to create pages for the Homonym Book during centers and add new words to the poster. I could see that students were becoming aware of the fact that word choice is important, that word meanings are multilayered, and, most importantly, that words are fun! During a reading of *Chocolate Moose for Dinner* (Gwynne, 2005), students discovered that some words can be spelled the same and still have different meanings. One line in the story says that the ruler was adored by his subjects and shows a picture of people bowing before a measurement ruler. Students enjoyed the fact that words could be funny, and so I took the opportunity to establish the Riddle of the Week routine.

Using Other Ways to Use Words

Creating Riddles

I started the Riddle of the Week routine by bringing in multiple copies of joke and riddle books for the students to read. I allowed students a chance to explore the books and learn the format and patterns of riddles. Then I posted a weekly riddle in the classroom. Throughout the week, students wrote possible answers on half-sheets of paper, along with an illustration, and placed their work in the Riddle Basket. I encouraged students to use spicy words in their answers. Then, on the final day of the week, I read aloud student guesses and give the correct answer. This routine was great fun for students and myself as well. I discovered excellent websites with puns and jokes and an entire subculture of elephant riddles that I never knew existed!

An example of a Riddle of the Week is "Why did the elephant wear red toenail polish?" The openness and absurdity of the elephant riddles lend themselves to all sorts of funny and creative answers. Charles wrote, "Because he was being ridiculous," and Curt wrote, "Maybe because she was trying to cheer herself up." Trenton and Carolina came closer to the mark by writing, "Because she ran out of green" and "Because she couldn't find the pink." Needless to say, the true answer, "Because she was trying to hide in the strawberry patch," got lots of laughs.

Through the games and word play, students are practicing using words for multiple purposes. They are learning how to manipulate word meanings and contexts. Most importantly, they are discovering that words are fun!

Writing Character Letters: Dear Despereaux . . .

Students wrote character letters as another activity that encouraged authentic use of spicy words and further developed word play. During one mini-lesson, I read aloud a letter my younger brother had written to me when I was in college. At the time, he was ten years old, the same age as most of my students. He wrote me because I was struggling through my first experience of being away from home and he was trying to cheer me up. I loved that letter and I saved it because it was so important to me. After I had given students this background, we talked about how I felt being away from my family—*miserable* and *melancholy* were words students used. Then we talked about how the letter had comforted me and brainstormed other "comforting" things. Some examples were making cookies with your mom, getting a present, and someone giving you a compliment. After this, we brainstormed a list of people and characters that might need some comforting. Making the list were all the characters in *The Tale of Despereaux*. Each character in the story has some sadness, and students picked up on this theme very easily. After we reviewed the brainstorms, students were released to center activities.

One center activity that followed this mini-lesson was Comforting Character Letters. Students chose a character from *The Tale of Despereaux* and wrote a comforting letter to him or her. As always, I encouraged them to use spicy words. Edgar's letter to the princess said he was sorry about the queen dying and he would feel miserable if he was her, too. He said she was fortunate that she still had the king and Despereaux to take care of her. Carolina's letter was equally creative. She, too, wrote to the princess, telling her she was more fortunate than she realized. She also included her own riddles in her letter to cheer up the princess. One of them, "How do you know when there is an elephant under your bed," I had used as a Riddle of the Week.

Comforting Character Letters provided an authentic writing activity for using spicy words. Using spicy words in the letters gave students practice and familiarity with them. The confidence they gained from this practice translated into using spicy words in Reader Response Letters as well. In Trenton's Reader Response for *The Stranger* (Van Allsburg, 1986), he used the spicy word *peculiar* to describe the main character. He then wrote in his learning log that he had learned how to use spicy words in his writing. By scaffolding authentic activities like Comforting Character Letters and encouraging use of spicy words, I could see a difference in my students' writing and awareness of the words around them.

"I Heard *Miserable* on American Idol!"

With their increased word awareness, I felt that my students were ripe for two activities that further promote instruction moving across settings: "Find That Word" (Richek, 2005) and word "sightings" (Graves & Watts-Taffe, 2002). These are activities in which students search for words they are studying in their environments. Students "collect" words anywhere—in parents' or siblings' conversation, on a television program or in an advertisement, or on a street map. These "collections" are then brought to class to be shared and discussed. I made a few revisions as I went along with this routine. At first, students could collect any spicy word just as described above. They earned one point for a collecting a word from television, adult conversation, or from a piece of print. They could earn two points for collecting a spicy word from other students' conversation. My hope here was to encourage students to use spicy words in their conversations with one another. What happened with the point system, unfortunately, was it became a management nightmare. Students were really excited about Find That Word, which was great, but there were so many students with so many collections every day that I couldn't keep track. I didn't want to discourage students' enthusiasm, though, so instead of calling it off, I gave students one spicy word per week to collect. One word versus twenty-five words was much easier to manage. Also, with the shorter list of sightings, students could post them on a small bulletin board for the class to see.

The one drawback that I couldn't figure out how to prevent was students "lying" about their sightings. For example, I was fairly certain George's brother did not wish him a *pleasant* day the week *pleasant* was the spicy word students were hunting for. What I decided, however, was that if George was so determined to earn an extra point, he deserved it. Also, he, and the other little fibbers in the room, were thinking about ways people could possibly use spicy words outside of the classroom, which was my goal anyway. So while they may have thought they were pulling one over on me when they brought in fake sightings, I believe I was the big winner in this game!

Some examples of sightings are listed below:

Carolina: The commercial said the candle had a pleasant smell.
Trenton: SpongeBob said Patrick was ridiculous.
Mariah: My mom said she was exhausted.
Mitch: Ms. Bryden told me to have a pleasant weekend.
George: My sister said she was miserable.
Donny: I saw the word *splendid* in the magazine ad.

Students were using their word knowledge to create word awareness. Now that I had resolved the original issues with Find That Word, the routine basically ran itself. Student posted their own sightings and I gave points based on what was posted. I even found myself hunting for the week's spicy word and sharing my sightings with students. It was another way that students could see how word play can be fun and words are all around them.

If You Build It, They Will Come

Deep processing of word learning is a fortunate by-product of meaningful activities that occur across settings and allow for play, practice, and connection making. By creating cohesion in my vocabulary program through linking two previously detached routines, I had developed such activities. Word knowledge introduced in Three R's was practiced, played with, and connected to morning literacy block. Sensory webs, Learning Logs, Character Letters, games, and riddles all demonstrated students' deep processing of spicy words.

It seemed like such an easy answer—be sure your instruction contains the themes of what has proven to be effective and your students will have better vocabularies. Unfortunately, it really is not this easy or this clear-cut. I cannot say for certain that students will make connections to words in their independent reading. Will they still skip unknown words in their reading? Will they continue to look for spicy words when they stop earning points for doing so? I wish I could say I was certain they would continue these good habits, but I cannot. What I can say is that at this point in time, they were more aware of words and were motivated to explore them. They had a positive view of word study and had increased their word knowledge. Considering where we started, I am happy with where we are.

Bumps—or How NOT to Conduct an Inquiry Project!

As I reread my paper, I am amazed at how pulled together I made it sound! You would never know how often I struggled, how much I questioned what I was doing, and how many times I wanted to start over. If I could do it over, I would start smaller than I did here. Vocabulary is such a huge, overwhelming topic. I think I could have done a better job with it if I had maybe focused on one routine—either morning literacy block or Three R's. As it was, I ran out of time, and energy, and did not include any guided reading material in my report. I spent so much time with the other two areas that I knew I could not do justice to the guided reading portion as well.

I also would have certain things in place before I started if I could do it all over. While the Comforting Character Letters were sufficient, it would have been more effective and authentic to have Pen Pals set up prior to beginning the inquiry. Even better would be to have Pen Pals that were reading the same book, such as *Despereaux*, for example, so that students could write about their experiences and thoughts using common spicy words.

One last bump was that I ran out of time to complete a post-test to gauge the effect of the change in instruction on students' comprehension, fluency, and word knowledge assessments. I had hoped to administer the tests prior to spring break, but due to ISAT testing and mandated five-week assessments at my school, I felt that students were tested out! I still plan to administer the end-of-year assessments in June and will compare scores to September and January scores. For now, I am confident that the quality of current student work is representative of their increased word awareness and demonstrative of their use of word-learning strategies.

References

Becker, W. C. (1977). Teaching reading and language to the disadvantaged: What we have learned from field research. *Harvard Educational Review, 47,* 518–543.

Blachowicz, C. L. Z., & Fisher, P. J. (2003). Best practices in vocabulary instruction. In L. Morrow, L. Gambrell, & M. Pressley (Eds.), *Best practices in literacy instruction* (pp. 87–110). New York: Guilford Press.

Cleary, B. (1965). *The mouse and the motorcycle.* New York: HarperCollins.

DiCamillo, K. (2000). *Because of Winn-Dixie.* Cambridge, MA: Candlewick Press.

DiCamillo, K. (2003). *The Tale of Despereaux.* Cambridge, MA: Candlewick Press.

Dahl, R. (1996). *James and the giant peach.* New York: Scholastic.

Graves, M. F., & Watts-Taffe, S. M. (2002). The place of word-consciousness in a research-based vocabulary program. In A. E. Farstrup & S. J. Samuels (Eds.), *What research has to say about reading instruction* (pp. 140–165). Newark, DE: International Reading Association.

Greive, B. T. (2000). *The blue day book.* Kansas City: McMeel.

Gwynne, F. (1988). *A little pigeon toad.* New York: Simon & Schuster.

Gwynne, F. (2005). *Chocolate moose for dinner.* New York: Simon & Schuster.

Hart, B., & Risley, T. R. (1995). *Meaningful differences in the everyday experiences of young American children.* Baltimore: Paul H. Brookes.

Klare, G. R. (1984). Readability. In P. D. Pearson, R. Barr, M. L. Kamill, & P. Mosenthal (Eds.), *Handbook of reading research* (pp. 681–794). New York: Longman.

Le Guin, U. K. (1988). *Catwings.* New York: Scholastic.

Pardo, L. S. (2004). What every teacher needs to know about comprehension. *The Reading Teacher, 25*(3), 272–280.

Richek, M. A. (2005). Words are wonderful: Interactive, time-efficient strategies to teach meaning vocabulary. *The Reading Teacher, 58*(5), 414–422.

Silverstein, S. (1974). *Where the sidewalk ends.* New York: HarperCollins.

Van Allsburg, C. (1986). *The stranger.* New York: Houghton Mifflin.

White, T. G., Graves, M. F., & Slater, W.H. (1990). Development of recognition and reading vocabularies in diverse sociolinguistic and educational settings. *Journal of Educational Psychology, 82*(2), 281–290.

Wishinsky, F. (2003). *Jennifer Jones won't leave me alone.* Minneapolis, MN: Lerner Publishing.

Chapter 11

Sandra Zanghi's Inquiry Paper

INTRODUCTORY HIGHLIGHTS

- Included references to others' ideas early in the paper.
- Used interesting titles of headings and sub-headings.
- Employed two focal small groups in her inquiry/paper.
- Used numbered discourse examples to be better able to refer to them when discussing her interpretations.
- Talked about the impact of standardized test preparation on her study.

Letting Their Voices Be Heard: Improving Literature Response Participation during Read-Alouds through Small-Group Discussions

Sandra Zanghi

Will the teacher like my answer? Will people think my thoughts are pointless? Will everyone think I am stupid? Darn it! Someone just said what I was about to say! Why can't I just sit in the back of the room and just listen?

I can remember the guts it took for me to raise my hand and speak in front of the entire class in elementary school. Questions and thoughts would race through my head every time before I would make that brave move to participate. Math was not as severe because I could calculate and see the answers blunt and clear before me. However, in reading class, there was no formula for making inferences and connections! How would I know I was right? As an adult, I gained the confidence to work past these fears. I also understand that there is value in how everyone responds to literature. Now, as a teacher, I find the need to pass on this understanding to my students.

During read-alouds, I noticed that the same six students continuously participate in whole group discussions. They understood the text, made inferences, asked questions, and connected to the text. These students demonstrated excellent responses to literature, yet the majority of my students rarely participated in read-aloud discussions. I wondered, "Do the students that do not participate have the same fears as I did as a child?" I could tell that even if they didn't participate, they were paying attention because all of my students were attentive and eager for read-aloud time. What I wanted was their responses to be heard and valued. I was also worried that if they just kept their thoughts to themselves, they would not be able to develop those thoughts and improve their understanding. Therefore, I came up with a plan to get all of my students more involved in literature discussions in responses to read-alouds.

My 5th grade classroom consisted of around 23 students of Mexican, Puerto Rican, or Latin American descent. The majority of my class spoke Spanish as their first language and ten students received ESL services. For three months, I tried implementing small group discussions following read-alouds. I would read aloud a chapter or section of a book. Following the read-alouds, students would respond by talking in small groups and writing in their journals. My research focused on how read-alouds followed by small-group discussions affected participation. Considering that improved participation may improve the quality of reading responses, I additionally looked at how small-group discussions during read-alouds would affect the quality of reading reflections.

Why Read-Alouds?

Read-alouds have always been part of the daily routine in my classroom. It is a special time of the day that the students enjoy, and it gives me an opportunity to model and teach many skills that the students can benefit from. Read-alouds help build vocabulary development and improve understanding of story structure. Students see how book language differs from oral language. I can model many reading strategies during read-alouds, as well as fluent, expressive reading. Also, read-alouds introduce children to the joy of reading and motivate them to read (Fisher, Flood, Lapp, & Frey, 2004; Rog, 2001; Sipe, 2000).

Other benefits of read-alouds include learning of factual information and encouragement of higher levels of thinking (Rog, 2001). Furthermore, students are enabled to express themselves as individuals (Fisher et al., 2004), as well as enhance knowledge of the convention of print (Rog, 2001; Sipe, 2000). In addition, an emotional attachment to the adult reader forms during read-alouds (Sipe, 2000).

Why Reading Responses?

While past researchers have found that read-alouds provide an opportunity for teachers to model reading strategies such as making text connections, it is also essential for students to take up these strategies themselves. When students make connections and other responses to literature, they are using a key comprehension strategy (Rog, 2001). Literature responses rely on the reader response theory. According to the reader response theory, "literary understanding involves the tracing of readers' personal responses and associations with a text" (Sipe, 2000, p. 260). Readers use their own experiences to shape their understandings of literature and then use literature to understand and shape their own lives (Sipe, 2000). Often, so much of literature instruction involves literal understanding, that students are not able to connect to texts and critically examine texts (Hart, Escobar, & Jacobson, 2001). The reader response theory supports my reasoning for having students respond to literature in ways *they* connect. While it is important for me to check for literal understanding and model reading strategies, read-aloud discussions should not focus only on my own thoughts on the literature. Instead, the discussion should center on how students make meaning of text.

Why Small-Group Literature Discussions?

Before I began this study, I had always conducted whole-group discussions during read-alouds. As I discussed before, I found whole-group discussions did not involve all of my students. Whether it was because certain students were too shy, or I'd run out of time for students to share their responses, I was not satisfied that only a few students were sharing and developing their responses to the literature. Small-group literature discussions seemed to be the best answer for my conflict.

Small-group literature discussion is grounded in Vygotsky's (1978) learning theories. Vygotskian ideas emphasize that learning takes place through social interactions. This relates to literacy instruction in that "as students learn how to interpret and critique literature within discussion groups, they are also learning how to understand differing views and interpretations of others" (Hart et al., 2001, p. 309). I hoped that by having students discuss read-aloud books in small groups, students would be more willing to discuss literature and learn from their discussions.

An Unexpected Beginning

When I first began collecting data, I wasn't sure if I should have students write before they discussed in small groups or after. My plan was to read the beginning of the story, have students write a response in their journals, and then have them discuss it. I predicted that students would not be sure of what to write about in their journals, so I gave them some open-ended questions they could answer from Fisher's (1995, p. 62) Inquiry List:

- What did you notice?   I noticed . . .
- What do you wonder?   I wonder . . .
- What did you think?   I thought . . .
- What did you like?   I liked . . .
- What did you learn?   I learned . . .
- What did you discover?   I discovered . . .
- How did you feel?   I felt . . .
- What did you consider?   I considered . . .

Next, I introduced the title of the short story I was going to read, "Lupe and la Llorona" (from *My Land Sings: Stories from the Rio Grande* [Anaya, 1999]), where the main character is challenged to find the truth about the ghost of la Llorona. As soon as I read the title, the majority of my students' hands shot right up and waved eagerly in the air. I had no idea that this story was so popular in Mexican culture. Going along with their enthusiasm, I had them write in their journal about the thoughts that came up in their head when I read the title. Meanwhile, I went to the video camera to record the discussion that was about to occur.

However, while I was distracted by video camera complications, the students couldn't hold in their desire to talk about the story. They ended up talking about what they knew about the story with the cluster of kids they sat with. I wish I had not been distracted by the video camera because I would have rather been listening in on my students' conversations. When I finally got the video camera to work, I didn't stop them from talking in their small groups. I figured this was what I wanted from the students in the long run! When time was running up, I had them wrap up their conversations and then they shared in a whole-group discussion. Students shared how they had heard about the ghost of la Llorona. As with many ghost stories, they had heard many versions of the story. They seemed fascinated to learn the true story. I had gotten them hooked! More importantly, they were engaged in literature discussions in small groups! This was my first indication that small-group discussions following read-alouds could get more of my students involved in responding to literature.

My students' eagerness to talk about the story made me reconsider having students write before discussing. I thought it might hinder discussions if the students had to hold back what they want to say until they were done writing. Still, I wanted students to write after they discussed because writing: (1) keeps students accountable for staying on topic during discussions; (2) gives students time to collect their thoughts; (3) gives them an opportunity to express things they may have not said in their discussion; and (4) serves as data for my study.

Bumpy Discussions

Now I was feeling more secure in my plan, which consisted of reading aloud, having students discuss in small groups, and then journal-write. I was still reading "Lupe and la Llorona" at this point. I tried to pay attention to how students participated within their small groups, using two groups as focal groups. I was only able to jot down the names of the students as they participated and a few notes. When I was observing one of the focal groups—Ashley, Mairany, Jessica, and Francisco—I realized that each member began by going around in a circle to share their ideas. I was concerned that they didn't really interact at first. They just stated comments that started with "I think" and then the next person would do the same. None of their comments connected to what another member said. At this point, questions began to arise. Should I do something to encourage more interactive discussions where students are responding to what others say? Or should I leave it be and see if more natural, interactive discussions would begin to occur naturally? After the third person in the group, Jessica, began to share, they started interacting more. They started commenting on group members' comments. Francisco didn't get his turn and was struggling to get his thoughts out. However, Jessica and Mairany dominated the conversation at this point while Ashley nodded and repeatedly said, "Yeah." Now I wondered if I needed to talk to students about allowing all group members to participate.

On the next day, I videotaped the same group. Again they went around their table in an orderly fashion:

1. *Ashley:*   I think ***
2. *Mairany:*   I really think that a different woman that when she goes to the river, she is going to get scared of a voice she hears, but then she's going to find out that la Llorona is not that bad, like not too scary. So she is going to be nice and that every day she is going to visit her.

3. *Jessica:*   I think that maybe Lupe is going to help la Llorona when she gets to know her better. She's gonna help her find her baby and that Lupe is going to go back to heaven and her soul is going to go back to heaven.

4. *Mairany:*   Lupe or la Llorona?

5. *Jessica:*   La Llorona.

6. *Mairany:*   It's your turn.

7. *Francisco:*   I think that Carlos is going to dress like la Llorona and he is going to scare . . .

8. *Mairany:*   Uhhh . . . It's possible. But, uhh . . . Carlos is going to say to everybody that he ran away. He's going to tell the truth. He's going to tell the truth. And then Carlos, and they will be best friends again, and join in games. And I think Carlos is going to be with her.

After each person had had a turn to participate once, Mairany again began to dominate the conversation similar to the previous day began. She did invite Francisco to speak (line 6), but then interrupted him before he could finish his sentence (line 8). I noticed that the students were mostly making predictions and beginning their predictions with "I think." Also, they were not responding to each other's predictions except when Mairany (in line 8) responded to what Francisco attempted to say about Carlos's action. Some of their predictions were confusing and random. I would have liked to see them question each other to clarify predictions and understand how they arrived at those predictions.

As I walked around the room, I noticed students were responding to the text in three ways. They were making the predictions about the story, discussing what they knew about la Llorona, telling what they had learned about the story of la Llorona, and debating whether la Llorona was real. I also noticed students were engaged in their conversations. The mystery of la Llorona seemed to intrigue them. What I was worried about was that students would continue to repeatedly discuss the mystery of la Llorona even though the plot of the story is moving away from the mystery.

Smoothing Out Discussions

To solve the participation problem I was seeing in the small-group discussions, I modeled a small-group discussion following a read-aloud of chapter 2 in *Becoming Naomi Leon* (2004) by Pam Muñoz Ryan. I had students volunteer to be part of a small-group discussion with me while the rest of the class observed. In this fishbowl-fashioned discussion, I chose two students who were often confident leaders in literature discussions and one student who was often quiet. While the three students and I discussed our responses to the chapter, I tried my best to act like a student, and not the teacher leading a discussion. Meanwhile, I modeled how a student could be a leader in a discussion by involving other students. For example, I tried to get the shyer student involved in the conversation by asking him questions such as "What do you think?" and "How would this make you feel?" In addition to modeling a discussion, I told students to be sure to include all of their fellow group members.

The fishbowl discussion also modeled various ways students could respond to the read-aloud literature. In this chapter of *Becoming Naomi Leon*, Naomi tells about how she hates her last name, Outlaw, because other kids make fun of it. In our fishbowl discussion, we discussed connections about how we have each been made fun of for our names. Students and I also analyzed characters and shared questions that we hoped to be answered as we read on.

Journal Writing

Mediocre Journal Writes

When students were done with their small-group discussions about the read-aloud book, I had them immediately write their responses in their journal. I noticed that some students would just list the things they talked about in their group, but not include their responses. For example, after a small-group discussion about the mystery of la Llorona and the main characters (Lupe and Carlos) in the story, Leo wrote, "We talked about how the current was to strong and the baby drowned and Carlos didn't think it was real but Lupa [Lupe] goes with Carlos to see if it's real." He focused on what happened in the text rather than his own thoughts and interpretations. I decided to target Leo in my study because he often has difficulty coming up with responses to literature. I realized that I had to keep the video camera focused on one group during a discussion because I was curious about what he said during the small-group discussions. Was he simply retelling the main events, or was he including his own responses to the story? I decided I needed to clarify to students that they should write their responses and not just a list of events that happened in the story.

Still, a lot of students were including thoughtful responses in their journals. For example, Desi wrote in response to "Lupe and la Llorona," "What we read so far is similar to another story about a man who drowns his wife and kid. People say you could hear him cry. I wonder if that story is true." I thought this was a good connection, although I would have liked to see her elaborate a little more and tell how the stories are alike. Larry also had many good responses on the reading, but also could have elaborated more. Larry wrote, "I learned another Llorona story. I wonder what will happen in the river. I noticed that Lupe and Carlos were scared." One factor that could have caused the lack of elaboration was time constrictions. During this time, my school was under a lot of pressure to prepare for the ISAT (Illinois Standards Achievement Tests), especially in math. Therefore, I could not spend as much time as I wished on my study and I may have rushed students during their journal writing. After discovering my students were not elaborating on their responses, I decided to manage my time better so they could have more time to write. I also realized I needed to talk to them about including more explanation for their responses and show an example of a written response.

While I was not completely satisfied with the journal responses, I saw some indications that small-group discussions may have been helping students respond to literature. For example, Randy often did not display confidence when participating in class, especially in reading. When I would ask him questions regarding an opinion, he often would tell me he didn't know the answer. He tended to participate more only when he could be sure he was right. However, he was able to give his opinion in this journal response to the book *The True Story of the Three Little Pigs* (1989) by Jon Scieszka: "I didn't [like the story] because the wolf never got a cup of sugar And the thing that I didn't get was why didn't they want to give the wolf the cup a sugar." Randy didn't understand that the pigs were probably too scared of the wolf to give him sugar because wolves eat pigs, yet I was happy to see that Randy was comfortable in asking about something he wasn't sure about regarding the reasoning of the pigs. He was also being a critical reader when he stated his reason for not liking the story. Again, I did not have the video camera on his group, so I did not know if the topic of his journal write came up in his discussion, and therefore affected his written response. However, I did know that his voice was now being heard through his journal writing. He most likely would not have shared this response if we had been discussing the story as a whole group.

Improving Journal Responses

In order to help students elaborate their journal responses and change the lists in their journals of what they talked about into well-written responses, I wrote an example of a response that would be written in a journal. I actually modeled the journal response after the fishbowl because I wanted the students to see how they could transfer what they talked about in their small groups into their written responses.

Modeling a discussion and then a journal response was time-consuming, but it was worth it. I saw fewer journal responses that were like a list, and more journal responses that displayed the writers' own thoughts, opinions, and connections to literature. For example, Leo, who had previously written lists of things he had talked about with his group, began writing his own thoughts on the literature. The day after I modeled the journal write, his response to *Becoming Naomi Leon* began with "I think that Skyla is acting werd [weird]. And not miture [mature]. She is acting like a kid." With this response, I can see that he is making an inference when he writes about Skyla, Naomi's mother, acting weird and immature. Also, he makes a comparison when he writes about the mother acting like a kid. Finally, I was beginning to see progress in my study.

Success for All

Generally, I was finding success in students responding to the read-aloud literature when they were allowed to discuss and then write a response. Following a read-aloud of a chapter in *Becoming Naomi Leon*, I saw a group of students of mixed ability levels benefit from a small-group discussion. In this chapter, Naomi's and Owen's mother suddenly shows up for the first time after the mother had left her children with her grandmother seven years ago. This is how a group of four students in my second focal group responded:

1. *Ruby:*   You wouldn't be really excited if your mom . . .
2. *Vernice:*—I'd freak out.
3. *Ruby:*   I'd be excited if my mom came home after a long time.
4. *Pat:*   But, you like hardly know 'em. You probably don't know what's good or bad about them.

5. *Edwin:*   ***
6. *Ruby:*   Well, I know, 'cause like you said.
7. *Pat:*   Well, yeah, like you don't know her, because, yeah.
8. *Ruby:*   But her grandma explained everything.
9. *Vernice:*   Well, I don't really know how I'd feel if I didn't really know my mom for seven years or something.
10. *Ruby:*   I'd be like she didn't really like me. She didn't want us.
11. *Vernice:*   If she left us alone and stuff.
12. *Edwin:*   I'd feel like she was a stranger to me.
13. *Vernice:*   That happened to my mom, her mom left her when she was like just born.
14. *Ruby:*   I was thinking of [the mom], that her mom should of came before seven years.
15. *Edwin:*   I couldn't believe they watched *Wheel of Fortune* that many times.
16. *Vernice:*—That was so funny. Their record . . . 744.
17. *Ruby:*   Now I am going to keep track of how many cartoons I watch.

If we look at this conversation, it is clear that Ruby and Vernice were the leaders of the discussion. Ruby was a natural leader when it came to most group work. She often had strong opinions that she liked to share. I found it interesting how her opinion changed about the mother returning to her children. At first, Ruby thought that it would be exciting (lines 1 and 3), but towards the end of the discussion she began to see the possible problems that might occur with the mother's return (lines 10 and 14). All four of the students were involved in the debate, which led them to a greater understanding of the text. Edwin and Pat often do not participate in whole-group discussions; however, here they voiced their opinions and were able to change Ruby's opinion about the mother returning (lines 4, 7, and 12). In addition to the debate, Vernice made a connection with her own mother's experience (line 13). Edwin expressed his amazement that the grandma had watched 744 episodes of *Wheel of Fortune* (line 15). Overall, I thought this discussion was an excellent example of how small-group discussions can improve student responses because students were able to have the chance to voice and develop their thoughts about the literature.

After the students had discussed the chapter, they wrote in their journals. Edwin, who often struggles with putting his thoughts onto paper, easily wrote a reflective response. He wrote, "I'm thinking what is the good and the bad about Skyla comeing to see Naomi and Owen and if my mom left me and came back to see me she would be like a stranger to me." I believe the opportunity to discuss these thoughts before he wrote them on paper helped him come up with this written response. Vernice and Ruby wrote journal writes similar to Edwin's ideas. Vernice wrote, "I think that Skyla didn't love Naomi and Owen because she had left them when they were little. I mean if my mom had left me, I would be scared if she came back." Ruby wrote, "If I was Naomi I would think that Skyla (Naomi's mom) didn't like them very much because she left them for 7 years. If Skyla really love them she would'nt have left them for 7 years. Skyla didn't call or write to them during these seven years." Pat wrote about Owen, Naomi's younger brother: "I think that Owen is very happy and excited the skyla has come back because Owen and Naomi hasent seen Skyla for seven years." Although Pat's journal entry was a retelling of the story, it was focused on Owen and about an interesting point in the book: Owen's eternal optimism became more apparent as the book went on. I wondered if Pat was beginning to understand Owen's character at this point in the book.

They Can "Get It" without the Teacher

When I first began giving students time to discuss the read-aloud literature in small groups, I was a little hesitant in giving up the control of discussions that I would have with whole-group discussions. I feared that without me asking questions, students would not make inferences and would miss important ideas in the literature. But that wasn't the case; they could do this on their own. During the following discussion, the class had just listened to the chapter in *Becoming Naomi Leon* where Skyla, Naomi's and Owen's mother, does not show up for parent–teacher conferences. When Naomi overhears a conversation by the school principal and her teacher, she learns that her mother had been in hospitals and halfway houses for alcoholism. Naomi also learns that her father wanted to have custody of his children, but her mother would not allow him to see Naomi and Owen. Below is how the same group discussed this chapter:

1.	*Vernice:*	If Skyla would have let him visit them at least.
2.	*Desi:*	And she said she would call court.
3.	*Vernice:*	Yeah, that she would have to go to court.
4.	*Desi:*	Yeah, but the dad has rights to see his own kids.
5.	*Leo:*	I know. Everyone does.
6.	*Desi:*	It's not like, it's not like . . . I'd understand if she called him to court if he was like stalking her and the kids, and threatening and stuff like that. But he's not. He just wanted to see his kids.
7.	*Leo:*	I bet Naomi is going to run away and take an airplane to Mexico.
8.	*Desi:*	But don't you have to be an adult to buy a ticket?
9.	*Vernice:*	Uh . . . I don't know. [pause]
10.	*David:*	I think . . . um . . . when Skyla took Naomi and Owen, maybe she was drunk and that's why she took them.
11.	*Leo:*	Oh! I know! Maybe she was drunk and that's why she didn't go [to the parent–teacher conference].
12.	*Desi:*	That's probably why.
13.	*David:*	But they said that she went . . .
14.	*Vernice:*	. . . she went to the hospital.
15.	*David:*	Yeah, they said she went to the hospital.
16.	*Desi:*	Yeah, but they said no one really knows. She probably could have been with Clive. And who knows what she doing. She could have been drinking.
17.	*Vernice:*	Wasn't she in a halfway house, right?
18.	*Desi:*	Yeah, but they said counselors watch you. But right now, she probably is not in there because she has to live there. But she is living with the grandma right now.
19.	*Vernice:*	Yeah.

The small group began by stating their opinion about the father's right to see his children (lines 1–6). Then Leo made a prediction that Naomi will take a plane to Mexico to find her father (line 7). Desi made a critical response to Leo's prediction, saying that children cannot buy plane tickets (line 8). After a pause in the conversation, David linked the children being taken away from their father to the mother's alcohol addiction (line 10). David's thought triggered Leo to come up with an explanation for why the mother did not go to the parent–teacher conference (line 11). Desi agreed that alcohol is probably the reason why the mother didn't show up (line 12), but David and Vernice state that it was because the mother was in the hospital or halfway house (lines 13–15). Desi then has to clarify that the mother was probably not at a hospital or halfway house because she was living with the grandmother (lines 16 and 18).

In this discussion, students stated their opinions, made predictions, were critical of predictions, made inferences about events that took place throughout the book, and clarified main events using textual evidence. All four students were able to express their own ideas that helped them make meaning of the text. If I were discussing this chapter with the whole class, I would have led the class to discuss the points that this group discussed. However, in a whole-class discussion, the four students in this group wouldn't have all expressed their ideas using critical reading skills as they did when they were in small groups.

Proof That I Still Need to Tweak Imperfections

In the previous discussion, students interacted well and responded to each other's ideas. Yet the group with Francisco and Ashley were still going around in a circle telling their thoughts. Francisco and Ashley's group had to switch Jessica and Mairany with Renaldo and Pat for reasons unrelated to the study. The group had some good ideas about the text and allowed others to share, but they did not respond to their group members' ideas. Here, they were discussing a chapter in *Becoming Naomi Leon* where Skyla announces that she wants Naomi to move to Las Vegas with her and her boyfriend, Clive. Also, Skyla yells and insults Owen when he defeats her at checkers several times. This is what each group member said when it was his or her turn to share:

1. *Renaldo:* I think Skyla and Clive are going to say that Owen doesn't know how to play checkers that much and they're gonna tell people he can't play good. Then people are going to play Owen and Owen is going to win. And then Clive and Skyla are going to waste the money that they bet on him.
2. *Francisco:* I think when . . . um . . . um . . . when they go to Las Vegas, she and her boyfriend are going to go out a lot.
3. *Pat:* I think Owen is probably mad at Skyla because Skyla was mean to him and he was probably scared. So, probably next time, when Skyla comes back to town, that he'll worry and he will start being mad.
4. *Ashley:* I think that . . . um . . . when Skyla and her boyfriend go to Las Vegas, they are going to go out a lot and that they are going to leave Naomi to clean the house and then they are going to come home late and they're gonna tell Naomi to do the food for them.

One possible reason that this group did not respond to each other's comments may be that they felt uncomfortable discussing when I was videotaping them, because I noticed they kept on looking into the camera when I videotaped them. Another explanation may be that they are all ESL students and their lack of English language skills might have hindered their ability to respond to each other's comments. In the future, placing a stronger discussion leader such as Ruby, Desi, or Vernice with this group could possibly improve this group's discussions. Also, I want to have more fishbowl discussions, with the class watching groups that have had interactive discussions.

After their discussion, each student wrote a response that reflects the thoughts that they expressed in their discussion. The following are excerpts from their journals:

Renaldo: I think Clay is going to housoul [hustle] people saing that Owen cant play right and hes going to bet money and hes not going to give Owen his part of the money.

Francisco: I think that when Skyla and her boyfriend and Naomis when there going to las Vegas Skyla and her boyfriend are going to go out a lot and their going to leave Naomi and Owen alone in the house because Skyla and her boyfriend said they were going to take Naomi and Owen to Las vegas.

Pat: I think that Owen is mad at Skyla because Skyla said bad things about him about the tape he wheres in his chest. And Owen is not gonna want the bike no more.

Ashley: I think that Clief [Clive], Skyla, and Naomi are going to go to Las Vegas and they are going to go out a lot and Naomi is going to stay at home. I notice that when Naomi stays at home she is going to cook, clean just like Cinderrela.

While their discussion wasn't perfect, they did get to express their ideas aloud and on paper, for what they shared in the discussion was more or less what they included in their journal writing—except, perhaps, Ashley's reference to Naomi being like Cinderella. However, they might not have had this opportunity if they had been discussing the chapter with the whole class.

Other Thoughts for the Future . . .

Now that I have seen all of the wonderful responses my students can come up with during small-group discussions on read-alouds, my next step would be to further improve their written responses in their journals. I would like to see them explain and elaborate more on their written responses. For a start, I could respond to their journal entries by asking questions that would encourage them to explain and elaborate their responses. Also, modeling more journal writes and using student examples might also improve their written responses.

I intend to continue to allow students to discuss read-aloud literature in small groups. Overall, I saw students who usually did not participate voice their ideas as active speakers. I also saw students of different ability levels expand their ideas and come up with inferences that they had not come up with in whole-class discussions. Some of their responses were very thoughtful, and I was excited to see them dig deep into their own personal experiences.

One drawback is that small-group discussions are somewhat time-consuming. In a whole-class discussion, the teacher can lead students to important points in a book quickly, but without a teacher leading the discussion the small groups need a little more time to express their ideas. Still, the small groups are worth the extra time, even if the small groups can only discuss a few times a week, because it gives everyone in the class an opportunity to share their responses to the read-aloud literature.

References

Fisher, B. (1995). *Thinking and learning together.* Portsmouth, NH: Heinemann.

Fisher, D., Flood, J., Lapp, D., & Frey, N. (2004). Interactive read-alouds: Is there a common set of implementation practices? *The Reading Teacher, 58*(1), 8–17.

Hart, S., Escobar, D., & Jacobson, S. C. (2001). The rocky road to grand conversations: Learning how to facilitate literature-discussion groups in fourth grade. In C. C. Pappas & L. B. Zecker (Eds.), *Transforming literacy curriculum genres: Working with teacher researchers in urban classrooms* (pp. 307–324). Mahwah, NJ: Lawrence Erlbaum.

Rog, L. J. (2001). *Early literacy instruction in kindergarten.* Newark, DE: International Reading Association.

Sipe, L. R. (2000). The construction of literary understanding by first and second graders in oral response to picture storybook read-alouds. *Reading Research Quarterly, 35*(2), 252–275.

Vygotsky, L. S. (1962). *Thought and language.* Cambridge, MA: MIT Press.

Children's Books

Anaya, R. (1999). *My land sings: Stories from the Rio Grande.* New York: HarperCollins.

Ryan, P. M. (2004). *Becoming Naomi Leon.* New York: Scholastic Press.

Scieszka, J. (1989). *The true story of the three little pigs.* New York: Viking Kestrel.

Chapter 12

Tara Braverman's Inquiry Paper

INTRODUCTORY HIGHLIGHTS

- Wove her references to other work within sections of her paper.
- Used interesting, theme headings.
- Included both running text quotes and separate quote sections.
- Used pre and post assessments.
- Incorporated some descriptive statistics.

What's This Word? Helping Sixth Grade Students Use Reading and Vocabulary Strategies Independently

Tara Braverman

I sat at my desk during silent reading time. With one reading conference finished and another one not yet started, it was the perfect time for a student to come to me with a question. I was happy to see Gloria approach my desk with her book in hand. Eager to help, I leaned forward to see her book, and was soon disappointed to hear, "What does this word mean?" Despite so many mini-lessons on different reading strategies, modeling, practicing with groups, completing homework lessons on making predictions, connections, inferences, and so on, the only question I was asked during silent reading time was, "What's this word?" I began my inquiry wondering how I could help my students become more independent readers during silent reading time. I wanted them to find out about new words without me prompting them to consult a dictionary, or to use the reading strategies they seemed so capable of implementing during whole-class instruction.

Although I had assessed students' reading abilities early in the year, I wanted to more accurately identify the specific strategies that helped students comprehend text independently, and I wondered how I could encourage, monitor, and adjust students' use of these strategies. Upon completion of this inquiry I hoped to see how students' reading processes changed once they were more aware of these strategies and also more in control of how they used them during independent reading time.

Do I Use Reading Strategies?

My students were all sixth graders in a sixth through eighth grade middle school in the northern suburbs of Chicago. I taught three eighty-four-minute blocks of reading/language arts. While I used the same procedures in all three blocks, I concentrated mainly on my middle block because they presented the most challenges to me instructionally. The class consisted of sixteen boys and seven girls, so I was constantly trying to make the girls feel comfortable sharing during class. For both boys and girls there was a wide variety of personalities, from the extremely outgoing to the painfully shy. Their reading abilities were also quite varied, from quick, efficient readers to those who struggled with grade-level text. Those who excelled at reading were often less than enthusiastic to complete the teacher-created assignments. I hoped that the new routines I was going to set up during silent reading time would help students feel more ownership over what kind of information they gained from their books, and also help direct their energy to more active reading.

Towards the beginning of the year, I had given students a "Meta-Comprehension Index," which surveyed students about what they did before, during, and after reading (Schmitt, 1990). The index checked for students' use and awareness of predicting, determining the purpose for reading, self-questioning, and summarizing. For example, to assess a student's ability to predict, one question asked the student to pick the best answer from the following:

Before I begin reading, it's a good idea to:
A. See how many pages there are in the story.
B. Look up all the big words in the dictionary.
C. Make some guesses about what I think will happen in the story.
D. Think about what has happened so far in the story.

(p. 348)

If students answered "C," they demonstrated some ability to predict before they began reading. The index consisted of twenty-five questions similar to the one above, separated into three groups: before reading, during reading, and after reading. The directions stated that there were no correct answers; students were to choose what they *thought* would help the most. Analysis of students' answers helped me assess which strategies students were consciously using or not using at all.

While I had scored these surveys and kept them private in the past, this year I decided to let students score them and see which strategies they did or did not use. The scoring sheet had a list of all the reading strategies as categories, and then it listed the number of each question that corresponded to the strategy. When a student found an incorrect answer, he or she circled that number. If they circled more than two numbers in a category, they circled the entire category to identify that strategy as one to work on during the year. During this process, Chris suspiciously stated, "But I thought there weren't any wrong answers." I explained, "You're right, it was just a survey to see what you think, and I'm not putting any score in my grade-book. However, this helps you see which reading strategies you are using very well, and which ones you should pay more attention to when you're reading."

During the first administration of this survey, I found that most students excelled at previewing, which was a relief since we had spent so much time in the first few weeks of school practicing this skill with every new fiction or nonfiction book we read, including students' science and social studies textbooks that are used in other classrooms.

However, I was surprised at the low number of students using predicting before reading. During whole-class reading, students often raised their hands, eager to share a prediction, without any prompting from me. I assumed they had all mastered that strategy, but according to the index most students did not utilize this strategy *before* reading. About half of the class actively determined the purpose of their reading and self-questioned as they read, and more than half indicated that they regularly summarized text in their head during and after reading. It was problematic to see that a very small proportion, only 16%, thought about their prior knowledge before they began reading. For my inquiry, I decided to encourage the use of predicting and drawing on background knowledge as ways to help students understand their texts.

In the past, I felt this analysis faded away and was eventually forgotten during the year, although I continued to model these strategies anytime we read either fiction or nonfiction as a class by performing think-alouds or pausing and asking students to tell me what they were thinking about a story. With the new routines I implemented (described below), students began recording their use of these strategies while reading. These records then became the foundation for a short written response to their texts. Through this process, students became more aware of their own reading styles.

After six weeks of my inquiry, I had students take the same survey they had taken in the beginning of the year. Again students scored them and recorded their answers on the same sheet from the beginning of the year, but with a different color. Many students saw a marked improvement in their use of reading strategies. After analyzing her answers, Isabella looked up at me beaming, and said, "I did a lot better this time!" I felt that giving students control of this process helped them see that the work I required them to do during their silent reading did help them become more independent readers. The post-inquiry meta-comprehension index showed a major gain (about twice as much from the pre-test) for all of the reading strategies assessed, except for previewing, which remained at the exact same level, which was already a very high 83%. Many more students indicated through the assessment that they now actively predicted, determined the purpose for their reading, self-questioned as they read, activated their prior knowledge, and summarized the text during and after reading. I believe these data may not necessarily show an increase in the *use* of these reading strategies, but more accurately reflect an increase in students' *awareness* of their use of these strategies. With this increased awareness, students consciously added comprehension tools to their repertoire, now ready to employ them as their academic reading becomes progressively more challenging.

How Do I Show What I'm Thinking When I'm Reading?

Now that students were aware of which reading strategies they did or did not use, I needed a way for students to make these strategies tangible during their independent reading time. I decided to use "coding," a system of making marks and abbreviations on sticky notes during reading (Harvey & Goudvis, 2000). In this way, students could quickly record a prediction, exciting moment, connection, or confusing word or phrase, and continue reading. I asked the class what kinds of things we should notice while reading, and they came up with ideas such as new words, connections, questions, poetic devices, character changes, literary devices (such as foreshadowing and flashback), and other ideas inspired by our previous studies throughout the year.

Wanting students to take ownership over their use of strategies, I helped the class come up with a code for quickly identifying strategies, connections, poetic devices, new words, and other noticeable occurrences. Each of my three classes created different marks for their codes. For example, in my first block, Kevin suggested writing "M.E." on a sticky note if he came across a major event. During my middle block, Steven suggested drawing a star on his sticky note for the same concept. I encouraged students to use codes they would remember and feel comfortable writing. Julie's text coding sheet included about 16 codes (e.g. *Pred.* for prediction; *?* for confusing, strange, out of character; *!* for shocking, crazy, unbelievable; *V* for visualizing—I can picture this!; and so forth).

After creating a class list of the code during the middle block, and explaining how I wanted students to implement this code while silently reading, Adam raised his hand and told the class, "I don't really like doing that because it, like, takes a long time and the book isn't fun anymore. "Wow," I responded, "Adam, I am so glad you said that! That is such a great point! Sometimes we can get so carried away with our Post-its, we lose track of the book, or we write too much down and it interrupts our reading. Let's try to keep it simple, and only mark what really strikes you." Adam still seemed a little skeptical, but instead of resisting the new method he went overboard and began placing two to three sticky notes on every page, filling them with his thoughts about the book. A few times, I caught him getting carried away, and told him, "Adam, it's impossible to record every single thing we learn about a character. Try to stick to what really strikes you. You don't need a Post-it on every page."

As students practiced going through the motions of keeping sticky notes handy during silent reading, and pausing periodically to make a note of something, I wanted to demonstrate for the class how I might code a book while reading. As a class, we were reading the Newberry Award winner *Maniac Magee* by Jerry Spinelli (1991). I used the think-aloud strategy to demonstrate my inner monologue to students, coming up with a connection to the story, jotting down "T-S" (Text to Self-connection) on my sticky note and placing it in the margin of the book. I then encouraged them to continue reading and let the class know if they came up with something else to code. Several students raised their hands and shared connections with themselves, books they had read, or movies they had seen. I promoted making connections as an important reading strategy to code, believing this would help students draw on their prior knowledge while reading and improve their comprehension. I also focused on making predictions, continually asking students what parts of the story seemed as though they might be important later, encouraging students to code this as *foreshadowing*. They also coded *predictions* when they made guesses about what might happen next.

For the next few days, I carefully monitored student behavior during silent reading. Overall, I was shocked at how willingly students accepted this new activity, and dutifully sat reading with their pads of sticky notes at hand. Although almost all students had sticky notes in their lockers, as it was on the school supply list, a few either did not have any or forgot to bring them to class. I decided to gather up all of my extra pads of paper filling up my desk drawers, placed them in a little container and set it out near the dictionaries and thesauruses in the room. I let students know that if they forgot their sticky notes there were extras available to them for that day. I did not want these additionally required class materials to impede learning, instigate an argument over borrowing supplies, or become an excuse for students to go to their locker during valuable reading time. I noticed after my announcement that when students asked to borrow sticky notes from each other, they were often directed to my supply.

Students were very enthusiastic to code at first, but I had to monitor their use of the new system carefully during reading time for several days. During the first week, I required students to keep their copy of the class code out on their desks during silent reading for a quick reference. I hoped to see students code text with abbreviations so that recording was quick and did not intrude on the reading process (Harvey & Goudvis, 2000). In the days just following our initial implementation of the new routine, I saw Joey copying sentences directly from his book onto his sticky notes, before placing them on the page. I told him, "No complete sentences. Let's just write down one of the abbreviations from our code." Later on I saw he was writing less on his sticky notes, but still taking helpful notes.

Paul often struggles with changes in the daily routine, and he approached the coding of text in a similar way. During the first day after our creation of the code, I saw Paul enthusiastically sticking little notes in his book. Peering over his shoulder, I noticed he had copied an exact sentence from the book, and placed his sticky note at the top of the page, nowhere near the actual text he was discussing. I held an informal conference at his desk:

Me: Oh, you found something to code already?

Paul: Yeah, I think this is really great description of the setting.

Me: What do think this is? Imagery? Character description? Setting?

Paul: Imagery.

Me: OK. Here [I took a fresh sticky note and handed it to him]. Let's write just the one word *imagery* and place it right next to the sentence. Let's write as little as possible on each Post-it so it doesn't interrupt your reading too much.

Paul: OK.

Thus, I found that many students wrote too much on their sticky notes at first; however, others wrote too little. Soon after my exchange with Paul, I noticed that Staci had an abundance of sticky notes protruding from her silent reading book. I asked her to show me what she was coding, and saw that she was only writing one- or two-letter abbreviations on each note. I asked her to tell me about what she had jotted down, and as she flipped through the pages, we both realized she had no idea why she recorded anything. I suggested that she write at least one word after the abbreviation to remind her of the connection she had made, or the poetic device she had found. She began to record her ideas in that manner, and a few days later proudly explained to me what all of her sticky notes meant. While I was convincing Paul, Joey, and Adam to write less on their sticky notes, Staci was not helped at all by coding until she added more. Students needed help striking a balance with their note-taking so they neither recorded so much information their reading became tedious, nor took so few notes they were unintelligible a day later.

Jamie was not the only student to feel some anxiety during the beginning of this process. When I walked past her desk to see how she was doing she looked up at me exasperated and exclaimed, "I can only find *setting!*" She was hoping to code all sorts of things and was frustrated that she was only picking up on one major element of the book. I smiled and told her, "I want you to enjoy your book. Relax about the coding; it's going to take time to get used to. Just read your book and enjoy. If something jumps out at you, great, but don't stress about it." I noticed other students had to be comforted as well when they couldn't find every element on the list we had created. This was a new type of activity for students. There was no set number of items to find, no time limit, and no assignment to rush to complete before the bell rang. Some students had trouble understanding a process

155

that was not designed to fulfill teacher requirements, but instead existed as a self-monitored guide to help students improve their own reading abilities.

Later that week Michael ran up to me and urgently explained that what was happening in his book was just like something that happened to his neighbor. I asked him what kind of connection that was and he said, "text-to-world." I asked him to code it with a sticky note. He did so, then looked at me and asked, "Now what?"

What Do I Do with All of These Sticky Notes?

Once students began finishing their novels, they started to ask me what to do with all of the sticky notes jutting out from the pages of their books. This led to another new routine to establish in the classroom. I wanted students to organize these sticky notes into categories and reflect upon the progression of their reading (Harvey & Goudvis, 2000). Students in my class had always kept a "Reader Response Journal," a spiral notebook where they wrote about their independent reading books. However, to get them to write, I posed a question to the entire class that they had to answer in their journals. Since my students were each reading a different book, my questions had to be very broad, such as "How does your character change during the story?" or "What is the major conflict in your book?" The previous year, I had worked with a few students after school on reading, and had been able to ask them questions specific to their book. I found their answers much more thoughtful and enthusiastic. I decided that this inquiry could give me the chance to allow students to write more meaningfully about their books, because through their coding, they could generate their own more specific and appropriate questions to answer.

I wanted students to engage in a written activity revolving around their book, one that was a natural extension of the work they did and strategies they used while reading (Blachowicz & Obrochta, 2005). We came up with a class list of questions to answer, based on coding. For example, if a student finished a book and realized he had drawn several exclamation points on sticky notes throughout the book, he could answer the question "How is this book shocking or exciting?" If another student noticed a lot of question marks in her coding, she might have chosen to answer "How was this book confusing?" I explained to students that they could modify these questions to suit their books.

Now that we had a long list of questions, I wanted students to take this process one step further. I asked them to group similar questions together, and the class eventually agreed upon three categories into which all of the questions fit: Reading Strategies (predicting, summarizing, questioning, etc.), Literary Devices (suspense, foreshadowing, flashback, etc.), and Poetic Devices (simile, metaphor, onomatopoeia, etc.). Students glued the new list of questions onto the inside cover of their spirals, and these became the new questions to respond to in their reader response journals.

Students now had many steps to follow with regard to silent reading. First, they had to code text during reading. Once they were finished with a book, they had to take all of their sticky notes and sort them into the three categories they had identified. After sorting, they had to decide, based upon their sticky notes, which category they thought was most important to them as they read: Reading Strategies, Literary Devices, or Poetic Devices. Once they decided on a category, they then had to choose a question from that category to answer in their journals, underneath or on the back of the page with all of their sticky notes. I roamed around the room, helping students code, sort their notes, choose appropriate questions, and write their responses. At first, so many steps seemed overwhelming to both the students and to me. Yet the process did help students develop an organized visual representation of the reading strategies they had used. This then helped them to develop a complex understanding of their book, as demonstrated through their written responses and subsequent teacher–student discussion. And after a while, the process became much simpler for students to understand and utilize.

During reading conferences, I read these responses along with students and used them as a basis for discussion during conferences. Surprisingly, some students chose to completely make up their own questions. During a reading conference with Julie, I noticed that she had answered the question "Why does Sheila trick all of her friends?" I asked her why she made up her own question and she replied, "Because as I was reading, I kept thinking 'Why is she tricking everybody?' and then my question was answered and I saw that that was really the main thing in the book." Here Julie was able to decide for herself what was important about the book, and in doing so expressed a more complex understanding of the story than if she had been forced to answer one of my generic questions. Her coding helped her come up with a question, and her written response helped her discuss her book with me during our conference.

Students became more active readers, using reading strategies in a manner more apparent to themselves and to me, successfully making internal reactions externally visible. Their responses to books became more in-depth, and their choices about how to respond to the text helped them focus on what they felt were the most important parts. Maria used to write pages of plot summary, without ever going into very much depth or expressing original thoughts about her books. As shown below, she used her coding and question list to help her create a concise but thoughtful response to her book. She reflected on how the character's actions represented human nature, demonstrating her close reading of this story: "This part was shocking because Daine can speak and turn into animals, and she always has control over it. This time it was different, she completely lost control and attacked a human. I think that was this only happens very rarely, and she has a lot of control over her powers. It also reminds me that when someone loses their temper they sort of lose control of their power like Daine. This was really shocking when it happened, in a good way."

When my students began actively coding text while they read, I felt they were paying closer attention to their own reading and asking more meaningful questions, focusing on the writer's style and not simply individual words the author used. Natalya came up to me during silent reading to ask about a potential typo in her book. The word was "wrassled." After I had explained the author's use of dialect, she quickly found more examples on the same page, and happily realized the author was creating more realistic characters through this literary device.

What Does This Word Mean?

In an effort to reduce the constant "What's this word?" question during silent reading, I also created a "Reference Corner" to encourage students to find answers themselves. Although students were aware of where the dictionaries and thesauruses were located in the room, there they sat, practically untouched, tucked on a shelf near the floor, exactly as I had found them when I first began teaching here. So I decided to dust them off and display them prominently in the room. In addition to the typical student dictionaries and thesauruses, I had finally found a place to display other interesting resources I had collected over the past few years, including rhyming dictionaries, tips for spelling, tips for writing, and other student-friendly reference books. I had noticed during my inquiry that I was often the "enabler" of student dependence, quickly responding to every question I was asked without thinking about the student's opportunity for self-exploration. The Reference Corner was not only a resource for the students but also a visual reminder for me to stop answering every question, and allow students to utilize the resources in my room to find their own information.

The day after I set up the Reference Corner, I explained its use to the students. They seemed slightly interested in the books they had not seen before, but were not sure how this would really change the way things worked in class. During a whole-class lesson, Adam asked what *commissioned* meant, because a character in his book had been commissioned to carve a statue. I announced that we had our first volunteer to go the reference corner and look up a new word. Adam looked up the word, found a couple of definitions, and read them to the class. Students decided on the one that fit into Josh's book best and Adam blurted out, "Oh, I get it!"

Mentally, I resolved to stop jumping in to rescue every child who did not under-stand a word. Almost immediately, I was tested with the dreaded question. When Thomas brought his book up to me and asked, "What's this word?" while pointing to the word *archaic* in his book, I opened my mouth to answer, then quickly caught myself, pointed to the new display on the table and responded, "Check the reference corner. Then get back to me, because sometimes there is more than one meaning to a word. Let me know what you find."

Later I noticed Thomas had continued reading, and I asked him, "Did you find that word?" He replied, "Well, yeah. It had a few meanings, but I think it was the one about being old-fashioned, because the girl in the book is complaining that her dad is, like, not with it, and he's not from ancient times or anything." I was impressed with Thomas's ability to choose the correct definition and place it back into the context of his book. A little remorsefully, I realized I had been underestimating many of my students by jumping in to help when I could have been fostering their independence.

Despite the typical reading strategies students were utilizing and the literary and poetic devices they were identifying in their books, I still had not addressed my original concern of helping students decipher new words found in context, and build meaning beyond the dictionary definition. I wanted students to recognize that a robust vocabulary could help their reading comprehension. I wished for students to investigate how interesting words enhanced their text, and wanted them to understand new words beyond the rote memorization of dictionary definitions. Often, when I had created a list of vocabulary words from the book the class was reading, students misused the word in later writings, demonstrating an inadequate understanding of both the word and what it brought to the text. I knew that children across ability levels were capable of choosing important words from their texts, and I wanted to explicitly develop this skill in my students (Harmon, Hedrick, Wood, & Gress, 2005).

To help students build deeper meanings with new words, I decided to utilize semantic maps (Bromley, Irwin-De Vitis, & Modlo, 1995). Students have been inundated with graphic organizers in every subject area, but I had never thought to use anything other than a horizontal chart to help record new words. With a semantic map, students were able to record more than just the definition, namely, connections they had made, other forms of the word, original sentences with the word, how it added to the story, and anything they else they found relevant (Blachowicz & Obrochta, 2005). Instead of memorizing a list of teacher-selected vocabulary words, students had the freedom to learn words they chose during their own reading. I hoped this choice would make their vocabulary development more authentic and therefore more meaningful (Harmon et al., 2005). I wanted students to become self-motivated "Language Detectives" so that instead of memorization, students investigated how certain authors used words differently to create a style of writing that may appeal to certain readers (Monohan, 2003).

Now that they were actively seeking answers to their own questions, I realized that I needed a common place for students to record and keep track of their new words. I had students take their old reader response journals and divide them up into two sections, using sticky notes as dividers and section labels. We called the first section "Reader response" and kept its original use as a place to respond to books. The second section became "Words." I explained that this was going to be where students would record new words from their silent reading books. Students did not yet understand what to record in this "Words" section, but they soon would learn.

Difficult vocabulary can be an obstacle to reading, but using an organizational strategy such as a semantic map can help students build a deeper understanding of vocabulary words beyond what they might develop simply reading the dictionary definition (Bromley et al., 1995). Traditionally, I had provided students with a vocabulary chart where they were required to record the new word, make a guess as to the meaning, record the dictionary definition, and then create a new sentence using this word. Students found these charts tiresome, and I found that completing this chart usually did not lead to students fully comprehending the new word. I almost always found errors proving students did not grasp how the word should be used.

Semantic maps are intended for teachers and students to use collaboratively, eventually leading towards students' independent use of them as a learning strategy (Bromley et al., 1995). I used butcher paper to create a generic word map with students. I put the phrase "new word" in the center of the map and asked students for suggestions of what we might want to learn about the word. They instructed me to create a place for the definition, the book title from where the word was found, and the sentence with the word from the book. I then added the part of speech, other forms of the word (verb tenses or inflectional endings), and connections. This poster then remained prominently displayed in the room.

To model this new strategy, I again used *Maniac Magee*. In the chapter we had just read, some of the characters had begun building a pillbox. I explained to the students:

> I hadn't seen this word before I read this book, so I'm going to record "pillbox" in the center of my word map. Now I can tell from the sentence that it's a thing, so I'm going to put "noun" on my semantic map. What else should I record to help me understand this word?

Students offered up the phrase from the book, and one student went to the Reference Corner and looked up the definition and read it aloud as I recorded it. Then I asked if anyone could make any connections to this word from other sources. A few boys in class informed me that pillboxes are often used by characters in video games that are set during wars, and they named a few. I made a section labeled "T-VG" for a text-to-video-game connection and recorded the titles of the games. This helped students understand that they could build meaning of new vocabulary by placing the word into the context of their lives. Students also recorded this map in the "Words" section of their response journals, so they had an example to use for future reference as they worked on their own word maps.

Throughout the following weeks, I monitored student selection of words and encouraged use of the Reference Corner to find information. During silent reading time, I walked around the room and discussed semantic maps with students individually. I tried to encourage students to push themselves to pick challenging words. Throughout this time, I noticed students visiting the reference corner often to borrow a dictionary while they explored a new word.

When choosing words, some students chose words I am convinced they already knew; while others really delved into the investigation process. For example, when Margaret was reading the fifth Harry Potter book (Rowling, 2003), she became confused at the British use of the word *queue*. Her semantic map included the phrase from the book ("as they joined the queue to climb out of the portrait hole") and a definition ("a line of people waiting for something"), but also other ideas such as "traffic jam" as a *Connection* and "it's from a liation word meaning 'tail'" under shown *Other Facts*. Her map showed how she gained a thorough knowledge of this word, which helped her understand what was going on in the book. My favorite aspect of the semantic map is that, unlike the traditional chart I had used previously, this format allowed Margaret to include as much information as she found important, including her impressive notation about the Latin root of the word meaning *tail*. If only asked to record the definition, Margaret could have easily glossed over this fact and never really understood how and why the word was being used.

Joey, on the other hand, chose to investigate the word *misunderstood* from his book. I asked him a few times, "Is this really a new word for you?" and he responded, "Well, it's being used in a way I haven't seen before." This was one of the ways I told students they could choose new words, so after much insisting on his part, I relented and let him use his chosen word. Even students like Joey, who I am certain *did* understand his word, learned a new way to organize information around vocabulary that challenged them to make personal connections and think about the words in more complex ways.

In the future, I need to set up more activities around student-selected words. Maybe publicizing new words would motivate some to challenge themselves with more advanced vocabulary. The variety and complexity of the words students chose was beyond the lists I had given students in the past. I truly believe they benefited from finding their own words in context to investigate, which in turn helped their comprehension of their chosen book (Harmon et al., 2005).

In addition to comprehension improvements, I noticed students' enthusiasm for new words increase, as did their use of new words in other contexts. About one month after a lengthy class discussion surrounding the word *infamous* and how it was being used in *Maniac Magee*, Kevin used the word in a completely unrelated assignment, writing a warning related to the book he was reading, "Watch out for the *infamous* leader of all the vampires, the Vampenze Lord." Recall, and therefore learning, improves when students create organizers and discuss them during reading experiences (Bromley et al., 1995).

During the entire silent reading time, students were actively participating in their learning, which has been found to be more productive for vocabulary acquisition than passive listening (Blachowicz & Obrochta, 2005). Student engagement and input are crucial when selecting vocabulary and using that vocabulary to make meaning from text.

Where Do We Go From Here?

My major objective for teaching reading and vocabulary strategies was to empower students to take control of their own learning, implementing reading strategies appropriate for them and their selected book. I wanted them to independently use strategies to help decide how to approach their text, track their own progress along the way, be aware of mistakes or stumbling blocks and find ways to overcome them, synthesize their new knowledge, and celebrate their success.

I began my inquiry naïvely thinking I could help students become more independent with a few mini-lessons, quickly implemented routines, and some practice. With each new step I realized how enormous this goal really was. Every time I tried introducing a new skill, I realized there was so much work to do just to set up the routine. Before we could code text, we needed to make the code, record it, practice using it, make mistakes, and adjust. Many students did not see the benefit of coding until they went to write their responses, and then regretted their lack of note taking and coded more in the next book they read. Before students could begin using word maps, we needed to make a place for them, so it took some class time to divide up their journal into two sections. Before diving into that strategy, I had to model the word map and practice it with them. It still took several attempts before students felt they had grasped the concept, and I was frequently answering questions about what to put in the map.

Once students became more comfortable with the maps and really showed a deeper understanding of the words, I realized I needed to add several more steps to the process, such as a place to display these words, time for students to teach these words to their classmates, and even more formal assessments of students' vocabulary growth through writing assignments. These next steps are still in development.

During most of this process, I felt time slipping away before I could really see for myself and also show students the benefit of these new practices. I kept wishing, "If only I had set this all up in September!" Although I now realize it was a bit much to take on in a six-week time period, I feel that each part of the process was interrelated, and students needed each part of the puzzle to see the big picture, and therefore the purpose of using reading strategies independently. In an ideal setting, I would have introduced each routine gradually, allowing students to become comfortable with one before adding another. Hopefully, I will be able to implement some more of these routines before the school year is over, but I know I will begin this process towards the beginning of the next school year.

Students made significant gains during this inquiry—they displayed a heightened awareness about the reading strategies they actually used; they demonstrated an increased ability to respond meaningfully to their novels; and they showed more enthusiasm for investigating the language used by their chosen authors. Although I could not do it all in the time given, I am relieved that I have finally begun to implement strategies that I have wanted to try for years. Both my teaching and students' learning were reinvigorated by these active and self-directed strategies to improve comprehension. With patient instruction, redirection, and support, my students have become more self-reliant during reading time. I am confident they are developing habits and skills that will benefit them far into their literate futures.

References

Blachowicz, C., & Obrochta, C. (2005). Vocabulary visits: Virtual field trips for content vocabulary development. *The Reading Teacher, 59*(3), 262–268.

Bromley, K., Irwin-De Vitis, L., & Modlo, M. (1995). *Graphic organizers: Visual strategies for active learning*. New York: Scholastic Professional Books.

Harmon, J. M., Hedrick, W. B., Wood, K. D., & Gress, M. (2005). Vocabulary self-selection: A study of middle-school students' word selections from expository texts. *Reading Psychology, 26*, 313–333.

Harvey, S., & Goudvis, A. (2000). *Strategies that work: Teaching comprehension to enhance understanding*. York, ME: Stenhouse.

Monohan, M. (2003). On the lookout for language: Children as language detectives. *Language Arts, 80*(3), 206–215.

Rowling, J. K. (2003). *Harry Potter and the order of the Phoenix*. New York: Arthur A. Levine Books.

Schmitt, M. C. (1990). A questionnaire to measure children's awareness of strategic reading processes. *The Reading Teacher, 43*(7), 454–461.

Spinelli, J. (1991). *Maniac Magee*. New York: HarperCollins.

Chapter 13

Libby Tuerk's Inquiry Paper

INTRODUCTORY HIGHLIGHTS

- Used an early "Theoretical Foundation" section but also included references to others' work throughout the paper.
- Included information from two surveys on independent reading.
- Used interesting headings.
- Used quotations both in running text and in separate sections.

Let's Read: Motivating Junior High Students to Become Lifelong Readers

Libby Tuerk

Over the past four years, I have come to recognize independent reading—time when students can read texts of their own choice and at their own reading level—as an important and valuable component of my junior high reading curriculum. I view independent reading not only as a time for students to practice and improve their reading skills, but also as an opportunity for them to develop a lifelong love of reading, to see as I do the pleasure that can come from experiencing the world through books. However, in reality, it remained a constant struggle to engage my often reluctant students in their reading. On independent reading days, I was repeatedly faced with students who had left their books at home, others whose eyes drifted off the page and stared into space, still others who tore through the pages of book after book at lightning speed yet could not recall anything about the books, and finally students who viewed independent reading time as nothing more than nap time or social hour. As I was not willing to give up independent reading altogether, I decided to conduct my inquiry project around the question of how to engage these reluctant readers.

Theoretical Foundation

There is widespread research to support the connection between independent reading and students' academic success. Reading independently increases students' fluency and vocabulary (Kasten & Wilfong, 2005). A study by the National Assessment of Education Progress found that students who read independently at home scored on average 25 points higher than those who did not on tests of reading achievement (Kasten & Wilfong, 2005). Conversely, according to Worthy (2002), when students do not choose to read on their own, "their general academic progress is in jeopardy" (p. 568).

Despite the overwhelming evidence that independent reading improves student achievement, there is a significant drop in the amount of time students spend reading when they enter middle and high school (Kasten & Wilfong, 2005). This is often tied to students' lack of confidence in reading and inability to see themselves as readers. As Wilhelm (1997) observed in his classroom, middle school students often had negative attitudes toward reading because they did not feel they were any good at it. Many of Wilhelm's students viewed reading as a passive activity rather than one in which they could actively engage in creating meaning. Therefore, they did not retain meaning from texts and were unmotivated to continue reading.

I saw many similarities between Wilhelm's descriptions of his students and my own students. By the time my students walk through the door of my classroom as seventh graders, many have already been labeled "low" or "remedial." Some have received D's and F's in reading for many years now, accepting the attitude that reading is just something at which they are not very good. Even when given the opportunity to read books of their own choice, they are not motivated. Wilhelm's explanation that students' lack of motivation is often caused by their inability to see their own role in actively creating meaning in texts resonated with me. Like his students, my own students seem willing to wait for someone else to explain the meaning of a book for them, rather than become a participant in the meaning-making process.

Wilhelm also found that many of the practices used in classrooms discourage rather than motivate student reading. According to Wilhelm (1997), most classroom practices are based on the literary theory of New Criticism, which emphasizes the notion that there is one correct meaning in a text. The focus in New Criticism interpretations is on literary elements, devices, and structure. Teachers who espouse this theory "often communicate that literature is not about the students and their most vital concerns, but about whatever some superior intelligence tells them it is about" (p. 15). The New Criticism approach to literature in the classroom is one of the reasons students begin to view reading as a passive activity in which they have no say in the creating of meaning.

Teachers need to move away from the practices associated with the New Criticism theory if they want their students to become truly engaged in their independent reading. An alternative to the New Criticism theory can be found in Rosenblatt's (1995) transactional theory, which says that meaning does not come from the text alone but from the reader's transaction with the text. Rosenblatt distinguishes between reading for information (efferent) and reading for enjoyment (aesthetic). She argues that classrooms have traditionally focused on the former but they should encourage students to take an aesthetic stance while reading so they can understand that literature is meant to be an enjoyable experience.

Context of Study

Throughout the course of my inquiry project, I used various activities and best practices associated with Rosenblatt's and Wilhelm's ideas to help my students see the "enjoyment" that comes from the experience of reading a book. In my data collection, I looked for signs that students were engaged in their independent reading, that they were excited about choosing and reading books, that they came prepared for and participated in independent reading, and that they saw themselves as an active participant in the meaning-making process of reading.

I conducted my inquiry in one of my seventh grade Reading classes at a small elementary (K-12) school located in a township west of Chicago. In this Reading class, there are 19 students (5 Latino, 10 African American, 2 Asian/Indian, and 1 Caucasian), and approximately 60% of them qualify for free or reduced lunch.

Choosing Books

During independent reading in my classroom, students are allowed to choose their own books. Kasten and Wilfong (2005) find that "student choice is a critical factor in encouraging student motivation to read" (p. 658). In her research, Worthy (2002) also found that students repeatedly indicated that choosing from a variety of reading materials is an important factor in making reading more appealing. However, prior to my inquiry, students in my class did not appear to see the connection between choosing their own books and finding something they would like. Many students simply chose the nearest book or a book with a "fun" cover when given the opportunity to pick their independent reading books. This was indicated by responses on a survey that students filled out anonymously during the first week of my inquiry. When asked, "What you do not like about Independent Reading," one student responded, "Sometimes your book can be boring if it's something you don't like." Another response stated, "A bad book you feel like you HAVE to read." Both these responses show that students were continuing to spend their time reading books they had picked out but did not enjoy, thereby compounding their already negative attitudes about reading. These students' feelings were unfortunately representative of many of my students who did not understand that independent reading was supposed to be an enjoyable experience.

One of the ways through which I hoped to increase student motivation to read throughout my inquiry was encouraging them to think more about their book choices. According to research, students should be able to choose books based on their own interests, but they also should hear suggestions from teachers and peers (Worthy, 2002). To encourage students to think more about what type of book they would actually enjoy reading, I asked students to fill out a Book Choice Survey at the outset of the inquiry. We completed the survey on a class visit to the school library. It asked students to list topics they were interested in, books or authors they had read and liked in the past, books they had heard about from friends that sounded interesting, and genres they liked. The survey also instructed students to use their likes and interests to guide their book choice and to get information about books they chose from a classmate, me, a librarian, or the Internet before making their final decision and checking out.

The use of the book choice surveys had mixed results. Many students were able to "choose wisely," while others continued in their old patterns. An example of a student who benefited from the survey was Anna. Anna was a very strong reader, probably one of the most proficient readers in this class, and she read regularly in her own time. She indicated on her survey that her favorite author is Jacqueline Woodson. During our trip to the library, Anna told me she had read all the books by Woodson that our school had but asked if I thought she could ask the librarian for a recommendation for another author who is similar. The librarian directed her to *Heaven*, by Angela Johnson (1998). Another student who used the surveys to his advantage was Danny. Unlike Anna, Danny was not a student who read much on his own. David was one of our ESL students, and although he has made great progress, he continued to read two or three years below grade level. He initially chose an *Artemis Fowl* (Colfer, 2002) book for his independent reading, but when he asked his classmate Jake about it, Jake told him those books were sometimes confusing and he should read the *Series of Unfortunate Events* (Snicket, 1999) books instead. Danny took Jake's advice and has since read four of the books in the series. Both Danny and Anna were able to use the surveys as a jumping off point for having conversations with others about their books before choosing them. I think this shows they were interested in finding a book they would truly enjoy.

Despite their successes, some students did not use the book choice surveys quite as I had hoped. For example, Andy wrote on his survey, "I liked the cover of the book, I showed it to Mike and he liked it too so I checked it out." On his own survey, Mike wrote, "I recommended this book to myself because I've read it before and it's pretty good." These were not exactly the types of recommendations and book conversations I had in mind!

As some students finished their books over the course of the inquiry and looked for new books to check out, they did not use the written book choice surveys again. However, they were informally using many of the ideas on the surveys. I observed many more conversations among students recommending books to each other and noticed students putting more thought into their choices. One example of this can be seen again with Anna. After the librarian recommended *Heaven* to her, she passed the recommendation on to a group of her friends. During a book talk, she told two girls, "I know for a fact you guys would like this book!" She then told a third girl in her group that she did not think she would like it because it didn't really have "any big adventures or wizard stuff in it like you like." This conversation showed that Anna understood the importance of different students choosing different books to fit their unique interests and likes.

Being Prepared: You Can't Read If You Don't Have a Book

One of my major frustrations with independent reading has always been students showing up unprepared. Students often came to class on independent reading days without a book. Reading time was then wasted for these students as they needed to go to their lockers to find their books or look through the classroom library for something else to read. Because it was often the same students who forgot their books week after week, these students were reading one or two chapters of a different book each week and never finishing any of them. It was quite clear that these students were not very engaged in their reading of any of these books. At its worst, prior to the official start of my inquiry project, nine of the nineteen students came to class without a book one day.

As my inquiry project progressed, I started to notice some improvements with preparedness. During the fourth week and every subsequent week of the project, at most only two students forgot their books. More often than not it was the same two students who were without books. In fact, my students knew that I was writing a paper about their independent reading and it became a joke in our class that the title of this paper should be "Andy and Camilla Forget Their Books AGAIN."

I don't know if the improvement in preparedness was related to the new activities with independent reading we were using or if the students were merely growing more acclimated to the junior high routines. Seventh grade is the first year students at our school have lockers and switch rooms for all classes, so in all areas, not just independent reading, they seem to have trouble being prepared. This lack of preparedness tends to improve gradually during the year, so it would not be surprising to see it change at this point in the school year.

Learning from Mistakes: No More Reading Logs

I am a big believer in accountability. I hold myself accountable for what I am supposed to do and I try to hold my students accountable as well. So for independent reading, I always worried about finding a way to hold the students accountable: to make sure that they were using the assigned time to read. I didn't just want a means through which to make students accountable; I also wanted a way to assess and assign a grade for independent reading. This year, I thought I had come up with a brilliant idea to do both: reading logs. Reading logs are worksheets based on Raphael's Book Club program. The reading log allows students to choose different ways to respond in writing to what they have read; they can write about reading strategies used, or vocabulary words they have found, or they can write more personal and/or creative responses to the literature (Raphael & McMahon, 1994). Although Worthy (2002) reported that students are less motivated to read when there are required worksheets or journal entries to complete, I justified the use of reading logs because they gave the students choice in their responses and were not traditional question/answer worksheets.

Unfortunately, my students did not agree with my brilliant view of using the reading logs. As is evident from the responses on the anonymous survey, my students did not enjoy completing the reading logs each week: Question on survey: "What do you not like about Independent Reading?" Some sample answers:

1 That we have to do reading logs every week.
2 Having to right [sic] about the information.
3 The reading logs because we have to stop and write when we are having a climax in the book.
4 I like the reading but I just don't like the reading log.

These answers are representative of many of the students' responses and feelings toward the reading logs. As I read the surveys, I realized the reading logs were working against one of my main goals for independent reading: allowing students to see the enjoyment in reading for pleasure.

Four weeks into my inquiry, despite my own attachment to them, I realized I needed to abandon the use of the reading logs. I knew I had made the right decision because when I told the class, the room erupted in cheers and applause.

Measuring Engagement: Enthusiasm during Book Talks

So with the reading logs a thing of the past, I shifted my attention to the use of students' oral responses to their books as the means of accountability and assessment. I decided to try book talks. Book talks are opportunities for students to meet in small groups to discuss their books. Kasten and Wilfong (2005) advocated a similar idea when they created a Book Bistro program to be used in middle and high school classrooms so that "independent reading was more like our favorite bookstore with a cafe, and we could linger over favorite books and share them with others" (p. 656). In the Book Bistro, the classroom was transformed, via tables, tablecloths, candles, and beverages, into a cafe where small groups of students met to share the books they were reading with each other. Different teachers made slight adaptations to this Bistro idea to fit their unique situations, but all kept the main goal in mind: that students are given a chance to talk about their experience of reading a book. Students were not required to answer questions with right or wrong answers, but rather given the opportunity to see the satisfaction in reading, sharing, and discussing books. Although I did not want to go so far as transforming my classroom into a bistro, I did like the idea of students getting together informally to discuss books.

The first time we tried the book talks, students met in assigned groups of four or five students after the silent reading time and were given fifteen minutes to discuss their books. As I walked around the room, most students were talking enthusiastically about their books and asking questions of each other. All of the groups were still talking at the end of the fifteen minutes but the school schedule prevented us from continuing. In a class vote the next day, all but one student voted to continue having book talks after independent reading time every Friday. To fulfill my own need for accountability and the school's need for assessments, I decided to develop a rubric students could use to evaluate each other during the book talks. Since it was the students who would be using the rubric, I wanted their input as to what should be included on it. Again, students met in small groups to write their own rubrics for the book talks. Each group was instructed to come up with four criteria and three grade levels for each of those criteria. We then met as a class to go over what they had written and to reach a consensus on what criteria to include on the final rubric. Developing the rubric produced some very lively discussion and strong opinions. I was especially interested in how strongly four of my male students felt about what to include. These were four students who did not usually get excited about anything in class, and especially not about independent reading. They wanted to make sure that the rubric included something about keeping the book talk interesting and knowing what you are talking about. One of these boys, Jake, told the class, "I don't want to sit and listen to someone keep going, 'um, um, um' and have to look up everything in the book. If you're going to talk about the book, you better read it!"

As I listened to the class's discussions about the rubric, I became concerned with how fact- and detail-oriented students wanted their rubric to be. Their focus was definitely on remembering literary elements rather than personal connections to the book and their own construction of meaning. Many of the students' comments illustrate how fact-oriented they were: "You have to know all the characters' names without looking in the book"; "And you should be able to know what's going on in your story without reading the back of your book"; "You need to be able to answer questions about your book for at least three minutes, or maybe only two."

Students obviously had adopted what Wilhelm identified as a New Critical approach to literature. The final rubric the class approved included four criteria: characters, setting, plot/events, and cooperation. With the exception of cooperation, all the criteria seemed to be a "test" of what the students could remember about their book.

Despite my concerns about their rubric, students did not strictly adhere to this during the actual book talks. They still gave high scores to their peers even if they couldn't remember every detail about the plot, setting, and characters of their books. And even though they were not included on the rubric, the personal connections and themes of the books were discussed regularly during book talks. For example, after telling his group who the main characters were in his book *Shark Bite* (Strasser, 1998), Carlos began to talk about the theme of his book, sparking a conversation about what different students had learned from their own books:

Carlos: The hidden message in my book is don't judge a book by its cover.

Andy: Your book does have a lame cover.

Carlos: No, because everyone thought Ian was going to be some regular rich kid. Like stuck up and not doing anything. But he's the one who took charge instead of panicking when the shark attacks. That's what I would have done too. Nobody saw that coming.

Jeff: Actually, it's the same message in my book. They all thought Junebug was stupid because he was black. But the Reverend teaches him how to ignore it. And he wasn't stupid. He got all A's on tests. [Referring to *Junebug and the Reverend* (Mead, 1998).]

Andy: They always think the black kid's stupid. Not just in books.

Jeff: Yeah. You should read this.

Carlos: I'll think about it.

Through their book talk, the boys discussed the lessons they were learning from their books, related them to their own lives, and made recommendations about books. None of these were specifically covered on the rubric, yet they all gave each other high scores. When I asked Carlos about his score, he said it was fair because he couldn't have known the lesson of the book if he hadn't read it, "and that's all the rubric is supposed to do, check that we read, right?" I found it interesting that the students saw the rubric as the worksheet or test—the written proof of who had read and who had not. Yet the book talks remained a time for the students to respond more personally and openly to their books.

Another group had a similar experience with their book talks. A group of four girls decided to start their book talks by describing the character they liked best. Donna, who was reading *Getting Near to Baby* (Couloumbis, 1999), enthusiastically volunteered to go first. She could not remember the name of the character she liked best but she described how the young girl had been sent to live with an aunt because her mother was sick. Her mother had just lost a baby and she needed some time alone. Donna described in detail how lonely and upset this character was and how she began to act out. Another student in the

171

group pointed out that this was similar to Donna's own situation. Donna's parents moved but she is living with her grandparents so she can finish the school year at our school. At first, Donna denied any connection because she saw her mom on the weekends and the character did not, but later she admitted that the parallel with the character could be "part of the reason I like this girl." Again, as with Carlos and Jeff, Donna was given perfect scores by her group on the rubric. The rubric clearly states that the student must know the character's name without looking back in the book, but Donna's classmates overlooked this. Students were beginning to realize there were more important aspects of reading than just memorizing characters, settings, and plots.

Measuring Engagement: Dialogue with the Book

One of the means through which I attempted to gauge students' engagement with their independent reading book was through student dialogue with the book. By this, I mean evidence that a student is putting him- or herself into the book: conversing with a character, sharing feelings about a plot event as it would affect them, or placing him- or herself into the setting. As Wilhelm (1997) noted, students' comprehension improves when they are able to see themselves as active constructors of meaning and as a part of the text. Rosenblatt (1995) also notes the importance of students putting themselves into literature in order to participate "in the experiences of others" (p. 88). Although I did not see this happening very often initially in my class's book talks, as the inquiry progressed, more and more students began to make comments that demonstrated their own dialogue with the book.

One poignant example of this can be seen in comments made by Marisa during a book talk during the sixth week of my inquiry. Marisa is a thirteen-year-old girl who moved to the United States from Mexico when she was in the third grade. She spoke no English and continued to speak only Spanish at home. Despite this, her English was quite good, although there were still occasionally some language-related comprehension issues. Marisa chose *Becoming Naomi Leon* by Pam Muñoz Ryan (2004) as her independent reading book. During a book talk, she showed that she was putting herself into the book when she told her group that Naomi "told us, well told me about her brother's disability problem." When her group asked her more about the brother's disability, she continued to talk about it from Naomi's point of view, saying how bad she felt for her that she had to deal with her brother. These comments showed that Marisa was looking at the book as a conversation between Naomi and herself and was able to empathize with Naomi.

Marisa showed further evidence of understanding the character of Naomi in a book talk the following week. She was describing for her group how Naomi watched the Posadas when she traveled to Oaxaca, Mexico. The Posadas are a Christmas tradition in Mexico where people go door to door with figurines of Joseph and Mary looking for a place for them to stay. It is meant to re-enact the Christmas story when Mary and Joseph could not find room at an inn.

Marisa: They sing and they come to your door.
Ayana: Are they dressed up like Mary and Joseph?

172

Marisa:	No, they have little dolls dressed up as them and they're asking for . . . I don't know the word, so they can stay there
Alicia:	A hotel?
Marisa:	No, but it starts with "h."
Karen:	A hostel?
Marisa:	No.
Anna:	Room at the inn?
Miss Tuerk:	Hospitality?
Marisa:	I don't know. Maybe it doesn't translate. But it doesn't matter. What matters is the Posada—I've done it and so has Naomi. They really do it in Mexico every year where I'm from.

This dialogue shows that Marisa realized that what is important in her reading is not always her recall of a word but her connection to it, her ability to make meaning of the text for herself.

Another example that demonstrated dialogue with the book took place during the SRI book talks. An SRI (symbolic representation interview) involves students being asked to bring in objects, pictures, or cutouts of shapes "to dramatize what they have read and how they have read it" (Wilhelm, 1997, p. 43). During an SRI, Lacey brought in a picture of a girl from a magazine to represent Carmen, a character from her book *The Sisterhood of the Traveling Pants* (Brashares, 2003). On the back side of the magazine picture, she had pasted a picture of herself. She explained to her group she did this because she understood how Carmen felt because they both have divorced parents. She became quite animated during her explanation when she described how Carmen had gone to visit her dad for the summer, expecting to spend time alone with him. Instead, she arrived and her father surprised her with the news he was getting remarried and had moved in with his fiancée and her children. Lacey told her group how upset she would have been if a similar thing happened to her: "My dad's coming out here for Spring Break and if he tells me he's getting married, ooh, I'd be sooooo mad. I just wouldn't talk to him. Ever." Again, like Marisa, Lacey showed an ability to relate to and empathize with a character. She put herself into the book to understand how a character was feeling.

Conclusions

Because independent reading is a year-long activity, I do not feel as though my inquiry has ended. I am continuing to look for ways to motivate and engage my students in independent reading. What I have learned from conducting this inquiry is the importance of dialogue and conversation in the classroom. I am aware of how important it is to challenge myself to come up with different ways to encourage talk about books in the classroom. The insights and ideas the students expressed in conversation with each other were much more valuable than anything they could have done with a question and answer worksheet or reading log. In their book talks, they were able to empathize with others, share experiences, and apply lessons to their own lives. However, I am not sure all my students were even aware they were doing this. I feel my next challenge is to make the students more conscious of what they are doing so they can make a rubric that more accurately reflects their role in the reading and meaning-making process. Hopefully, as the students become more aware of their importance in making meaning, and all they can learn from and relate to in books, they will be hooked, and my goal of developing "lifelong readers" will be achieved.

References

Kasten, W., & Wilfong, L. (2005). Encouraging independent reading with ambience: The Book Bistro in middle and secondary school classes. *Journal of Adolescent and Adult Literacy, 48*, 656–664.

Raphael, T. E., & McMahon, S. I. (1994). Book club: An alternative framework for reading instruction. *The Reading Teacher, 48*, 102–116.

Rosenblatt, L. (1995). *Literature as exploration*. New York: Modern Language Association of America.

Wilhelm, J. (1997). *You gotta be the book: Teaching engaged and reflective reading with adolescents*. New York: Teachers College Press.

Worthy, J. (2002). The intermediate grades: What makes intermediate grade students want to read? *The Reading Teacher, 55*, 567–570.

Children's Literature

Brashares, A. (2003). *The sisterhood of the traveling pants*. New York: Delacorte Press.

Colfer, E. (2002). *Artemis Fowl*. New York: Hyperion Books.

Couloumbis, A. (1999). *Getting near to Baby*. New York: Puffin Books.

Johnson, A. (1998). *Heaven*. New York: Simon & Schuster Children's Publishing.

Mead, A. (1998). *Junebug and the Reverend*. New York: Dell Yearling.

Ryan, P. M. (2004). *Becoming Naomi Leon*. New York: Scholastic.

Snicket, L. (1999). *A series of unfortunate events*. New York: HarperCollins.

Strasser, T. (1998). *Shark bite: Against the odds*. New York: Aladdin.

Chapter 14

Meg Goethals's Inquiry Paper

INTRODUCTORY HIGHLIGHTS

- Described an inquiry conducted in a colleague's eighth-grade classroom.
- Used pre and post surveys.
- Used quotations in running text.
- Used interesting headings.

"Books That Have Ghetto Feelings": How Reading Workshop Increases Inner-City Eighth-Graders' Motivation, Engagement, and Comprehension

Meg Goethals

Introduction

"How can I motivate my students to read?" "Why aren't my students reading on their own?" "How can I best foster their reading comprehension?" These were the questions my colleague (who is also my roommate), Sally, continually asked me as she attempted to teach reading to her class of eighth graders. She would often lament that students weren't "doing the reading" and therefore would fail the class. She longed to assist her students in seeing themselves as "readers," in knowing how to read effectively, and in finding the joy in reading. Her school was departmentalized and she taught math to the junior high students, but also taught her own home-room class reading, an area in which she felt she had little discipline knowledge. She had communicated her frustrations about this class, so when I needed to conduct an inquiry for a literacy course, she invited me to work with her in her reading class. We established our general questions. "How do we get students to a deeper level of comprehension as they read?" "How do we get eighth graders motivated to read and enjoy reading?" I found a section, "Teaching Comprehension in a Reading Workshop," from a book by Harvey and Goudvis (2000). Sally had mentioned this approach to me in our discussions because a teacher she knew and admired suggested it to her. She wanted to try Reading Workshop herself, but felt it would be too much to take on alone. I was unfamiliar with the exact components, but was more than willing to do the research. Thus began my inquiry: In what ways does Reading Workshop aid student comprehension?

The first, and perhaps most powerful, component of a Reading Workshop is providing students choices in what they read. When students can choose a book they want to and, more importantly, *can* read, they will be more likely to engage in that text. Giving students control in what they do is highly motivating. Every student, even struggling readers, should be able to find a book they will enjoy. In effect, students will read more. With more reading practice and exposure to different kinds of texts, learners will deepen their understanding of literature and how it works. When implementing our Reading Workshop, we hoped allowing students to choose their texts would increase motivation and engagement.

Reading Workshop also includes direct strategy instruction to guide students as they engage in literature. Researchers like Harvey and Goudvis (2000) promote teaching specific strategies chronologically, but I now feel *students* should direct the instruction. Teachers should plan mini-lessons based on what students show they know and what they still need to learn. It will ensure that students continue to grow, improve, and build on what they already know, rather than learn arbitrary strategies in an arbitrary order. Meaning is made by the reader, so the teacher should act as a guide in discovering this meaning rather than force-feeding students his or her own ideas. The teacher should be available as a resource rather than an all-knowing figure, and should learn from his or her students just as the students learn from the teacher. Direct instruction is still necessary in a reading classroom, but only if that instruction is based on student need.

Since meaning is made by the reader, reader response drives Reading Workshop. Dialogue journals are an excellent medium through which to give students daily response opportunities along with teacher guidance. In our dialogue journals, students and I wrote letters to each other about their reading. I posed questions to foster deeper thinking about their texts, and they responded with additional thoughts or questions as well. Sally and I hoped this would create a private forum for students to explore their identities as readers and reflect not only on what they were reading, but also on what they were learning.

Conferencing is another way to monitor student response, strategizing with them about concerns or questions in their reading, and setting individual goals. Students should share these responses with classmates as well. This can be done through literature circles, book talks, or PowerPoint presentations, or creatively by writing a poem or an alternative ending to their book. It is important for students to share their ideas and thoughts with peers and teachers. Engaging in discussion or creative response will urge students to think deeply about what they read, which will promote further comprehension.

My vision for our Reading Workshop was to create a literary community in which students and teachers would collaborate to create an understanding of the text and of ourselves. We hoped students would discover themselves in what they read, and, in their responses, reflect on who they were and what they believed. We also hoped to provide the unique opportunity to glimpse other perspectives of which they might have little knowledge. We hoped that getting them excited about reading, discussing texts, and validating their own meaning making would deepen their comprehension not only of literature and how it works, but also of themselves and the world. As we began our inquiry, I was shocked by how little students read and how difficult it seemed to engage them. By the end, however, students' attitudes were transformed as they found books they enjoyed, related to, and learned from.

Creating a Literary Community

When Sally invited me to work in her classroom, while excited and hopeful I felt somewhat apprehensive. This is her second year teaching 8th grade and she has shared with me her various frustrations with her teaching. To implement a Reading Workshop in Sally's classroom, I researched extensively not only about the method itself but also about adolescents and, in particular, inner-city African American adolescents. The Pope John Paul II Elementary School [code name] is located in the Englewood neighborhood on the southwest side of Chicago. According to the U.S. Census in 2000, of the approximately 3,000 residents in this community, 43% live below the poverty line. Violence and crime terrorize the community. In recent news it had been the setting for a number of shootings, two of which killed young girls. More than 700 murders have taken place in the past ten years. The population of the school was 100% African American, the majority of whom lived in this neighborhood. Most of Sally's students lived in single-parent homes, mostly headed by mothers, with others also living with relatives or a group home. To meet the needs of our students, we wanted to know what would engage and motivate them.

Although I began my inquiry with focal students, I quickly resolved to follow every student because I noticed such important and interesting comments, journal entries, and changes in all of them. I did not want to put greater importance on any one student's ideas or actions. They completed an initial reading survey so we could gauge their attitudes about reading, the amount they read in school and at home, the literacy practices they engaged in at home, and what reading activities they liked or disliked. We also discussed with them what types of books they liked to read. We then implemented our Reading Workshop routine. It took place over a three-month period, from 9:00 to 10:00 a.m. Monday through Friday (except for days having special school events). The 60 minutes consisted of a 10- to 15-minute read-aloud connected to a mini-lesson, 30–35 minutes of independent silent reading, and 10–15 minutes to share responses to their reading. I recorded my observations during all three time periods. I noted student participation, or lack thereof, student behavior, and student comments. I documented our teaching as well. Sally and I alternated teaching mini-lessons, which I discuss further in the subsequent sections. In their dialogue journals, we corresponded about their reading. The first page was a Reading Log, where they recorded books they started, finished, or abandoned. I observed and analyzed what we wrote to each other and how many books they finished or abandoned. We also took notes during student conferences, some of which I tape-recorded. I documented other student response activities, such as book talks or discussions. When we ended our workshop, we gave them an exit survey. This survey attempted to capture how their attitudes toward reading had changed, how they used the reading strategies we taught them, how they felt their comprehension had improved. It also documented how many books they had finished, and what book was their favorite and why. Although Sally and I taught together and I discussed the data with her, I collected and analyzed these data alone. I did, however, discuss the analysis with her. In the following sections, I discuss the results inquiry on the Reading Workshop in three sections: the beginning stages, problems we observed and changes we implemented, and the final outcome.

"This Book Got Me!": Engaging in the World of Literature

What We Learned about the Beginning Survey

Student responses on their initial surveys showed that students weren't reading. Moreover, twelve out of eighteen students in our eighth grade classroom said that reading was boring, they hated school reading activities, and they simply didn't like to read. For example, when asked about the reading they did in school, Keisha wrote, "So far I feel that I don't like the reading in school because it's just boring and I don't have patience for it." Another student, Richard, said, "I think reading is OK because some of it is easy and the rest is too confusing. Me, I just hate reading." This student, Sally told me, had failed reading the previous two quarters. The other six students said reading is just "OK," or, as Alicia wrote, "It's cool if I'm into the book." The majority of responses, however, were negative. For example, Christina wrote, "Sometimes when I get a book I feel like going to sleep because it's that boring." William and John also noted that reading was boring, and Darius, Andrea, and LaKendra commented that they didn't like it. Sally and I wondered what might have created these strong and mostly negative feelings about reading.

On the reading survey, we asked them about literacy practices in their homes. We found out many of them do not own many books. Five students said there were fewer than ten books in their homes, and all of these students said they hated reading them. The other students said they owned anywhere from 25 to 100 books, but also answered that they personally owned very few of these books. We wondered if the number of books in their households reflected the value their families placed on literacy, or if it perhaps simply indicated the number of books they could afford. More research in this area would have to be done to know for sure, but regardless, students overall expressed a general indifference toward, or even dislike of, reading. We hoped Reading Workshop would change this.

Another survey question asked students what types of books they like to read. We discussed this with them further so we could fill our library with books that would interest them. The majority of students expressed a desire to read books they could relate to, or realistic fiction. In our discussion, Jacquelia said she liked to read "books that have ghetto feelings!" In other words, she wanted to read books that portrayed life in her urban environment. The rest of the class expressed their agreement. On her survey and then in our discussion, Alicia shared her favorite book, *The Coldest Winter Ever* by Sister Souljah (1999). This comment caused an uproar among the girls in the class. All of them became excited and animated. Having never heard of this book, I read it to see what might have caused this reaction. What I found might have scared some teachers because of the explicit language and content, but as I continued to read I realized why the girls might have reacted that way. It is a novel about a teenage girl, born in the ghetto to a drug-dealing, wealthy, and powerful father. It paints an extremely raw and real portrait of life in the ghetto. The book also provides a Reader's Guide in which the author answers questions about the novel. When asked if it is based on a true story, she writes, "No. My novel is not based on a true story. However, it is based on real events that happen every day. That's why it feels so real. After all, drugs are real. Drug dealers are real. Drug wars are real. The ghetto is real" (p. 435). Sister Souljah explains that her reasons for writing the novel were to counteract the often romanticized world of drug empires in Hollywood. She wanted to expose the myth that the drug world is perhaps a justifiable alternative to poverty. She also explains her choice to tell the story through the eyes of a teenage girl. She writes:

> I felt that Hollywood completely missed the real story of black girls and women. They had created female images that for me were simply figments of their imagination. They were not authentic. The sounds of their voices, the depth of their thoughts, their manner of speech, their style of dress, the gravity of their hearts, the varying levels of love, the challenges they faced, and their attitudes had been all wrong. Writing *The Coldest Winter Ever* for me was to set it straight, to capture an array of black female personalities, to explore the many psychoses, the real strengths and weaknesses. To allow female characters to speak free from cultural domination or projections of how others thought we are. To get it right, finally.
>
> (p. 438)

Reading this, I realized why many of the students wanted to read books they can relate to, books that evoke "ghetto feelings," books about real life. Our students were tired of reading about unfamiliar characters, stories of which they had little or no experience, and themes irrelevant to their lives. In a world in which they often feel misrepresented or underrepresented, our students were expressing a desire to see themselves or their neighborhoods in the literary world. Books such as *The Coldest Winter Ever*, to which they could perhaps relate, would foster the very active, critical, and reflective learning we had hoped to create.

Talking with Students about Their Books

To build a literary community in which our students could begin to engage in text and discover their identities as "readers," we developed individual relationships with each child. We attempted to achieve this through dialogue journals, conferences, and informal conversations. Their journals began as an assignment. We gave them prompts based on the strategies we taught them. For example, when we taught making connections, we assigned students to write a connection they made to their book. During conferences, I assessed whether the comprehension of their books was based on their summaries of the events, their discussions of the characters, their predictions and personal thoughts about the book. I conferred one day with Mya, who I felt to be disengaged. She switched books a couple of times, would not read during class, was not responding in her journal, and would often roll her eyes when I walked in the room. I held a conference with her to probe the problem. I asked her what types of books she likes to read and she responded, "I like books about killing, violence, rape, date rape." When I asked her what made her like those types of books, she answered, "Because it relates to my block." I asked her if she had read any books like that and she answered, "I read Sister Souljah, I forget the name of the book." After our conference, I noticed a change immediately. I had given her the book *There Are No Children Here* by Alex Kotlowitz (1991), a nonfiction account of two young boys growing up in the Henry Horner Homes Projects in Chicago. Although this book could be considered primarily an adult book, Sally had read some of it to them previously and Mya mentioned

181

that she enjoyed it. That day, she read longer than the time we allotted and began responding in her journal. At first, I was disappointed with her journal entries because while other students would summarize their reading that day and tell me their thoughts about it, she kept her entries short and answered my questions only briefly. One day I asked her, "So with all that shooting, what do Pharaoh and Lafayette do? How do they live?" Mya answered, "They get on the ground like an ordinary African American person would do. All they do is get on the ground. I guess they're used to all the shooting. I am used to shooting around my house and I be outside playing." When I took a closer look at her response I saw her making connections to her own life and also realized she was sharing a part of herself with me. The following day I asked her how the shooting affects Pharaoh, Lafayette, and herself. She answered, "The shooting doesn't affect me." It amazed me how nonchalantly she seemed to write about the violence in the novel and in her own neighborhood. It further suggested to me the need to discover more literature that reflects these themes.

We deepened our individual literary relationships by expressing interest in what they were reading, asking about their books, and checking for understanding. On his reading survey, William had written that reading was boring, and I noticed that in the beginning he would read silently for about 20 minutes and then draw in his notebook. As I showed more interest in what he was reading, he became more engaged. The book he chose, *Silent to the Bone* (Konigsburg, 2000), is a mystery about a boy who is accused of putting his baby sister into a coma. Instead of claiming innocence, he refuses to speak. Most days, I walked into class and asked William if he had discovered any new information yet. He would explain anything he'd found, and I would express my interest about what was to come. As I continued to do this, I noticed him reading more and more. He no longer stopped after 20 minutes to draw. Responses in his journal also began to show more engagement in his reading. On February 6 he wrote, "I read the first five chapters of *Silent to the Bone*. The relationship of Branwell and Connor Kane . . ." but he didn't finish. I noticed him that day stopping to draw instead. I wrote, "What do you think about the book? Tell me more about it." The next day he raised his hand to share about the book after independent reading time was over. I wrote to him that night, "Your book sounds extremely interesting! I love that you say you can see what's happening as you read. That's what we call visualizing. I do that all the time when I read so I can really understand what's happening. So what happens next in the story? I can't wait to find out!" On February 8 he wrote, "The book's suspense grows more and more each chapter but no questions are being answered so it forces you to read on to see what will happen. At this point anything goes." Then on March 6 he wrote, "The book is getting even better. I can't wait to find out what happens at the end, but they are only giving little pieces at a time which makes it impossible to figure out what will happen." Our informal dialogue led to a more formal response in his journal. All students appreciate and desire guidance and encouragement as they grow, learn, and deepen their understanding of themselves and the world. Either informally or formally, teacher interest motivates student engagement.

Motivation is perhaps the most vital component of a quality reading curriculum. Without it, students will be less likely to read, and furthermore will be less likely to read effectively. By giving them choice in the texts they read, we hoped to further motivate and engage our students in the literary community. We filled our classroom with books we felt they would enjoy: books about characters like them, books that have "ghetto feelings." We chose books to put in the library based on recommendations from other teachers, books referenced in *Children's Books in Children's Hands* (Martinez, Temple, & Yokota, 2006), books from the International Reading Association website, or books we ourselves had read and enjoyed. We slowly began to see student engagement increase as they took control of their learning.

The change in student engagement, while in some cases not immediate, was both hopeful and exciting. Some students jumped at the chance to read right away. Grace, who Sally told me completed little work, finished her first book in the first week. Richard, mentioned earlier, who was a slow reader and hated reading, chose *Shooter* by Walter Dean Myers (2004), and although it took him a couple of weeks to read it, he loved it. On more than one occasion, he raised his hand to share what was happening in his book. He would also give me updates informally after class. "This book is really interesting. I think it really happened. I was looking on the internet and found the actual story," he commented during a conference. Walter Dean Myers wrote the book as a real trial, including court documents, transcripts from interviews, and newspaper clippings. Richard and I discussed authors' craft: what authors do, and how they do it to create a better novel. Richard had gone so far as to research the topic on the internet! He later realized it was a different story he read about on the internet, but this experience indicated that student engagement fosters a deeper thinking about the story.

Other students took more time to find a book they enjoyed. I noticed in the beginning that some students were not reading during independent reading time. As I discussed with them why this was the case, all of them expressed a lack of interest in their books. We searched together for books they would enjoy. It was difficult to provide enough books for everyone. In a school with an already low budget, the only books we could supply came from the library. With two library cards we could only check out 60 books, but we found a only limited number of books at the library that we felt our students would read. Keisha, who said she hated reading and had no patience for it, was one such student. She had started and given up on three books already. In her journal she wrote, "Reading is just not interesting. I sometimes enjoy reading, but it is very RARE to catch me reading a book . . . I just don't like READING PROBABLY!" I remembered a book I had read as a beginning teacher called *Our America: Life and Death on the South Side of Chicago* (Jones, Newman, & Isay, 1997). It is a radio documentary that was put into a book about two young boys describing life in Ida B. Wells Projects on the South Side of Chicago. Although I thought she might enjoy it, I wasn't expecting the reaction she had. The first day she read the book, she read for the entire period. When silent reading time ended, she showed her book to another student and said, "This book got me!" In her journal that day she also wrote, "This book is VERY GOOD! I think or I KNOW that I am going to enjoy this book . . . This is the book I was waiting on!!!" Imagine our excitement! It was that day I realized the importance of not only giving students choice in the books they read, but also providing them with enough books so everyone can find something with which they'll engage.

Using Mini-lessons to Promote Comprehension

Although students seemed to be more engaged in books, we wondered how best we could foster reading comprehension in our instruction. Our first mini-lessons were mainly procedural. We outlined and taught our expectations during Reading Workshop. During independent reading, we expected them to choose a quality book, actively engage with the text, code the text with Post-it notes, use their time wisely, use strategies to better understand the text, and enjoy reading the books they chose. When sharing, we expected them to make eye contact with the person who was sharing, participate in discussions, use appropriate language, demonstrate listening skills, and give appropriate and constructive comments to classmates. During conferences, we expected them to demonstrate an understanding of the text by summarizing, using strategies, and engaging in discussion with the teacher. In their journals, we expected them to respond every day, to complete anything assigned, and make personal responses. We also discussed how to choose a book.

Reading instruction prior to this consisted primarily of students reading the same novel, answering questions constructed by the teacher, and completing a novel chart. On the novel chart they identified characters, point of view, conflict, climax, resolution, themes, and symbols. There were right and wrong answers. Thus, after we established our routines and procedures, we then planned to teach reading comprehension strategies as outlined by Harvey and Goudvis (2000) in *Strategies That Work*. As is suggested in that book, we decided to use picture books to guide students in using these strategies. Picture books can provide an excellent anchor experience for learners because they are short and can demonstrate reading strategies. The six we planned to teach were: making the three types of connections, text to self, text to text, and text to world, followed by questioning, visualizing, making inferences, determining importance, and synthesizing. By guiding students in the use of reading comprehension strategies, we hoped students would learn to use them on their own and flexibly as they needed them.

Addressing Issues and Concerns: Changing Some of Our Plans

Concerns about Assessment

Although students were becoming motivated and beginning to understand comprehension strategies, I was growing increasingly frustrated. In the beginning of our Reading Workshop, both Sally and I were excited, motivated, and hopeful. However, Sally raised a couple of important issues. Her main concern was assessment, so she could know what she would write on their report cards and explain to their parents. She was also concerned about their behavior during Reading Workshop. She felt there should be consequences for students who didn't read during independent reading time. Another concern of hers was how students could change books at any time. She thought students would do this simply so they wouldn't have to finish a book. Because of her concerns about grades and standards, we decided to give students a self-assessment each week. For each student, we would complete the same assessment. The questions were based on the expectations we gave them in the beginning. They include understanding of the concepts, participation during mini-lessons, reading independently, using time wisely, their discussions in conferences, and journal assignments. For their report cards, we would look at these weekly assessments and transfer our observations onto a Reading Workshop Rubric. The rubric outlined the same components of the self-evaluation. We looked at their evaluations and for each component decided whether students demonstrated it "always," "sometimes," "rarely," or "never." For example, a student participates in mini-lessons always, sometimes, rarely, or never. In this way, Sally would have a concrete assessment to show parents at their conferences and we would both have a solid idea of how the students were progressing. She and I felt this would also help with behavior during independent reading because they would know they would be held accountable. I expressed to her again how important it is to find the right book for each student. As we had seen, when students engaged in a book, they read more. This not only would decrease the number of times students gave up on books, but also would decrease behavior problems.

Using a Novel for Strategy Lessons

To improve our teaching of the reading strategies, we made some important adjustments. In the beginning, we used short picture books for mini-lessons, but Sally felt they were not appropriate for 8th graders. She argued that perhaps using a novel would prove more beneficial because it would be closer to the type of texts they were reading. So we planned to read aloud *Acceleration* (McNamee, 2003), a recommendation she heard at a reading conference.

Although we were teaching specific comprehension strategies, we felt students were either already using them or using them simply because we assigned them. For example, during one of our first mini-lessons, Sally explained that the objective of teaching these reading strategies was not for our benefit, but for theirs. She then asked them why they felt they were making connections as they read and William answered, honestly, "Because you told us to." Other students, however, expressed a belief that they already understood what they were reading so they didn't need to use strategies. Jacquelia said, "Why do we have to use the strategies? I already understand everything I read." Later, I conferred with her about this comment, asking her what she thought about as she read. She said she pictured it in her mind sometimes and she rereads parts she didn't understand. I explained to her that those are comprehension strategies, and I realized that she was using them as she needed them. Another student felt the same way. In her final survey Fiona wrote, "I learned that I was using the strategies before I learned about them." So Sally suggested that we show them the PowerPoint presentation I had created, outlining all six strategies. This way, they would have a name for strategies they were using, and it would create a common language in our classroom. It would also allow students more control in their use of strategies. And, in their final surveys, they mentioned a range of strategies that they used.

185

Making Journal Entries Open-ended

In trying to increase student control, we resolved to allow them to use more open-ended responses in their journals. In the beginning, we forced them to document the strategies we were teaching. For example, the first strategy we taught them was making a connection to the story. Some of their responses showed that either they couldn't make a connection or the connection they did make wasn't meaningful or wasn't aiding their comprehension. William wrote, "I can almost relate to Connor's and Branwell's relationship with me and my cousin." When I asked him how this helps him understand the story better, he replied, "I don't know." Damon made a text to self-connection also. "In the book a man named Little John helps a mole that is walking across the pasture alone because he says it's easy prey. That is how I helped this puppy that was walking down the alley because I believed it would be easy for bigger dogs to attack it." Although both of these entries could be insightful, neither boy seemed to think it helped them understand the story better. Andrea, on the other hand, could not make a connection at all. When the assignment was to make a text-to-self connection, she wrote, "I could not make a connection to the book." When told to make a text-to-world connection, she wrote, "Text to World: I don't have one idea." Her response wasn't helping us learn what she *was* doing as she read, only what she wasn't doing. These entries and those like it directed us to allow them to employ more open-ended responses. We hoped it would increase student participation and would be a way to assess what students knew and what we still needed to teach. It would give us a glimpse of what students were doing and thinking about as they were reading. Perhaps most importantly, it would place student rather than teacher response in the driver's seat, where I had wanted it all along.

Considering Book Talks and Other Possibilities

Also, I had a desire to create more opportunities for student response, to better understand students' thoughts and ideas. I thought students should complete book talks, which I thought not only would deepen student thinking about their books, but also would further create a literary community. Students would learn from each other. I also wanted students to respond creatively, which I felt would increase motivation and deepen student understanding. Since students had just gotten into the routine of Reading Workshop, we decided to start with book talks and move from there.

To foster increased comprehension, I wanted more opportunities for students to work in cooperative groups. I had a couple of ideas I wanted to add to our Reading Workshop. To deepen students' understanding of reading comprehension strategies, I felt it would be beneficial for our 8th graders to teach some of the strategies to students from younger grades. It would provide an authentic experience for students to think reflectively and critically about each strategy. They would be forced to think about their audience, the reading strategy they were teaching, and how best to teach it. They could choose the text they wanted to use for guided practice and the means in which they wanted to relay the information. They could use poster board or PowerPoint presentations. It would also provide an opportunity for students to work together. When working cooperatively, students have an opportunity to reflect on their own thinking while also hearing others' perspectives. It is vital we learn to share our ideas confidently while also being receptive and respectful of other opinions. We predicted our changes would allow students more control of their learning, teach us what they know and still need to learn, and increase motivation, engagement, and comprehension.

"This book shows you how people like us can make it in the world today": Changing Student Views and Responses

In the final week of our workshop, we gave students surveys to assess their feelings about Reading Workshop, their use of reading comprehension strategies, and what they'd learned about themselves as readers. Below I talk about the changes that occurred regarding students' views and response in the various Reading Workshop activities. Students' post-survey remarks are integrated in this discussion.

Changing Attitudes

Fourteen of the eighteen students felt that their attitudes toward reading had changed. As William, mentioned earlier as a student who previously had said reading was boring, wrote, "I can enjoy reading better." Richard, who had said he hated reading, wrote, "I learned that reading can be fun if you put effort in to it." Keisha was one of the students who felt her attitude had not changed, but her answer interested me and I wondered if I should be disappointed or hopeful. Prior to our Reading Workshop, she felt she had no patience for reading, hated reading, and, as we began, had difficulty in finding a book she enjoyed until I introduced her to *Our America* (Jones et al., 1997). On the survey, she wrote, "I still feel that reading is not the subject for me, but if I *have* to read I will be happy to." She also said, however, that "I learned that books are not all the same, and that I might like the book or might not." Her goals for the future are to "[s]tart reading a little more, as long as I find the right books to read, I am sure that I would complete a lot of books." I concluded that we had succeeded in motivating her to read more and in opening her eyes and mind to the world of literature. We had at least showed her that reading *can* be an enjoyable experience and that there are books she *would* want to read, which will best prepare her for adult reading. I certainly do not enjoy every book I read, so we should expect the same from our students. However, if we expose them to various texts and instruct them in strategic reading so they can better understand what they read, students will be more likely to discover books in which they engage and enjoy.

Also on the survey, we asked them which component of Reading Workshop they liked the most. Three students answered they liked everything, three students wrote that they liked to hear the teacher read aloud, two people answered book talks, and one students said journals. Half of the students (nine out of our eighteen students) said that independent reading was their favorite part. Some of them said they liked it because they could read at their own pace, some said because it was quiet and peaceful. Fiona wrote, "I liked independent reading because, it helped me get into reading independently which

I hardly ever did." The amount students read and engaged in books increased because we found books they would enjoy. I noticed students exchanging and recommending books in the final weeks. *Speak* (Anderson, 1999) made an impression on Katrina, and she then passed the book on to Nikki and Alicia. *The First Part Last* (Johnson, 2003) also changed hands, first with Monique, then to Katrina and Jacquelia. Some other books the girls exchanged were *Romiette and Julio* (Draper, 1999) and *Bronx Masquerade* (Grimes, 2002). Some of the boys exchanged books like *Tears of a Tiger* (1994) and *Forged by Fire* (1997) by Sharon Draper, and *Slam* (1996) and *Shooter* (2004) by Walter Dean Myers. As students became engrossed in books, we felt their attitudes toward reading improving.

By allowing students to write open-ended responses in their journals, we were able to better understand what students were doing and thinking when they read. I realized that students were thinking deeply about their books and using comprehension strategies. If I felt they needed assistance, my questions in our letters would drive this forward. Grace, who my colleague Sally had said hated school and did not complete work, wrote about *I Am the Cheese* by Robert Cormier (1977). On February 13, she wrote, "The boy in the story is traveling by bike. (which I think is crazy!) I just read chapters three, four, and five, and found out that his father is in a hospital. I don't know what for but I'll find the reason . . . This book is really interesting which is what really makes me want to continue to read." She gave personal commentary and created questions to push her reading forward. I also noticed Monique reading *Monster* by Walter Dean Myers (1999). The first couple of days I saw her close the book after the first fifteen minutes of independent reading, and in her journal she told me she didn't really like it. She tried another book, but gave up on that one too. I gave her *The First Part Last* by Angela Johnson (2003), about a teenage father raising his daughter alone. I asked her if she liked it, and in her journal she responded, "Yes, I do like my book. It's really good. It can and do give good information on teen pregnancy. It influence me not to have a baby at a young age." Sally also told me she read the book during free time. Monique had found a book that she enjoyed, engaged in, and learned from. Sally had expressed how hard Darius was to engage and motivate. She had said that his behavior often interfered with his work. When he was reading *Forged by Fire* by Sharon Draper (1997), I noticed he wasn't responding in his journal. I discussed with him in class how I'd love to hear about his book in his journal. I asked him every day how his book was and what was happening so far. He kept his answers short, responding, "Good," or with a short explanation of the plot. Then, one day, he wrote in his journal, "This book relates to me because it was a time I had not seen my dad for a long time then he just popped up like Gerald's mom." He made a valid and thoughtful connection that would deepen his understanding of the character's feelings. Books in which students could engage provided them the opportunity to reflect not only on the plot, theme, and characters, but also on their thoughts, on the deeper issues in the text, and on their own lives.

Fostering Comprehension

As student engagement and motivation increased, we began to learn what they knew and what we still need to teach. As already noted, we connected our instruction to a read aloud of the book *Acceleration* (McNamee, 2003). Sally read to the students for the first

15–20 minutes of the class period. We conducted mini-lessons on making predictions, questioning, and characterization. Before she started the novel, she asked them what they knew about the word *acceleration* and what they thought the book would be about. After reading the first chapter, we made a class list of questions we had so far. We had questions such as "How old is he?"; "Why does he work at a lost and found?"; "Why does he have nightmares?"; "What is the diary?"; "What is he going to do with it?"; "Why doesn't he take it to the police?" As the novel progressed, we added to our list, and added answers to our questions if we could. We also created a character chart, listing character traits of the main characters. When making predictions or inferences about characters' actions, we used this chart as a reference. We felt this modeled most effectively how to better understand a novel. They could then utilize these strategies in their own reading flexibly and only as they needed.

Individually, Sally and I guided comprehension through our dialogue with students. We noticed this deepen our individual relationships with them and increase student motivation. In the final survey, Christina wrote, "I like journals most because I like to talk one-on-one and not to the whole class, another is conferences because that's one-on-one." We know students love individual attention. On one occasion, I had mistakenly missed Andrea's journal. This is a student who Sally had said hates everything related to school. She asked me during class why I had not written her and seemed concerned. I explained that it was a mistake and apologized. She never failed to write to me in her journal—and this was a student Sally said rarely engaged in class. On one occasion, Andrea wrote about *Bronx Masquerade* (Grimes, 2002), "In their poetry now the students share the same things, but now they are sharing things that are personal and they don't like to talk about. So far I have learned that people look at ways in different ways." This was one of her less detailed entries, but it should be noted that she was not only engaged with her book but also engaged in a dialogue with me about her reading. She expressed her likes or dislikes and in this entry revealed to me what she was learning. Sally also relayed to me that on a day I was not there, many students received their journals and opened them right away to see what I had written. Through our literary relationships, we could provide more specific instruction and encouragement.

Book Talks

To provide more opportunities to demonstrate their understanding and comprehension, we allowed students to share their responses. The most telling project students completed was their book talks, which they gave after they had completed a book. They were to give the title and author, a brief synopsis without revealing the ending, and its point of view and format; to say why they chose the book and how they had heard about it, who they would recommend the book to, and why they liked it; and to share an important passage from the book. We could tell students took these book talks seriously and enjoyed sharing their book with their classmates. It also gave us a glimpse of how students were thinking and learning. Grace gave her book talk on *Bronx Masquerade* by Nikki Grimes (2002). She said, "My opinion about the book is that I feel the book was really deep because it talks about what real teens are going through and the author is making it seem very similar

189

to the world today. I recommend this book to those who like to rap or those who like poetry . . . because this book shows you how people like us can make it in the world today without violence and you can just write and express how you feel through poetry. This book can inspire us to mature up, if not it's at least telling us how young people like us can make it in the world today." In her final survey about Reading Workshop, Grace wrote, "I enjoyed book talks the most because I get to tell my classmates how the story can change people."

Nikki also showed that she enjoyed reading about real issues. She gave her book talk on *Ophelia Speaks* (Shandler, 1999), a collection of short stories about young girls. She said, "I liked it because it's kinda deep. You had to feel something or there had to be something you would connect to. I would recommend it to everyone because there's many different topics like rape, abuse, gangs, everyone who reads it can get something out of it." After reading *Speak* (Anderson, 1999), another book about rape, Katrina gave us her book talk. She said, "The excerpt I'm going to read made me think it was her fault what happened to her." I was shocked to hear this and wanted to hear why she felt this. After she had read the excerpt, she said, "When he touched her butt, she didn't say no . . . by her not answering it made me think it was her fault. I would've said something! I would come out and speak! I wouldn't have let it happen no matter how good he look!"

Students realized that to give a book talk they had to think about the book deeply and critically. Not only did we see student comprehension in their book talks, but also we noticed that audience questions during the book talks reflected a deeper understanding of literature. When Katrina gave her book talk on *Speak*, Alicia, who had previously read the book, asked, "Did the cover speak to you?" The cover shows a girl's face behind a tree. Katrina answered, "Yeah, I feel the one side is the real Melinda and the other side is the hurt side. The tree is a part of her." Other students during book talks raised their hands to ask questions like "What kinds of connections did you make to the book?"; "Who do you recommend it for?"; "Why did you pick it?" When Grace gave her book talk, Alicia asked her, "Why is it called *Bronx Masquerade*?" Grace said it was set in the Bronx, but didn't know about the masquerade part. James explained that a masquerade is a party where people put on masks. We asked everyone why the author would call it this. Grace explained that "some of the characters were trying to cover up deep issues they were dealing with." During John's book talk, Andrea asked him a similar question, wondering why it was called *Tears of a Tiger*. He didn't know, so Katrina, who had also read it said, "Andy is the tiger. He pretends to be real strong, but in the end we see he's not." These book talks and discussions taught us an important lesson. Many of the questions they asked were similar to those I asked them in their journals or conferences. They also reminded me of questions Sally asked herself or the class as she read aloud. In modeling strategic reading, we had fostered critical thinking about literature, how it works, and how to make meaning. We felt we had created a successful literary community.

Teaching Strategies to Other Students

To provide more opportunities for cooperative learning, our students worked together to teach reading strategies, which not only increased engagement, motivation, and understanding, but also strengthened our literary community. Students chose a partner and then ranked (first, second, and third) the strategies they wanted to teach. We allowed them to choose strategies that we had previously taught them: making connections, visualizing, and questioning. Three groups taught the 3rd grade, three the 4th grade; and three the 5th grade. Before they taught the strategies, each group practiced their lesson in class while their classmates and Sally and I provided constructive feedback. One group, William and Darius, chose to teach making connections to the 4th graders using "The Black Pledge of Allegiance." After reading "I pledge allegiance . . .," William explained the meaning of *allegiance* and asked them if any of them had ever made a promise. He continued, stopping momentarily after "I give my life and love to my people," to connect to sacrifices that they might have made during Lent. He also stopped after "To stand up for what is right," and asked them if they could think of a time when someone had stood up for what was right. One student answered, "Martin Luther King, Jr." William told her that was a good example and said, "See, that would be a text–world connection." Another group created a skit to demonstrate questioning. Fiona and Christina created a PowerPoint presentation to define and explain the strategy. They then modeled the strategy using an *Arthur* book. Christina read the story, while Fiona acted as Christina's brain. As Christina read, she stopped from time to time and Fiona would ask questions such as "Now why did that character do that?" or "Will Arthur ever find the diary?" or "What do I think will happen next?"

While they prepared their lessons, Sally and I could tell who had a deep understanding of the strategy and who needed further assistance. Damon and John, for example, taught visualizing. When practicing it, they defined it correctly and explained very well how it helps us, but were confused in how to actually use it. They read a picture book about Michael Jordan and asked students to visualize it as they read. After each section John asked us what we pictured. When some of us volunteered answers, John asked, "Was it like this?" He then showed us the picture in the book. "If so, you're right," he said. I explained to both of them that we all visualize differently and there is no right or wrong answer as long as what we visualize can be supported by the text. This project motivated students, engaged students, and encouraged students to think deeply and critically about reading comprehension. This project also demonstrated to us what students had learned or still needed to learn about the strategies we had taught. We also felt a sense of community as students expressed to each other strengths of their lessons and suggestions for improvement.

Conclusion

Reading Workshop allows students an authentic experience with text. It not only increases student motivation, engagement, and comprehension, but also provides a genuine context for teacher and students to deepen their understanding of the world and their place in it. Allowing students to choose what they read enables them to find a book they *can* and *will* read, which reflects the reading we do as adults. Providing an authentic context gives students an opportunity to practice real-world reading. This will better teach and prepare them for the future, which, in essence, is the purpose and goal of schooling.

Fostering a literary relationship with students not only further motivates and engages students, but also encourages them to think of themselves as "readers." In the beginning of our workshop, most of our students hated reading. Through our dialogue journals, informal conversations, and conferences, we created an environment in which students began to feel and think like a reader. In their final surveys, many students expressed a positive view toward Reading Workshop and explained how their feelings about reading had changed. Katrina wrote, "I like independent reading, journals, conferences, I like them all because it's something that I've never experienced and it's fun!! Nothing ever got me into it like Reading Workshop." Alicia commented, "I love all of it because it just let us read a book of our choice and at our speed and it help us share what we learn. I learned that reading can be fun and easy if I read books on my level that I could understand." Jacquelia explained how her attitude towards reading had changed. "Now I am reading at home. I just started reading a book yesterday and I have two more pages to go. My comprehension is good now because I focus more and read a lot more than before."

By allowing students to create their own responses and to generate their own meaning from what they read, the teacher can base instruction on their prior knowledge. This was perhaps the most important and most difficult lesson for Sally and me. We often expressed our concern with what they were doing or not doing. Since we hadn't read some of their books, we wondered if they would fully comprehend their texts. What we realized and concluded was that we needed to focus on what students were doing and move from there. We needed to give them more control. That's not to say, however, that we weren't teaching. Rather, it simply put students in the driver's seat. We looked at what they knew, what they were doing, and planned from there. We asked ourselves, "What are they showing us they need to learn?" In a sense, then, we created the curriculum together.

Although we saw tremendous improvement in student engagement and student understanding, we wish we had had more time to implement all we had learned. First, we provided more student response activities only at the end of our workshop. I would also have liked to provide more opportunities for student discussion. When the students were working in groups, Sally felt they were less productive, so we didn't give them many group activities. In the future, I would group students in literature circles of about four students who had read books with similar themes. They could compare and contrast themes, authors' writing styles, characters, and genres, and make text-to-text connections. We could create literature circles around genres. Students could each choose a book within a particular genre and discuss examples of the genre and aspects of genre, and perhaps attempt to write their own piece in the genre.

I would also increase the use of technology in Reading Workshop. The use of multimedia in the classroom is becoming not only desirable, but necessary in order to better reflect the world in which students live. The school owns a mobile laptop station that it acquired through a grant, but Sally wanted to keep use limited due to behavior issues. We allowed students to respond to their reading through email using e-pals. This is a website that provides students and teacher email accounts to correspond to each other only. We did this only once so they could write me when I was in California, but Sally observed that students became excited and engaged during this experience. It would be interesting to see whether and how responses changed, improved, or led to a deeper understanding while providing them an authentic experience with technology.

Finally, our students directed instruction only toward the end of our time together. I would like to implement Reading Workshop in a classroom over the course of a year, planning mini-lessons around what students need, and see how that might further increase comprehension. Releasing control proved the most difficult for me, but I learned that it is perhaps the most important and necessary part of effective instruction and learning. I wonder whether if they had been given more time, more response options, more opportunities to work in cooperative groups, and more control in their learning, the four students who said their attitudes toward reading had not changed would have answered differently.

By the end of our Reading Workshop, student rather than teacher response drove our classroom. We realized students engaged more when the subject interested them and instruction built on their existing knowledge. We learned that to foster reading comprehension we must motivate students to participate in a literary community in which they take risks, explore their identities as readers, and discuss their thoughts with peers and teachers. We came to understand that comprehension means more than simply mastering texts. Students need the opportunity to discover themselves in literature so they can reflect on who they are and what they believe, and begin to think more deeply about their position in society. Ultimately, by immersing them in literature, Reading Workshop transforms students into more active, critical, and reflective participants in the world beyond the classroom.

References

Anderson, L. H. (1999). *Speak*. New York: Penguin.

Cormier, R. (1977). *I am the cheese*. New York: Dell Laurel-Leaf.

Draper, S. M. (1994). *Tears of a tiger*. New York: Aladdin.

Draper, S. M. (1997). *Forged by fire*. New York: Aladdin.

Draper, S. M. (1999). *Romiette and Julio*. New York: Atheneum Books.

Grimes, N. (2002). *Bronx masquerade*. New York: Dial.

Harvey, S., & Goudvis, A. (2000). *Strategies that work: Teaching comprehension to enhance understanding*. Portland, ME: Stenhouse.

Johnson, A. (2003). *The first part last*. New York: Simon Pulse.

Jones, L., Newman, L., & Isay, D. (1997). *Our America: Life and death on the South Side of Chicago*. New York: Scribner.

Konigsburg, E. L. (2000). *Silent to the bone*. New York: Aladdin.

Kotlowitz, A. (1991). *There are no children here*. York: Anchor Books.

Martinez, M., Temple, C., & Yokota, J. (2006). *Children's books in children's hands*. New York: Pearson Education.

McNamee, G. (2003). *Acceleration*. New York: Wendy Lamb Books.

Myers, W. D. (1996). *Slam*. New York: Scholastic.

Myers, W. D. (1999). *Monster*. New York: HarperCollins.

Myers, W. D. (2004). *Shooter*. New York: HarperCollins.

Shandler, S. (1999). *Ophelia speaks*. New York: HarperCollins.

Sister Souljah. (1999). *The coldest winter ever*. New York: Pocket Books.

Chapter 15

Dawn Siska's Inquiry Paper

INTRODUCTORY HIGHLIGHTS

■ Provided a separate "Theoretical Framework" section, as well as referred to others' work throughout the paper.

■ Included information from pre and post surveys.

■ Included internet exchanges between student and teacher.

■ Used quotations in running text and in separate sections.

■ Used interesting headings.

Challenging the "I Quit!": Going Round and Round with Literature Circles in a Secondary Reading Classroom

Dawn Siska

In my inquiry, I wanted to capture the climate and personalities of both students and teachers that are entangled in the many classes that pass through my door each day. I heard many comments indicating that students dreaded and even hated reading; I heard nothing but complaints and pangs about many of the novels selected for use in this classroom. Unfortunately, it seemed as though reading was being used a punishment for our students and we were dampening any sort of spirit or draw they might have towards books. We, as teachers, often feel dejected when our own enthusiasms for reading are rejected by students; imagine how students feel when their desire for reading is stifled before it even begins.

I am one of the Lead Literacy Teachers (LLTs) at a Chicago public school on the city's Northwest Side, one of the city's most diverse areas. Of the school's over 1,900 students, more than half of them speak a language other than English at home (over 50 different languages are spoken). Over 80% of the students were born outside of the United States and almost 90% of them come from families below the poverty line. My job description is way beyond that of the typical LLT. I am primarily responsible for the curriculum within the school's Freshman Academy or Reading in the Language Arts classes. Of the 20 sections of Freshman Academy, there are 20 various content area teachers—ranging from P.E. and Math to Science and History—with whom I interact and support. Because there are usually two classes in the room in which I teach, there are two teachers (besides myself) present to facilitate classes that range in size anywhere from 25 to almost 70 students. The initial purpose of Academy, as I understood it, was to help students to become acclimated to a high school environment by providing support for these students in regards to their content area classes. It was a class where students had the opportunity to "read for pleasure," but at the same time also seemed to force them to read pre-selected texts that were mostly irrelevant to their lives. Before I began my inquiry, the class consisted of general crowd control and was primarily "taught" in a way where students read a novel along with the rest of the class and answered study questions or recorded responses in a reader response log.

It seems as though most of the students had an "I quit!" type of attitude when it came to trying something new and different. They seemed to pride themselves on the rote completion of random worksheets and almost seemed disappointed when the latter was unavailable. While implementing my inquiry, I had to be precise regarding the learning experiences I challenged my students with and what I wanted the outcomes to be. We needed to find a way to motivate students not only to read but also to read for pleasure (Williams, 2004/2005). As a literacy educator it was my job to teach these students not only to read but to want to read; it was to instill in them an understanding that their "reading identity" reaches far beyond the classroom and is applicable to their daily lives (Kasten & Wilfong, 2005). Strommen and Mates (2004) emphasize the importance of acknowledging that although *I* recognize the benefits of being motivated to read, students must "see *themselves* as participant readers in a community that pursues reading as a significant and enjoyable recreational activity if reading is going to become a lifelong endeavor" (p. 199).

Theoretical Framework

Much of my inquiry intervention was based on the social constructivist theories of Vygotsky (1978), who described several factors that inform the study of literacy learning. First and foremost, learning is socially constructed. Turner (1995) expounds upon this idea and says that the "society or culture of the classroom determines how literacy is defined, instructed, and evaluated. Patterns of social interaction such as discourse, organizational practices and sanctioned activities and routines foster shared understandings about meanings, forms, and uses of literacy" (p. 410). Students' experience of reading in school forms the foundation for learning both how to read and reading to learn—classroom context influences students' ideas pertaining to literacy and especially impacts their motivation to engage in literacy rich activities (Pflaum & Bishop, 2004; Turner, 1995). Many of my students came from elementary school environments where learning is surrounded by games and play and moved into the secondary school where the focus immediately shifts to competencies and assessments. My students needed just as much encouragement and collaboration now, in high school, as they had in elementary school. Vygotsky (1978) also emphasizes the importance of social contexts as appropriate settings for developing literacy skills. Therefore, as Turner (1995) states, "literacy is socially constructed by teachers and students as they engage in activities and participate in classroom discourse . . . To motivate students, learning environments must offer opportunities that will invite students' efforts and participation" (p. 413). My class allows for the kind of classroom environment that could optimize student interactions that could be collaborative, changing both student and teacher roles. Students were already organized into groups at tables, so this arrangement afforded the possibility of student–student and teacher–student collaborations.

With this inquiry, I was out to change my students' perceptions of reading. I wanted to change their thoughts about their current views of reading as "boring" and something they did because they "have to" or because "there is nothing else to do" (comments from pre surveys; see below). By providing students with an authentic learning experience, namely, literature circles, I sought to convey the idea that conversations around a text could be beneficial to them as individuals. An ultimate goal of such authentic tasks, according to Turner (1995), is to "create classrooms that are 'cultures of practice' in which students learn skills within their social and functional contexts" (p. 415).

Tell Me about Yourself

Students in all my classes completed a reading/interest survey (i.e., responding to statements such as "The things I'm great at as a reader are . . .," "I use these strategies as I read . . .," "I enjoy responding to books in discussions because . . .," and so forth) and answered eleven questions about reading (e.g., "Why do you read?"; What benefits do you see in reading?"; How do you think reading helps you in your daily life?"; "What do you do well as a reader?") at the beginning of the school year. Students were asked to respond honestly to these questions and were given an entire class period (46 minutes) to do so. I took a random sample of these responses to analyze for my inquiry project to get a better idea of the kinds of ideas students were bringing with them to the classroom, and specifically the ones from the class I was focusing on in my inquiry.

Overall, I was pretty impressed with the responses from most of the students, especially regarding the questions I was most interested in for my inquiry. This is what they said about their views regarding responding to books in discussions:

Why they enjoyed responding to books in discussions/enjoyed talking about books:

- "I like to persuade people to read the book."
- "I want people to know how interesting the book is."
- "We get to see what everybody has learned to the book like a moral."
- "We learn of other opinions of the book."
- "I want to share interesting things."

These responses allowed me to see where these students began (back in September) and gauge where they might end up and how involved they might be during the inquiry process in their literature circle groups.

Let's Get Down to Business

My classroom housed twelve round tables with at least six to seven chairs around each table and was also home of the Athletic Office. My focus class, 8th period, contained 50 students and was taught by both a Math teacher and a P.E. teacher with an English background. To give students a heads-up on the literature circle process, I asked them to collaborate and select one of the seventeen short stories in *Join In* (Gallo, 1995), a collection of multi-ethnic short stories. After reading their chosen story, students were directed to create a "Billboard"—a visual representation of their story. The directions stated:

Where do you get information when there's no available person to point you in the proper direction? Billboards. Billboards are the cheapest and easiest way to reach more people than any other form of advertising medium.

Your task is to create a billboard for the short story your group selected. You will be graded on its attractiveness, originality, and your knowledge of the story. Be creative!

I wasn't too surprised by how students responded to this experience. As expected, most groups were off task and rushed through both the story and the project. I heard the phrase "I don't know what to draw" at least fifteen times as students balanced markers on their hands and laughed at each other's jokes. Nevertheless, I thought I got a sense of group dynamics and felt that I would be better informed about interactions when it came time to form and enact literature circle groups. However, as it turned out, I had no idea what I was getting myself into.

After students had completed their short-story projects, I took Daniels and Zemelman's (2004) advice and tried out a fishbowl demonstration to show students what participation in a literature circle looked like. Well, with 50 students in the room this was a difficult task. I used a newspaper article that I thought would hook students; it focused on school violence, particularly a school shooting incident. I was right. It did hook students, but apparently it wasn't enough to get them talking. I got many questions from them regarding as to whether or not the event actually happened. I used this as a teaching moment, asking students to ask their peers what they thought about the text—"Don't talk to me, talk to those around you." Eventually, conversations began (in about 30 seconds) and I asked for volunteers to be in the "fishbowl." I had five students sit around one table and have a conversation about the text. They sat there and stared blankly at one another until Anna spoke up:

Anna: "Well, this kinda reminded me of how unsafe our school is."
Murray: "Yeah . . . and um that shooting at Schurz?"

I interrupted to point out that relating the text to your own lives was a great starting point for any conversation. Unfortunately, the rest of our fishbowl was not so successful. Students became restless at their tables and the lesson shifted to focus more on developing criteria by which students should guide their discussions—that is, specific social skills that could be beneficial during the group process. As a class, we generated a list of guidelines for groups:

- Be responsible and read up to the pages agreed upon.
- Be able to discuss the reading.
- Everyone must participate and share ideas.
- Ask questions to clarify parts you don't understand.
- Respect each other.

My hope was that by coming up with these criteria, students would abide by the rules they had set for each other—as well as enforce them within their group.

Taking the Plunge

I was in search of an activity for my students that wasn't assignment driven and would provide a genuine opportunity for students to exchange ideas (Lloyd, 2004). Because people find pleasure and interest in activities over which they feel they have both competence and control, my hope was that with the implementation of literature circles my students would be faced with a challenge they could confidently meet, helping them to thereby gain control and independence through genuine conversations around a text (Lloyd, 2004; Turner, 1995; Williams, 2004/2005).

There is no mystery about why students respond differently to literature of their own choosing. They are more motivated and willing to partake in activities where they have some say. Turner (1995) points out that students who showed more interest in an activity "processed texts more deeply; used more elaboration, critical thinking, and information-seeking strategies; invested more time and effort; and reported higher intrinsic motivation, self-esteem, and skill in those subjects" (p. 416). The first day of literature circles was quite surprising. Although I was hopeful about getting a positive response, I was also prepared to get the same kinds of reactions I normally get when we start something new—moans and groans. I got quite the opposite reaction, however. Once the students received the summaries handout detailing the twelve books that were being offered to them for them to choose, their eyes seemed to light up. They spent a good twenty minutes perusing the titles and ranking their top ten choices. After ranking the books, they were asked to respond to two questions for their choices—why they chose the books and what made the books so interesting to them. I prefaced this question with the idea that they were to convince me to assign them the book; the more interesting the responses, the more likely it was that they were going to get their first choice.

When students were assigned to their groups, they seemed generally excited about books. I have to mention that I purposely did not allow students to see the books beforehand, knowing quite well that they might have chosen the book with the smallest number of pages. With this in mind, one group was quite discouraged by the size of their book and envious of others who had "less work." One student, Janie, said, "I want to cry" and proceeded to put her head down on the table when she saw how "long" *Born Confused* (Hidier, 2002) was.

After receiving their assignments, students completed a literature circle planning worksheet for the following week. Students were asked to confer with their group members and to come to a consensus concerning the number of pages they were to read each day and what was expected of each group member on discussion days. After looking over their planning worksheets, I was surprised by some of the groups' plans. I felt that they seemed to drastically overestimate the number of pages they could expect to read in one class period. For example, some aspired to reach page 45 in a 46-minute period— which, on the basis of their past reading experiences, didn't seem a legitimate target.

Along with two other teachers in this class, we were able to pinpoint which groups could present problems, namely, the groups reading these three books: *Coach Carter* (Jones, 2004), *Friday Night Lights* (Bissinger, 1990), and *The Last Book in the Universe* (Philbrick, 2000). Each of the teachers volunteered to participate in the literature circles and to kind of "push along" the struggling readers or anti-readers in these groups, and my two colleagues seemed to be just as excited about the books and the prospect of the literature circle activity as were the students!

I Quit

I thought literature circles would give my students the opportunity to engage in discussions that were relevant to them and allow them to construct responses that were meaningful (Maloch, 2002). I assumed that grouping students in this way would afford students leadership opportunities and give them more time to talk about text. I wanted these circles to give me an insight into how a book might move students, the connections they would make, how the book might reflect their own personal experiences, as well as enable me to discover their interpretations of and views on a book (Samway & Whang, 1996). All of this happened . . . to a certain extent.

Following the first literature circle meeting, I was quite discouraged concerning how my inquiry might continue. I knew from the onset that getting students to work independently would take much time and coaxing, especially when it came to producing discussion topics and getting students to use various discussion techniques, but I didn't think students would be so pessimistic and unwilling to discuss their book within their groups. Overall, students seemed to be under the impression that they could get away with the "bare minimum." Mostly, students would kind of sit and stare at each other blankly, or they they'd raise their hands after five minutes of "discussion" to say that they were done with their conversations and asked, "What do we do now?" It was really frustrating to hear students say that everything was either boring or stupid. I actually had to sit with a few groups and challenge them to look for something in their books that wasn't boring, something that they actually enjoyed.

Before the first discussion, I had to come up with a new plan. Students would independently read two days a week, discuss two days a week, and spend a day planning. I had a difficult time deciding on exactly how to structure the literature circle activities; I was being pulled in a few different directions. Daniels (2002) is big on using some kind of role sheet within the literature circle-oriented classroom. He describes the role sheets as a "temporary, getting-started tool" (p. 99), recommending them as a kind of intermediate support structure while acclimating students to the collaborative climate of the classroom. However, I didn't want what Daniels (2002) described as a "business-as-usual worksheet in disguise." But whatever I came up with had not only to work with the range of students in the class but also to provide students with more of an open-ended way to respond. I was looking for a means to foster more productive conversations, which I thought would more likely occur from students' own questions and wonderings regarding the texts (Lloyd, 2004). I decided to use inquiry questions that wouldn't undermine the goal of the student-directed nature of literature circle discussions. Kasten and Wilfong (2005) present an intriguing case for using a three-part form, similar to a threefold brochure. So, I created a response sheet (what I called a *threefold*). In the middle section I included discussion questions borrowed from Fisher's (1995) inquiry list (e.g., "What did you notice?"; "What did you wonder?"; "What did you think?"; "What did you learn?"; "What did you discover?"; "How do you feel?"; "What did you consider?"). Low-level tasks, such as study guides, often emphasize recognition or memory skills more often than problem-solving processes (Turner, 1995). I thought that Fisher's open-ended type of questions would steer students' thinking in a different direction—giving them the opportunity to use higher-order thinking skills by helping students to become more proficient, critical readers.

I hoped that such questions would also foster an elevated level of motivation, as well as a more positive outlook on literacy (Lloyd, 2004; Turner, 1995). In the left- and right-hand sections, I incorporated a peer evaluation of group members' participation in discussion and their own evaluation of their own participation, respectively. These two sections consisted of students rating (from superior to weak) members and themselves on several levels: their participation in discussion; how they kept the group focused on the task; whether they contributed useful ideas; and the quantity and quality of the work. There was also a box where they could include additional comments by providing reasons for their ratings.

As the day started, students were given 15 minutes to look over and respond to the middle section on the threefold. When discussions began, the members of one group in particular, who were reading *Bottled Up* (Murray, 2004), were quite participatory in their discussions. They talked at length about the reasons why the main character might have ended up the way he did. Moreover, they allowed me to sit with them and listen in without their getting anxious and looking to me for answers. Another group, however, began discussing only when I was standing next to them—fidgeting and shuffling papers about as if to look busy. Edgar would say, "So, what do you think of John?" and the other group members would look to each other and laugh. At this point, I realized that I needed to figure out how to get students more involved in their discussion groups and to actually care about having the discussions. I had *thought* that the peer evaluations would have helped me to judge where students were at and how they were participating in their groups. They did quite the opposite, actually—they confused me. For example, students said their peers "did a good job," "did everything on the list," "participated and read," and "participated and helped." These rating responses did not seem to be aligned with what I was actually seeing in the discussion groups. I didn't know what to do next.

Oh Yeah? Try this Hot Shot

I tried a few different tactics to refocus student attention to participating more in discussions. First, for round two of literature circles, I asked students to generate at least five questions pertaining to their novels and inserted them on the threefold. Students then took the first ten minutes of class to respond to these questions. After responding to these questions, students began their discussions, while I proceeded to move around the room to meet with each group individually. Since some groups just ran through the list of questions as quickly as possible, I prodded them for more detailed responses to their questions by asking them what they had talked about in their group. Most of the groups just pointed to the questions and didn't have much to say about those questions. However, I was generally excited about the responses I did get when I prompted them. For instance, the *Curious Incident of the Dog in the Night-Time* (Haddon, 2003) group discussed their superstitions in response to the main character Christopher's idiosyncrasies.

After the not-so-great results regarding group discussion, I tried another approach. I asked each group member to select six scenes that he or she believed were important to understanding the story thus far. After about fifteen minutes, they discussed in their group to pick out the six scenes they thought would be best depicted in a comic strip format. I couldn't believe it: not only were they talking about the text but also they seemed interested in what other members thought. Overall, most students worked diligently—deciding on which scenes to choose and who would draw. Thus, with this assignment, I noticed that students worked better on group projects than they did when they were just supposed to discuss their books. In subsequent discussions, I thought about how I might incorporate a "project" aspect to subsequent literature circle activities.

Focusing on the Good, and Not the Bad

Successful Discussions

I felt that I was concentrating too much on the negative aspects of literature circles in my classroom. I think I was letting the pessimism of some groups affect my outlook on the process more generally, so I refocused my attention on one of the groups—the *Born Confused* group—that seemed to be successful in its discussion. *Born Confused* is about a New Jersey teen, Dimple Lala, who has been confused about her identity since she entered the world. She has spent her entire life trying to fit in. Darla, Janie, Ellen, Karen, and Sheila were initially shocked by the size of their book—all 512 pages of it. They were at first discouraged, thinking that they wouldn't be able to finish the book. This group seemed to have a very different dynamic than the others. They worked together to support each other and clarify ideas without concern for embarrassment. I decided to figure out what seemed made their conversations interesting, things that essentially persuaded members of the group to participate. The group was very nervous at first and didn't know where to start. Below is an excerpt of discussion using the inquiry questions from the threefold, where Darla posed them for the group discussion:

1. *Darla:* So what did you notice about the book?
2. *Janie:* I noticed like when Dylan and Gwyn broke up and like when they are going on the train station and she saw Dylan—Gwyn—and, um, she saw Dylan and then she saw the girl with him and she got really pissed off and when she asked him why he was with another girl he was like, um, "'cause I want a girl with culture" and I thought that was really rude cause she has culture. Everybody has culture . . . just like Dimple Lala.
3. *Darla:* Just like Janie [laugh].
4. *Janie:* Oh, but I noticed that like, you know, how like from the, um, first few pages of the book, you know, how she's like confused? The main character? 'Cause she don't know how's she's going to fit in with a crowd because sometimes she's like too Indian-ish and sometimes she's like too American-ish.
5. *Sheila:* Why does she think that?
6. *Karen:* I dunno, because she's like a whole . . .
7. *Darla:* Because sometimes people are making fun of her . . . that's why.
8. *Sheila:* She doesn't know what to do sometimes like . . . around people . . . the only person she has is Gwyn and that's the only person that really understands.
9. *Darla:* So what did you guys, um, wonder?

10. *Janie:*   I wonder why she be like that . . . because she doesn't fit into the crowd. I mean, why does she care, seriously?

11. *Karen:*   Who cares what people say? It's how YOU feel. If they think you're stupid, who cares!

12. *Sheila:*   She's probably the type of person that wants to know . . .

13. *Darla:*   To impress.

14. *Sheila:*   Yeah, that doesn't want to be talked about or anything . . . she takes everything that everybody says and just adds it in and adds it in and it never comes to work out.

15. *Janie:*   And doesn't like sometimes she says she wants to be like one of those cheerleaders in her school . . . those white girls.

16. *Karen:*   No, she said she wanted to be like Gwyn or something like . . .

17. *Sheila:*   Gwyn is a lovable person, that's why. Remember when she used to talk to her grandfather all the time and he used to understand her more than Gwyn did and he was like the second-most person she would go and talk to about everything.

18. *Ellen:*   She loved her grandfather but then he died . . . she felt like she had a hole in her heart, like she had a missing part of her.

19. *Janie:*   OK . . . next question . . .

20. *Darla:*   What did you think about?

Darla took the lead at every silent interval (or when prompted by Janie) to ask the next question on the sheet. All five girls were involved in the conversation, although Ellen offered only one remark in the above excerpt. However, her response in unit 18 was a thoughtful contribution to Sheila's ideas about the important role of Gwyn's grandfather in her life: Ellen talked about Gwyn feeling "like she had a hole in her heart, like she had a missing part of her" when he died.

Other responses were also interesting. For example, Janie's reaction to one of the character's (Dylan's) reason for being with another girl ("'cause I want a girl with culture") was strong (unit 2). She stressed that "everybody has culture," and laughingly Darla commented, "Just like Janie." Another interaction occurred in units 4–8, where several of them tried to figure out why the main character (Dimple Lala) was confused and didn't know how to fit in. This topic was continued even after the Darla posed the second inquiry question about what "you guys, um, wonder" (unit 9). Janie wanted to know why Dimple Lala cared about not fitting in, and Karen, Sheila, and Darla (units 11–16) offer— sometimes with passion—various possibilities to understand the feelings of this character.

From the start, I honestly thought Janie wouldn't push herself to finish the book; she was after all, was ready to cry when she received it. But overall she was one of the most active members of the literature circle group—making connections between herself and the novel and proposing ideas pertaining to the main character. Janie consistently made worthwhile contributions to the group that would cause a stir among the other members.

Janie: You know what I think about Dimple Lala? She's like . . . no offense or anything, she thinks, she's all that . . . like why's she like judging Karsh . . . she doesn't even know him, you know?

Sheila:	No . . . because she knows her type . . . so I'm saying why's she gonna say that Karsh is too geeky and like what people think about him, how about if they say she's too geeky? And like why's she gonna say a guy is too geeky?
Janie:	I know she just likes revenge like because people are doing it to her . . .
Darla:	But Karsh didn't do anything.
Janie:	I know, but she knows that Karsh is like nice, so it's like "oh," it's like taking advantage of him.
Karen:	Yeah, it's like because the people that say things about her face she doesn't say anything but she wants to see like . . .
Janie:	How it feels when you're the one making fun of people.

Janie brought up several ideas for other group members to consider about Dimple Lala and her behavior—how this character was acting towards others. Janie brought up Dimple Lala's judging Karsh, who is "too geeky," and how she is revengeful, taking advantage of Karsh. In the last unit, Janie argues that the motivation for these behaviors is that Dimple Lala wants to see what it "feels when you're making fun of people."

Online Discussion Board Discussions

So Janie and her *Born Confused* group members were able to discuss candidly what they felt about their books. However, there were other students who seemed afraid of looking interested in their books for fear of criticism by fellow group members. For instance, when I spoke to students on an individual basis, they lit up when asked about their literature circle selections and expounded upon ideas that were never really discussed in their group discussions. Andrea, for example, was reading *The Curious Incident of the Dog in the Night-Time* and I didn't recall hearing her communicate once with her fellow group members. I opened up an online discussion board where students could respond about their selections and post questions pertaining to each of the books to the students in those groups. Andrea was one of three students who e-mailed me for about a week discussing the novel. (Note that our messages have not been edited.)

> *From andrea:*
> not to sound cocky or anything, but this book is kinda too easy. he doesnt really talk about the main subject which is the dog, he basically goes off in his own world.

> *From ms. siska:*
> Yes, the book is written in very simple language. I was reading over your discussion question responses from Tuesday and noticed that you think that the character is mentally challenged—which he is to some extent. He is autistic. If the book is "kinda too easy" right now, I challenge you to look beyond what Christopher is saying and to look closely at his behaviors and actions and how they are so very different from MANY other people; look at how his own world differs from your world.
> Thanks for the response!

From andrea:

It's funny that you mentioned that because I actually did notice how he is smarter than most people even though he is "mentally challenged" he is really good at math and also good at noticing very small things that normally people would point out. I'm really enjoying this book.

From ms. siska:

His aversion to people touching him is also part of his being different. Did you notice how he 'hugs' his father or those people that he loves? A teacher-friend of mine works with severe and profoundly handicapped students in a special school and actually deals with autistic students on a regular basis. When she read this book she said that Christopher's 'hugs' reminded her of the students that she dealt with who interacted with her the same way! What do you think of all the pictures and maps that are inserted into the story? Do they help you see more from Christopher's point of view? Or do they give you a glimpse into the way he thinks? This is one of my most favorite books!

From andrea:

It's awesome how they show him working out the math problems and gives us a picture of what he is thinking in his mind. I also noticed the grownups in the book swears alot even the people you'd expect not to swear at christopher. And who is siobhan? is that like his teacher or counselor or something? I think some of christopher's neighbors are so mean to him and so anti social. I am also enjoying this book.

From ms. siska:

Autistic kids often attend special schools. Siobhan is Christopher's teacher and kind of like a case worker who works directly with him and his parents to develop some sort of direction for Christopher's life—like set goals and things. I think Christopher's neighbors kind of remind me of my neighbors! Everyone just kind of keeps to themselves and gets upset when people intrude or even get anxious when you attempt a conversation. I also think that they really don't know what to do with Christopher b/c of his handicap. A lot of people are nervous around people that seem different than themselves.

Andrea definitely opened up while communicating with me via the Internet but was still quite silent in her group, maybe because she felt that her peers weren't interested in discussing the book within the group. In our exchange, it was clear that Andrea had interesting ideas to bring up, which I could build on. Thus, an alternative to the in-class discussions made a voice heard that would have otherwise been silent.

The Final Countdown

I came to a few conclusions while wrapping up my inquiry. The first is that a literature circle atmosphere would be much easier to establish at the beginning of the school year so that students and teachers have time to get accustomed to both the social context and the academic level of the activity. Second, class size definitely might have affected the outcomes and quality of discussions. Smaller class sizes could allow for better management and student engagement. Third, most of my students seemed to talk about the text more when participating in an activity that wasn't only centered on discussion. They needed to do something hands-on to establish themselves as readers of the text and to recognize that they all had something to share with the others in the group.

I used these conclusions to structure the final project, which is in process. Each group had to create something to present that recognized the various components of literature (e.g., plot, summary, theme, and setting) found in their novel. The only stipulations were that they had to entice the audience to read the novel and that they couldn't give away the ending. Overall, these projects weren't exactly what I was expecting but involved every member of the group and focused their attention on a task that would improve their understanding of the circumstances in the novel.

What I found most useful at the end of my inquiry was reading student responses to the literature activity as a whole and what they thought the purpose of the activity was:

- "How to understand the story."
- "How to work in groups together."
- "To learn how to work together and discuss about the book."
- "What I think that we supposed to learn from these was to participate, help each other, open our minds, and agree, help partners, and work together."
- "I'm supposed to learn to communicate, understand how to read a book, and participate."
- "I think I am supposed to learn what the other people from my group read, and think about the book."
- "Working together is better than working independently."
- "I think that I am supposed to learn that with doing literature circles, people get a lot out of the book, and everybody has to share their own opinion about what they think about the book and all that."

I was shocked from these comments that despite all the problems I thought I had had with my students, trying to get them to do literature circles "the right way," they at least got the main point out of the activity—that is, that working together and discussing a text socially helps you to understand it better; constructing social meanings positively affects your comprehension. At the end of it all, I realized that there is no one right way to do literature circles in the classroom—every class is different, as every individual student is different—and that as you work your way through the activity, you find different ways to go about achieving the goal, teach the lesson, and affect students' understanding and motivation.

Hausfather (1996) states, "[T]oo often classroom discourse shuts down students through interrogation instead of dialogue" (p. 6). Activity structures in schools need to support and engage students in instructional conversations. In terms of literature circles, students are given the opportunity to expand their competence through their social interactions focusing on conversations. Because students seem to be capable of performing tasks with peer collaboration that would not be achieved alone, I challenged my students, with this inquiry, to not quit, but to work together to create meaning in their text and to share that meaning with those around them—and in some way, shape, or form, they succeeded.

References

Bissinger, H. G. (1990). *Friday night lights: A town, a team, and a dream*. Cambridge, MA: Da Capo Press.

Daniels, H. (2002). *Literature circles: Voice and choice in book clubs and reading groups*. Portland, ME: Stenhouse.

Daniels, H., & Zemelman, S. (2004). *Subjects matter: Every teacher's guide to content area reading*. Portsmouth, NH: Heinemann.

Fisher, B. (1995). *Thinking and learning together: Curriculum and community in a primary classroom*. Portsmouth, NH: Heinemann.

Gallo, D. R. (1995). *Join in: Multiethnic stories*. New York: Laurel-Leaf Books.

Haddon, M. (2003). *The curious incident of the dog in the night-time*. New York: Vintage.

Hausfather, S. (1996). Vygotsky and schooling: Creating a social context for learning. *Action in Teacher Education, 18*, 1–10.

Hidier, T. D. (2002). *Born confused*. New York: Scholastic.

Jones, J. (2004). *Coach Carter*. New York: HarperCollins.

Kasten, W. C., & Wilfong, L. G. (2005). Encouraging independent reading with ambience: The Book Bistro in middle and secondary school classes. *Journal of Adolescent and Adult Literacy, 48*, 656–664.

Lloyd, S. L. (2004). Using comprehension strategies as a springboard for student talk. *Journal of Adolescent and Adult Literacy, 48*, 114-124.

Maloch, B. (2002). Scaffolding student talk: One teacher's role in literature discussion groups. *Reading Research Quarterly, 37*, 94–112.

Murray, J. (2004). *Bottled up*. Toronto: Penguin.

Pflaum, S. W., & Bishop, P. A. (2004). Student perceptions of reading engagement: Learning from the learners. *Journal of Adolescent and Adult Literacy, 48*, 202–213.

Philbrick, R. (2000). *The last book in the universe*. New York: Scholastic.

Samway, K. D., & Whang, G. (1996). *Literature study circles in a multicultural classroom*. Portland, ME: Stenhouse.

Strommen, L. T., & Mates, B. F. (2004). Learning to love reading: Interviews with older children and teens. *Journal of Adolescent and Adult Literacy, 48*, 188–200.

Turner, J. C. (1995). The influence of classroom contexts on young children's motivation for literacy. *Reading Research Quarterly, 30*, 410–441.

Vygotsky, L. S. (1978). *Mind in society: The development of higher psychological processes*. Cambridge, MA: Harvard University Press.

Williams, B. (2004/2005). Are we having fun yet? Students, social class, and the pleasures of literacy. *Journal of Adolescent and Adult Literacy, 48*, 338–342.

Chapter 16

Courtney Wellner's Inquiry Paper

INTRODUCTORY HIGHLIGHTS

- Used a focus group.
- Used separate sections of classroom discourse.
- Included both surveys and interviews, the findings of which were depicted through descriptive statistics.
- Wove in references to others' work throughout the paper.
- Used interesting, catchy headings.

"But This *IS* My Final Draft!" Making Peer Writing Conferences More Effective for Struggling Ninth Grade Students

Courtney Wellner

Welcome to the Monkey House . . .

Metal desk chair legs scrape across the floor, orphaned loose-leaf papers flutter to the ground, and the incessant unzipping sound of opening backpacks across the room accompany my ninth-grade students' excited chatter. Their eagerness to get into their assigned small groups would please me, their freshmen English teacher, if I actually believed that their class experiences would lead to a whole 45-minute class period designed to allow them to talk to each other without my having to ask them to be quiet and pay attention. It is February, it is a survey English I course at a large public high school on the South Side of Chicago, and on this particular day, it is the classroom activity that every English teacher I know finds most difficult to teach successfully: the peer writing conference.

When I began teaching at my school three years ago, I agreed to comply with the newly written curriculum for the freshmen English course, which regarded as its focus the improvement of basic writing skills for all freshmen students. For the past three years, I have stretched myself to the ends of the pedagogical earth to find authentic, engaging, and relevant writing activities to help all of my students become more successful and confident writers. I have had many triumphs during this process, but I have also faced consistent obstacles in my quest to make even my most struggling students proficient and independent writers. And without a doubt, the component of the writing process I have the least success with—year after year, with both my advanced and my novice writers—is the art of effective revision. Therefore, when I began to consider topics for an inquiry project focusing on a troubling aspect of my own teaching and my students' learning (or lack thereof), the peer writing conference seemed the obvious choice for study.

And Now Let's Hear from the Contestants . . .

As indicated above, I teach at a large urban high school on the South Side of Chicago where the majority of students are Mexican, either recent immigrants or first-generation Mexican Americans, who live in the nearby communities. The majority of students are bilingual (Spanish and English) and most use only English at school. Class sizes range from 30 to 40 students per class, and of those students, a minimal percentage enter their freshman year reading or writing at grade level. This is also true of my other students, most of whom are either Chinese or African American.

After much deliberation, I decided to focus my inquiry on only one of my freshmen English classes, my ninth period class. This class consisted of 31 students and met late in the afternoon, the second to the last class of the day. I chose this class for several reasons: I thought the students represented the best diversity in terms of ability levels, motivational levels, experience with writing, and personality traits. This was also the class that I found the most difficulties with whenever I tried to incorporate peer writing conferences into the curriculum; in fact, until my inquiry began, I had stopped using peer revision altogether with this class because I found it be so chaotic and stressful that it became virtually useless for them (and extremely frustrating for me).

Taking into consideration the diversity of languages and backgrounds in my classes, the large class sizes, and the relatively low skill levels of the majority of my students, the overarching focus of my inquiry at the beginning of my project was simply this: *How can I make peer writing conferences more effective for all writers in my classroom?*

Underneath that umbrella question, several other issues surfaced that I thought I would need to consider throughout this action research process:

- What role does student grouping play in the effectiveness of peer writing conferences?
- How do the questioning prompts or techniques I use to guide peer revision help and/or hinder students' ability to revise each other's writing effectively?
- How can I harness students' strong verbal skills and transfer those abilities into effective conferences on writing?

On Your Mark: Setting Up the Teams

When I initially began this inquiry into peer writing conferences, I allowed my students to choose their own groups of four peers to work with during the revision process. My pedagogical basis for this decision was my belief that students would feel safer and more comfortable sharing their writing with people they trusted and knew from outside the class. But after about ten minutes into the first peer revision session, I realized that this decision had been a huge mistake. As students grouped off into isolated circles with their closest friends, my fieldnotes captured the chaos:

- All of my best writers are huddled together in one corner of the room, trying to escape the noise and laughter from other groups near them.
- Of course my five consistent class cutters, all of whom are failing miserably, have managed to find each other—none of them has his rough draft; in fact, I'm pretty sure

only one of them even knows what assignment we've been working on for the past three weeks. That group is going to be *really* productive.

- A few lost souls sit alone in the middle and edges of the room—they don't really know anyone in the class and feel too shy to ask to join another group. I should have thought about the fact that this might make some kids feels alienated.
- Who just threw their notebook across the room?
- Four kids just interrupted my note-taking to ask what they're supposed to do now— even though I just modeled it AND spend ten minutes explaining their tasks, with handouts that they've already managed to lose.

Two days later, I had let go of my frustrations and regrouped my thoughts, which meant regrouping my students as well. De Guerrero and Villamil (1994) argue that teachers need to provide many opportunities for students to interact with peers of various skill levels to take advantage of every student's ability to be the learner and the mentor. So I decided to reread the initial surveys I had given students a week earlier to try to group them into four different ability categories as self-selected by the students. One survey question asked students to rate their own helpfulness for their peers in the context of writing revision, and the four choices were: extremely helpful, sometimes helpful, rarely helpful, or never helpful. After reviewing these surveys, I discovered that I had a wide range of perceived ability levels in my class, and, following the advice of the experts, I reorganized students into groups that contained one student from each category (due to uneven numbers of students in the most extreme groups, some groups had two students with the same perceived ability level, but there was always a mixture of higher and lower levels in each group).

I also chose a focal group, a mixture of four students who I concentrated my research on when performing more detailed data analyses. I placed Edgar, Monica, Erica, and Lorenzo (all pseudonyms) in the same peer conferencing group because I felt they best represented the spectrum of student traits, including writing abilities, motivational levels, experiences with writing, and personality differences, found in the class as a whole. They were also four of the first students to return their parent permission letters for participation in this study, so I was able to begin working with them immediately. The newly organized peer conferencing groups were the ones that I used for the remainder of my inquiry, which began at the beginning of the second semester of the school year—around the end of January—and concluded during the last week in March.

Get Set . . . Explaining the Rules of the Game

During those eight weeks of my inquiry, my students worked on three major writing assignments, all of which involved multiple opportunities for peer writing conferences. The first assignment was an original fictional short story, created and written completely by each individual student. Then, we began our study of Shakespeare's *Romeo and Juliet*, and students were required to complete two separate writing assignments: a creative writing piece involving informal letter writing between several of the characters from the play; and a formal six-paragraph essay that analyzed the complexities of different types of relationships in the play, particularly the romantic relationship between Romeo and

Juliet. Students were required to write several rough drafts of each writing assignment, meet with their peer conferencing group twice for each draft, and eventually prepare a final draft, using their peers' feedback, for a final grade. On average, students met in their conferencing groups twice each week.

Throughout the inquiry process, I asked students to complete two separate surveys and two questionnaires. Students were asked to complete a general survey at the very beginning and the very end of the inquiry; on these surveys, they were asked to give their honest opinions about their own writing skills and processes, to define specific terms related to writing revision, and to give an assessment of their own experiences with peer writing conferences in the past. In addition, students were given multiple short questionnaires during their peer revision sessions, which asked them to evaluate both their own and each other's performances and effectiveness in helping to improve their writing assignments. Finally, students were asked to complete both a feedback sheet and a goal sheet towards the end of the inquiry, which required students to think meta-cognitively about their own revision abilities and reflect on their future goals for improvement. In addition, more specific and individual data were collected from my focus group of four students. Each of this group's peer revision sessions was audiotaped with a handheld tape recorder, and these tapes were analyzed by the focus students themselves and by me to look for patterns, trouble spots, or new insights from conference to conference. I also met with each focus student three times during this eight-week inquiry process, which gave me the opportunity to probe further into their individual strategies, struggles, and successes throughout this process. I watched and listened to my students participate in the revision process of multiple drafts of all of their assignments. I also analyzed several student writing samples—from all three writing assignments and from various stages of the writing process—to support many of my findings from this inquiry.

The Good, the Bad, and the Ugly . . .

After my inquiry project got under way and I began to analyze the data, I found much to be excited about and some things to be disappointed by—perhaps the battle cry of all teachers who are willing to take a truthful look at their own classrooms. Throughout these eight weeks, I saw students who had not completed an assignment yet that year working to rewrite several drafts of one letter to Juliet—and I also watched sadly as other students simply ignored their peers' revision comments and printed out another exact copy of their first drafts. I witnessed students engage in meaningful, thoughtful conversations about their own writing, and I observed other groups go through an entire class period without once looking at or talking about their writing.

By the end of the inquiry, however, three overarching pedagogical and theoretical findings clearly began to come to the surface:

1 Writing is inherently a social process, especially for novice and/or struggling writers.
2 Students are most motivated to learn and improve their own writing when given authentic, personally meaningful activities with which to engage.

3 There is an important connection between students' self-efficacies and their actual performances in the context of the writing conference.

Despite the definite problems I was still seeing as my students struggled with peer writing conferences, these three findings shed a positive and helpful light on the way these conferences could be much improved in my own classroom.

"How d'ya get yours to sound like that?": Students Using Each Other as Writing Models during the Peer Revision Process

Whenever I attempted to use peer writing conferences with my students, one of my biggest frustrations was that even if I got students to share their writing and give constructive feedback to each other, only rarely did they actually take that feedback to heart and go back and revise their own drafts. In the past, this has always led me to say to myself with disappointment: So what's the point? However, when I stepped back and more carefully observed students during their writing conferences, I discovered an unexpected, yet consistent, occurrence: students were using each other's writing as informal models to improve their own drafts. Even if they never looked at what their partners had written as feedback on their drafts, they were taking it upon themselves to examine both the form and the function of another's draft and were often transferring those modeled ideas to their own writing, a skill I had never explicitly taught them but one that they chose to engage in as novice writers.

Vygotsky (1978) would be so proud. According to him, communicative collaboration with more skilled peers helps struggling students, through dialogue, towards completion of a particular task that could not be accomplished alone—in this case, the revision of a short story draft into a more mature, well-written piece. For example, when my focus group of students met for their second peer revision session about their original short stories, both Erica and Lorenzo focused on the structure and organization of Edgar's short story and took back various ideas from his draft to revise their own original stories:

1. *Edgar:*   Are you finished with mine yet?
2. *Lorenzo:*   Yeah, almost.
3. *Edgar:*   What d'ya think of it?
4. *Lorenzo:*   Good . . . yeah, it's good. How did you know how to make it into chapters?
5. *Edgar:*   What do you mean? I just broke it into different chapters.
6. *Lorenzo:*   Did we have to do that?
7. *Edgar:*   No, I just wanted to make it look like that. And did you see how I made each chapter from a different character's point of view . . . perspective? Did you get that part?
8. *Erica:*   What did you do? You made different chapters?
9. *Edgar:*   Yeah. I made four chapters, and all of them were from a different character's point of view. I thought of that on my own—you didn't have to do it that way.
10. *Erica:*   That's cool. I could do that too, maybe. Would that work for mine?

214

11. *Monica:*   I don't know. You only have one main character. Who else would tell the story?

12. *Lorenzo:*   That would work for mine. I have the one guy, the brother, the guy he kills, and that guy's dad. I could have the dad talk about how he felt after his son was killed, like in the last chapter.

13. *Erica:*   Yeah, that's good.

14. *Edgar:*   Erica, you could just use different chapters to show the different days in the story since it jumps around so much, but just all from that one girl's perspective.

15. *Erica:*   Oh, yeah. That would be good. Yeah, I like that better than it is right now.

Through this kind of peer talk and social interaction, both Erica and Lorenzo were encouraged to challenge themselves as writers by changing the form of their stories to include multiple perspectives from different characters. To judge by my experiences with both Erica and Lorenzo throughout the year, neither student would have come up with this higher-level writing strategy on his or her own. These skills were just at the edge of their zones of proximal development in English writing, however, and encouraged by collaboration with Edgar, a more skilled peer.

At the conclusion of this inquiry project, I asked students to complete a survey about their emerging opinions about peer writing conferences, and several of their responses also supported this finding of students using each other as writing models. In response to the final survey question, "What part of the peer writing conference do you think most helped you to improve your writing?" the following responses were given by various students from the class:

- "getting to read someone else's ideas for plot and characters";
- "seeing how my partner put dialogue in so I could do it that way too";
- "getting ideas for titles and characters' names";
- "getting ideas from someone else's story or letter when I got stuck";
- "making my story longer when I got new ideas about what to put next";
- "when I got to read someone's story who's better at writing than me so I could see how they wrote it and then copy some of their ideas";
- "learning how to use tricks in my story, like making flashbacks or it's all a dream or tricking the person reading it to think that someone is dead who really isn't."

These last two comments again capture Vygotsky's sociocultural ideas of learning, or, as Atwell (1998) refers to one of his terms, mediated learning. Struggling writers learn best from dialoguing with more skilled peer writers during the revision process as they continuously improve their writing and revising skills to match those of their more highly skilled peers. As part of this inquiry, I tried to provide many opportunities for students to interact with peers of various skill levels to take advantage of every student's ability to be the learner and the mentor, with the hope that eventually, all students would be able to perform those tasks as individual, confident writers on their own. Students' responses to this survey question seemed to support the fact that they were indeed becoming more confident, independent writers after using their more skilled peers as writing role models.

"I already wrote it once—isn't that enough?": Motivating Students to Participate in Peer Writing Conferences through Authentic, Personally Meaningful Activities

By far the most difficult aspect of the peer writing conference for me was convincing my students that writing is a *process*, not a one-shot deal. For many students, pounding out that first draft is so painful that they can't even imagine having to go back and rewrite parts of it over again. And for many teachers, including myself at one point, this ambivalence towards the revision process is often easily chalked up to pure laziness on the students' parts. But through my observations and interviews with students during this inquiry, a second finding began to emerge that offers up a much more insightful—and dare I say much more constructive—explanation for students' lack of enthusiasm over the peer revision process. Simply put, students don't want to waste any more time than they have to on boring pieces of writing that are meaningless to them. And even as their English teacher, I couldn't say I blamed them.

And neither do the experts. De Guerrero and Villamil (1994) argue that when students are given opportunities to work on authentic, original pieces of writing that they have a personal attachment to, they will feel involvement in the revision process and will want to put forth their best effort because the task is meaningful to them. Support for these ideas can be found throughout my data. For example, at the conclusion of this inquiry, I engaged in one-on-one interviews with my focal students concerning their thoughts, opinions, concerns, and suggestions about their individual writing and participation in the peer revision conference. In one way or another, three of the four students mentioned that they were more willing to put the work into revision and into the writing conference when they felt personally connected to both an authentic writing assignment and meaningful revision activities. Erica, one of the four members, firmly argued that she puts her best effort forth in all assignments, regardless of her personal connection to the work. The three other members had other things to say in the interviews I had with them.

Edgar's Interview #1

1. *Me:*   So which writing assignment was your favorite? Or maybe I should ask, which one do you think showed off your best writing?
2. *Edgar:* Oh, definitely the short story. Yeah, definitely that one.
3. *Me:*   Why "definitely that one"?
4. *Edgar:* Because I spent the most time on that one because I really liked my story. I wanted to make it really good so all that time didn't get wasted for nothing.
5. *Me:*   What do you mean "get wasted for nothing"? Were you worried about not getting a good grade on it?
6. *Edgar:* Oh, I didn't really care about the grade. I wanted to show it to Lorenzo in my group after I made it better each time because he really liked reading the changes I made. I liked having him read it.
7. *Me:*   Do you think you would have liked writing it as much, or would have spent as

much time revising it, if I had given you the topic and made you write about that?

8. *Edgar:*   No, probably not. No offense [laughs] but you probably wouldn't have picked something I'm interested in. I mean, you don't really like stories about aliens eating people and taking over the world, do you?

9. *Me:*   [laughs] Well, they're not my favorite. You're probably right, I would have picked something that you thought was boring.

10. *Edgar:*   Yeah, then I probably wouldn't have even done it.

Edgar's final comment sums up the importance of giving students opportunities to write authentic, personally meaningful pieces in order to encourage them to put forth their best efforts throughout the writing process. Street (2005) also discusses the importance of using student-initiated writing assignments—those assignments that students have choice and control over—because the inherent stake they have in the choices they have made will also motivate them to produce the best results possible. Edgar, a student who probably wrote one of the best short stories in all four of my freshmen classes, stated that he probably wouldn't have even attempted to write one if he hadn't been interested in the assigned topic. And what a waste of a valuable learning experience for him it would have been.

Monica's Interview #2

1. *Me:*   So tell me, which of these three pieces of writing do you think show off your best skills?

2. *Monica:*   Oh, I don't know . . . probably the letter from Juliet to Romeo breaking up with him after he killed Tybalt. Yeah, probably that one's the best.

3. *Me:*   Why do you think that's your best? Did you revise that one the most times or spend the most time on it?

4. *Monica:*   Yeah, both I guess. I don't usually revise my writing. Sorry. I know we're supposed to, but usually I don't see any difference between the first time I write it and the revised one, except maybe I fix the spelling.

5. *Me:*   Sometimes I don't see any change in your drafts either [laughs]! So why did you take the time to revise your letter to Romeo?

6. *Monica:*   Because we were reading them in front of the class and I didn't want mine to sound stupid or boring. I wanted to impress everyone with one that was different, not the same like everyone else's.

Nystrand (1997) supports what Monica described here: peer writing conferences were effective in promoting motivation because the small-group setting allowed students a great deal of autonomy to work out their own interpretations and responses to open-ended tasks, such as the revision of a letter from Juliet to Romeo. When Monica's main goal was to make her text more enjoyable for members of the peer revision group or for the class as a whole—as when she was required to read her writing aloud to the class—the task now became motivating by the situation. She was now willing to make the necessary revisions and improvements to make that piece of writing more accessible to the peer audience. This was exactly what both Monica and Edgar described as their motivation for revising their writing.

Similarly, Lorenzo's interview showed that the pressure to perform for his peer conferencing group was the main motivating force behind his writing and revision efforts:

Lorenzo's Interview #3

1. *Me:* So how do you feel about your efforts on these three assignments? Do you think the peer conferences helped you at all?

2. *Lorenzo:* Um, yeah, I think so.

3. *Me:* How's that?

4. *Lorenzo:* Well, I don't usually like to revise because it's boring, but when I knew that I had to let Edgar and Erica read my assignments, I tried to fix them so they didn't have to keep telling me the same things over and over every time.

5. *Me:* Can you explain a little more what you mean?

6. *Lorenzo:* Like Erica would always show me when there were parts that were confusing for her and she would tell me I had to fix them. And if I didn't and she read the same confusing stuff over again the next time, she would get mad and ask why I didn't fix it like she already said. So I tried to make sure it was always better for her the next time.

7. *Me:* Oh, I see. And did you help her with her writing, too?

8. *Lorenzo:* Not as much, because she's better at it than me, but sometimes I would catch her not fixing her mistakes from the last time and then I would get to tell her the same things she was always telling me about not listening at the conference.

Lorenzo's comments were particularly intriguing because they illustrated how students become much more motivated when they actually feel like they have an important role to play in the classroom—or in this case, in the peer writing conference. Street (2005) argues that students need to view themselves as active participants, not just observers, of the construction of knowledge during the writing process. In line 4, Lorenzo admitted that he usually didn't participate in the revision process, but now that he had been paired with Erica, a more skilled and confident peer, he felt an obligation not to disappoint her, and therefore he became motivated to put time and energy into his work outside the conference. Lorenzo obviously felt pressure from Erica to come to the writing conference prepared to impress her and not waste her time, and that pressure was motivation enough for him to continue to work to improve his writing.

"I ain't a good writer, Ms. Wellner—this is as good as it gets": Improving Students' Performance during Peer Writing Conferences by Improving Their Self-Efficacy and Confidence

Earlier, I mentioned an initial survey I gave my students before this inquiry even got fully under way that asked them to rate their own peer revision skills on a scale of 1 to

4, with each number representing a higher level of ability: (1) Never helpful, (2) rarely helpful, (3) sometimes helpful, and (4) extremely helpful. The results were not encouraging. The 31 students in my ninth-period class assessed themselves as the following: 9 considered themselves never helpful, 11 were rarely helpful, 6 were helpful sometimes, and 5 students claimed to be extremely helpful during peer revision. This initial survey data immediately alerted me to the extremely low self-efficacies of the majority of my students when it came to supporting peer revision.

In addition, as I began to read over students' comments and revision remarks on their peers' rough drafts, the extremely low self-efficacy of several students became painfully evident. For instance, in this excerpt from Ruby's original short story—see Excerpt 16.1 below—her peer conferencing partner, Mayra, obviously understood that the introduction to Ruby's story was lacking adequate character and setting details, but each of her comments is followed by a disclaimer, showing her lack of confidence in her own skills as a peer reviser.

Excerpt 16.1: Ruby's Story Draft

It was a dazzling Saturday afternoon in Chicago. If you haven't notice Chicago is cut into two sides. The unfortunate lived in the south side and the wealthy live in the north side. The most attractive fine looking girl, named Judy who was only 16, lived with her parents and wicked step-sister in a beautiful mansion. Besides being beautiful she was also one of the richest girls in the world. This same day Judy and her peers had decided to go to the mall. As she was walking through the mall Mark noticed her. Her eye caught his, they stay there for an extended period of time. Some how they both had founded out that there were made of each other, like love at first side, but on the pate of his stomach he thought that he didn't had a chance with her. But this girl was the girl of her dreams: he wouldn't let her leave out of his life.

For example, Mayra suggested to Ruby that "maybe you want to describe Judy a little more" but then added, "but only if you want to!" This added remark showed that Mayra was not confident in her own skills and allowed Ruby to ignore her comments if she chose. Mayra also seemed apologetic throughout her revision, adding "Sorry!" when she pointed out a part of Ruby's introduction that was confusing for the reader. Both of these examples demonstrated how Mayra's low self-efficacy during the revision process might hinder Ruby's chances of obtaining unbiased, authentic feedback for her story—and she definitely needed it!

Another example of a student demonstrating low self-confidence in the revision process can be seen in Manuel's peer feedback on Jesse's short story—see Excerpt 16.2. Manuel's lack of confidence showed itself in a slightly different way from Mayra's—instead of being apologetic about pointing out places that need improvement, Manuel's comments tended to sound harsh and slightly irritated.

219

Excerpt 16.2: Jesse's Story Draft

It starts off when four teenagers attend John Adams High School. Jackie, Daniel, Fernando, and Anna all go there. They're the best friends and are always hanging out together. There is this flyer going around the whole school and it ways [*sic*] that there is going to be a party and Daniel picks it up and says, "What do you think guys, do you to go?"

"I don't know, and the place seems too far and I've never heard of it."

"And besides I don't know if my parents would let me go." Anna said, "Don't worry I know how to get there." Daniel responded.

So they all decided to that they would go, not knowing the consequences that they would encounter. All of them were going to meet at Jackie's house.

"Hey everyone ready!" Daniel said.

For example, Manuel started off by commenting that Jesse's opening sentences are boring, but added that he didn't know how to "fix them." He also cut out a sentence towards the end of the page, but then casually remarked, "Never mind—put back in." Both of these examples seem to show that Manuel had some idea that this introduction needed work, but he seemed tentative to offer his own suggestions, perhaps for fear that his ideas wouldn't be any better. He seemed to feel comfortable as the criticizer, but not the reviser, and I attributed Manuel's somewhat callous remarks to low self-confidence as a writer himself.

These examples struck me because I had not anticipated that students' lack of confidence in their own abilities as writers and revisers would be such a major obstacle in creating successful peer writing conferences. I knew I needed to make a concerted effort to try to improve my students' self-efficacies with regard to their own writing skills if I was ever going to find success during these peer conferences. And so, in the spirit of the classroom community and peer dialoguing that I had been encouraging throughout this process, I decided to have students complete both self-evaluations and peer evaluations regarding their individual performances during the peer conferences. Students were asked to respond to three major prompts: (1) What is this student's biggest strength during the peer writing conference? (2) What is this student's biggest weakness or area that needs the most improvement during the writing conference? (3) How do you think this student could improve on this weakness in the future?

After students had evaluated themselves on these criteria, they were allowed to read the evaluations of themselves completed by their peers. My reasons for this next step were important: I wanted students to know the honest opinions their peers had of their effectiveness during the writing conference, and I also wanted students to use these comments to come up with specific goals for improving their own participation in the few conferences remaining for this inquiry. Street (2005) argues that writing is ultimately a relationship among people, and without the ability to work closely with trusted peers, reluctant writers may never develop the ability to become independent, confident writers. I wanted my students to see their peers not as critics or bullies, but rather as guides to help them become more confident by pointing out their strengths and advising them on how to improve on their weaknesses during the peer writing conference.

For most students, their self-evaluations of their own strengths and weaknesses almost exactly corresponded to the evaluations given by their peers. This occurrence had both positive and negative consequences for students' self-efficacies with regard to the writing conference. I had a good number of students who took their peers' comments to heart, set realistic goals for themselves for future writing conferences, and saw some definite improvements in both their efficacies and their performances as a result. But I also had students with less positive experiences from this activity.

Mario, for example, noted as his biggest strength his creative ideas and use of language in fiction writing, and all three of group members agreed with him. However, Mario also noted that his biggest weakness was his writing mechanics, or, in his words, "I don't know how to fix the punctuation and spelling and all that." His group members all strongly agreed, with perhaps a little more energy than was necessary: "You always change my grammar and spelling even though I was already right and you make it wrong." Another student, responding to how Mario could improve on his biggest weakness, commented, "You don't know how to do the punctuation, so you should just leave mine alone."

After reading his group members' evaluations of his performance, Mario seemed to feel even more proud of his creative abilities, but his doubts and lack of confidence when it came to writing mechanics were only intensified by his peers' negative comments. On his goal sheet for the next writing conference, Mario had this to say: "I will only write things that I know are right and give ideas about the story but not say anything about the spelling or punctuation or any of that."

Taking into consideration Mario's peer evaluations, his goals should not be surprising to anyone; however, his comments do show that this activity somewhat backfired for me. My intention was that students would receive positive feedback to make them feel more confident about their contributions to their groups, while at the same time facing the truth about their own weaknesses and setting goals to improve on those weaknesses, and then, once those goals were starting to be reached, their self-efficacies would soar even higher. This did not happen with Mario, however—and he was not the only one. Instead of concentrating on the good comments he received from his peers, he concentrated on the negative ones, and I am afraid to think that his self-regard may have even decreased as a result.

Coming Full Circle: Revisiting My Initial Inquiry Questions

I began this inquiry with a question that I thought, at the time, would be fairly simple to find answers to: *How can I make peer writing conferences more effective for all writers in my classroom?* Using the research and the advice of the experts, I started off focusing on three tangible, measurable criteria for accomplishing that goal: student grouping, questioning techniques, and transferring verbal skills to writing skills. It all seemed so clear, so focused . . . *so easy.*

The first day of my inquiry arrived, and I, armed with a fancy overhead transparency with some new clip art pictures demonstrating the peer revising focus of the day, sat back smugly, pen in hand and ready to take fieldnotes. But my students weren't buying it. They had been forced to go through this process many times before, and even though for me there was a new and exciting twist—taking fieldnotes for my inquiry—for them it was the same meaningless activity.

It was at that moment that I realized that if I was going to find authentic, practical answers to my inquiry question, I was going to have to let my students discover those ideas for me. After all, they were the reason I was creating this entire project in the first place, so wouldn't it make sense to let the findings, positive or negative, subtle or obvious, come from their own needs, experiences, and goals? So, I shifted my focus away from the three tangible criteria I started out with and decided instead to ask my students to complete an initial survey to gauge their opinions and thoughts on a variety of topics related to peer writing conferences. Their responses worked to guide me down a new, virtually unknown path, and I tried my best to follow their lead throughout the remainder of my inquiry.

The data I collected from my students—through field notes, interviews, surveys, transcripts of conferences, and writing samples—forged past the more tangible criteria I began with and moved towards three new meaningful standards for peer writing conferences in my classroom. And significantly, it was the students themselves who brought these ideas to my attention, through their candid remarks and honest responses to questions and situations I posed to them. They took it upon themselves to use each other as writing models, examining both form and function of a peer's draft and transferring those modeled ideas to their own writing. Through their one-on-one interviews with me, they were the ones who reminded me that their motivation to perform in these writing conferences was based almost entirely on their perception of how meaningful and authentic that effort was going to be for them. And it was through their straightforward—if at times too frank—remarks both about each other's writing and about their own that taught me I needed to find ways to improve their self-confidence during this process, as both writers and revisers.

As I reflect on these findings, two important insights have revealed themselves to me: first, in any study or inquiry into teaching and learning, the *students* are the real experts to learn from, not the people who write the articles or books *about* the students. While I don't deny that educational experts have a great deal to offer in terms of research or theory, they don't know my students, and they certainly don't understand the subtle complexities involved in improving the motivation and performance of my particular students. My most significant "ah-ha" moments came not as I read an article or researched peer writing conferences online, but as I discussed with individual students their thoughts and opinions about what we could do together to improve my teaching and their learning in our classroom.

My second insight was this: the three major findings I have discussed in this inquiry are not specific to peer writing conferences; in fact, these pedagogical ideas transfer across curricula, across disciplines, and across student populations. Students involved in any type of learning, from solving an algebraic story problem to designing a website, who live in rural, suburban, or urban neighborhoods, all desire and need the three criteria for learning described here: they need to be able to work together and learn from each other as models and mentors, they need to find the activity meaningful and authentic to their own lives, and they need to build the confidence in themselves that they can be successful.

So it is with great enthusiasm that I go back to my classroom, armed with this new set of pedagogical standards. It is not as if these ideas are completely new to me—of course, I often consider the authenticity and significance of my classroom lessons—but this inquiry has helped to remind me that these principles of teaching and learning should be found in every activity I ask my students to engage in, and I should be reflecting consistently on if I'm meeting these goals for my students. And more importantly, I re-enter my classroom now with a new view of my students—they are no longer the "problems" to be overcome or dealt with, but rather they are a room full of experts teeming with wisdom and advice for making our classroom a more successful space for both teachers and learners.

References

Atwell, N. (1998). *In the middle: New understanding about writing, reading, and learning.* Portsmouth, NH: Boyton/Cook.

De Guerrero, M., & Villamil, O. (1994). Social-cognitive dimensions of interaction in L2 peer revision. *The Modern Language Journal, 78*(4), 484–496.

Nystrand, M. (1997). *Opening dialogue: Understanding the dynamics of language and learning in the English classroom.* New York: Teachers College Press.

Street, C. (2005). A reluctant writer's entry into a community of writers. *Journal of Adolescent and Adult Literacy, 48*(8), 636–641.

Vygotsky, L. S. (1978). *Mind in society.* Cambridge, MA: Harvard University Press.

Chapter 17

Shannon Dozoryst's Inquiry Paper

INTRODUCTORY HIGHLIGHTS

- Included an initial survey (described in the Appendix at the end of this chapter), with its findings (using percentages) and interpretations early in the paper.
- Used a focus group at the end of the inquiry/paper to gain insights on students' perspectives.
- Provided a description of how she coded her students' conference sheets.
- Talked about limitations of the study throughout the paper and not at the end.
- Used interesting headings.

Using Writing Workshop to Guide Revision

Shannon Dozoryst

Starting from Scratch

In the summer before the year of my inquiry, I was faced with the somewhat daunting task of developing a creative writing curriculum from scratch. After lobbying for the past four years to have this course included in the English curriculum at our school, my wish had been granted. I was both excited and overwhelmed at the same time.

Over the course of my summer vacation I thought a lot about what I wanted the students who took this class to achieve. I thought back to the creative writing class that I took in high school. Although we produced a huge quantity of writing and were given the opportunity to try our hands at a variety of types of writing, we rarely shared our work with others in the class and there was no revision of our work to speak of. My experiences in college-level Creative Writing classes were much more positive. These classes were directed as standard writing workshops where within the course of three hours several students would have their writing critiqued by the class of approximately fifteen students in a roundtable-type format. Although each of the class members received a lot of useful feedback, it was difficult, even as a college student, to learn to take constructive criticism. I knew that I wanted to create a class environment that would include a combination of direct writing instruction and writing workshop. My goals were to get my students to write about a variety of topics, experiment with form, learn to give and receive constructive criticism, and learn to use peers' feedback to revise written work.

And so I began the semester with my instructional goals guiding the way. Student choice in topic selection is essential (Larson & Maier, 2000). My predominantly African American urban 11th and 12th grade students were excited to have the opportunity to write about subjects that mattered to them. They were so used to writing academic essays, required in all subjects at our college preparatory high school, that they fully embraced the opportunity to write about less formal topics that centered on their own experiences, ideas, and opinions. It was not difficult for me to muster their enthusiasm to write about themselves—their favorite topic!

Helping students realize that they can belong to the literary world by becoming authors boosts students' confidence and encourages positive student writing practices such as accepting criticism and revising work (Street, 2005). By establishing that we were all novice writers who were allowed to make mistakes and learn from them, I was able to encourage an atmosphere in which my students felt comfortable sharing their work with other students. I allowed students to establish writing workshop groups of 4–6 students at the beginning of the school year. Though I had planned to change these groups every ten weeks, it turned out that my students became very close to the members in their groups and asked for these groups to be kept for the entire school year. They had established a safety zone of people whom they could bounce their ideas off without any fear of malicious criticism.

I decided that writing workshop would become an important part of the Creative Writing curriculum. Krogness (1994) found that her students needed social interaction to become better writers. She instituted an after-school writing workshop for students who wanted to share their work with others and learn to improve it. "They were all involved in thinking and helping; they did not feel left out" (p. 176). Like Krogness, I was interested in providing this kind of opportunity for my students. Each week I provided students with a prompt and a series of prewriting activities. They would then write drafts during the week, which they would bring in for review during writing workshop on Fridays. Nancy Atwell (1998) promotes the use of Vygotsky's (1962) principles in her approach to writing conferences. Her goal was to foster what Vygotsky termed "mediated" learning. "What the child can do in cooperation today he can do alone tomorrow" (Vygotsky, 1962, p. 104). I also applied Vygotsky's principles to my writing workshop sessions by modeling a process for writing workshop in which students would take turns reading their writing aloud, making verbal comments about each other's work, and marking written comments either on Post-it notes or directly on the drafts. I started out by modeling the process with the whole class. We then broke into groups and I guided them through the process. Then I had one student in each group lead the workshop. Finally, students were comfortable enough to take turns. Toward the end of first semester, this process became very natural for my students. Some of my students even began to adapt the workshop process to fit their own needs. Through observation, I found that each group had established its own routine for proceeding with the writing workshop sessions.

Toward the end of first semester, I began to introduce students to the revision process. I asked students to review comments their peers had made about their writing and use the useful comments to help guide their revisions. I found that my students needed more structure than I was providing them. I noticed that many of my students were not providing specific suggestions for improving the piece of writing. Instead, I was seeing a lot of "Good job," "I like this," and "Great!" One reason that they may not have been providing useful feedback is that they themselves were inexperienced readers and writers (Krogness, 1994). I was going to have to figure out a way to provide the structure that they needed and guide them to provide the quality feedback that I was looking for. I also discovered that although my students were happy to provide their peers with feedback, they were very reluctant to use the constructive criticism they received in order to make concrete changes to their own work. Perhaps, I thought, this was because the feedback they were receiving was not very useful to them in the first place.

My inquiry questions for this study emerged as a result of this. How could I encourage my students to write comments that included the reasons why they liked or disliked a piece of writing or suggestions for how a writer might improve a piece of writing when evaluating written work in the workshop setting? In what ways was workshop helping or not helping my students revise their own work?

Assessing What Is Working and What Is Not

It was difficult for me to admit that there were some aspects of my carefully planned writing workshop sessions that were clearly not working. Instead of trying to figure this out on my own, I decided to survey the students in one of my most diverse Creative Writing classes. The reason that I selected this class as the focus of my inquiry was that I had a unique combination of three special needs students, two honors-level students, and twenty regular-level students. Eight of the twenty-five students in this class were also juniors, while the rest were seniors. I felt that this class had the widest representation of students of any of my classes and would be the best indicator of feelings about writing workshop in general. I felt that a survey would be the best way to collect important initial information about my students' overall attitudes regarding what was or was not working when they participated in writing workshop. This would give me a basis for what I should pay attention to in this study.

This was an anonymous survey (see Appendix, p. 238) completed by twenty-five students. Each student answered a total of sixteen questions: ten questions rated on a 1–5 scale, four yes or no questions, and two short-answer questions. The results of this data collection were extremely important in helping me select focus areas for the study and validating my hypotheses that guided my inquiry.

Seventy-six percent of students said they always or almost always felt confident about their abilities to critique others' work. This was surprising to me because after investigating the comments that they were providing each other I found that their critiques were generally superficial (remember the aforementioned "Good job," "I like it," and "Great!"). I decided that one of my challenges in this inquiry would be for me to convince them that they needed to work on their critiquing skills, since most of them already believed that they were doing well in this area.

Ninety-two percent of students said that they did not want to change workshop groups, and 88% said that they would prefer to select their own group members rather than have me assign groups. Eighty-eight percent of them also stated that they felt that their current group members performed at a level that was comparable to their own. This information did not surprise me because I had already noticed that they had grown comfortable in the groups that were established at the beginning of the year. I initially thought that I would have students switch groups for the second semester of school; I was afraid that they might be getting bored with their current group members, and I felt that it would be a good experience for them to get the fresh perspectives of other students. However, as a result of the information I collected in the survey regarding groups, I decided to abandon my idea to reorganize groups unless a problem were to arise or I noticed a group was consistently not on target. I must admit that I was also somewhat resistant to changing groups immediately before collecting data for this inquiry project because I was afraid that my students would lose their level of comfort with sharing their work in writing workshop, and I would then be back at square one trying to establish positive group dynamics.

Only 60% of my students said that they felt the comments they received from their group members were helpful. This information was key to my inquiry because it indicated that although they might feel confident in their critiquing abilities, the results of their efforts did not match the feedback that they were providing their peers. I was encouraged by the fact that 72% of my students reported that they almost always read the comments that their group members provided. It became one of my goals to sustain and hopefully increase this percentage by the end of the study. Based on my observation and a focus-group interview of several students at the end of the inquiry, I was able to sustain the number of students who read their peers' comments, and I considered this a success.

A New Strategy for Criticism

I was now armed with data to support my hypothesis that although my students felt comfortable working with their peers in their writing workshop groups and felt confident about the feedback they were providing their peers, the feedback that they were receiving was not "useful" in the sense that it provided specific suggestions for improvement or reasons for why they liked or disliked aspects of a piece of writing. I also suspected that the main reason why they were not demonstrating results in their revisions was that they were not receiving useful suggestions for improvement from their peers.

Through observation and data I collected while taking field notes, I discovered that my students were employing many methods for providing their group members with feedback. I had suggested at the beginning of the year that students might want to write comments on Post-it notes for the peer whose writing they were critiquing. Although I did not mandate this procedure or monitor it, I found that two of the five groups were using this method. One group was actually using Post-it notes, while the other was writing comments on strips of paper and attaching them to the drafts with paperclips or staples. Other groups were providing written feedback directly on their peers' drafts. Although I found all of these methods to be good writing workshop strategies, I knew that it would be difficult for me to analyze data without some kind of standardized method in place. I also wanted to see if implementing more structure would help some of my students provide more specific suggestions for improvement.

I decided to implement a structured way in which students would respond to their peers' writing. I speculated that this "Writing Workshop Conferencing Sheet" would not only provide my students with some focus for providing feedback to their peers, but also be a systematic way to help me keep track of any progress made with writing critiques. There are a few important components to this conferencing sheet. Writers are first supposed to record what type of feedback they would like from their group. Then, group members review the writing and write both a positive and a negative comment on the chart. Finally, on the back of the form, the writer reviews the comments and answers a follow-up question about how they might implement their peers' suggestions in their revised writing.

Before we began using the conferencing sheet regularly, I modeled on the overhead the quality of feedback that I would like to see. Emulating some of my students' own comments, I wrote several examples on an overhead transparency of the conferencing sheet. I asked my students to review the comments, which ranged from "Good job" to

"I like the way that you described the couch positioned by itself in the middle of the living room to show how lonely the setting was." I then asked my students to explain which comments would be more useful for the writer and why. This provided them with some expectation for how they should use the sheet to gain the most benefits from it. I explained to my students that they would be using this conferencing sheet on a regular basis to record comments for each writer during writing workshop sessions. I also explained that a conferencing sheet must be completed after a writer had completed a draft and before he or she had written a revision. While my students were using the sheets in a writing workshop session for the first time, I circulated the room and prompted them to follow the instructions that I previously modeled for them. This was critical because they were not used to responding to their peers in such a manner.

Writing Workshop Conferencing Sheets: An Effective Tool for Revision?

As I read the first round of peer conferencing sheets, several categories began to emerge from the analysis: quality of the feedback request, quality of the peer criticism, ratio of positive to negative feedback, group response to the feedback request, and the author follow-up.

For the quality of the feedback request, I coded written responses in the following manner. The sheet scored "none" if no feedback was requested by the author. The sheet scored "vague" if the feedback requested was very general—if, for example, the student wrote "positive" or "the good kind" for the type of feedback that he or she was requesting. The sheet scored "medium" if the feedback requested was more focused—if, for example, the student wrote "Check my grammar" or "Are my characters good?" for the feedback that he or she was requesting. The sheet scored "detailed" if the feedback requested was very focused—if, for example, the student wrote "How can I make my dialogue seem more realistic?" or "How can I expand the end of my story?" I found that seven of the sixteen students provided a vague request for feedback. In my estimation, this was critical because it is the feedback request that is supposed to inform the peer review. If an author did not provide a specific request for feedback, how would it be possible for his or her peers to determine what it would be important for them to comment on?

For the quality of peer criticism, I coded written responses in the following manner. The sheet scored "poor" if the criticism consisted of responses such as "Good job" or "I didn't like it." The sheet scored "detailed" if the criticism consisted of responses that identified a specific problem, but offered no suggestions on how the writing might be improved. The sheet scored "very detailed" if the criticism consisted of responses that both identified specific problems in the writing and offered suggestions on how the writing might be improved. In analyzing the quality of peer criticism, I found that ten of the sixteen sheets showed detailed comments. I was pleased with this finding because it demonstrated that the implementation of the conferencing sheets was causing my students to become more aware of the quality of the feedback that they were providing their peers.

For the reviewer's ability to match the feedback to the writer's feedback request, I coded written responses in the following manner. The sheet scored "N/A" if there was no relationship between the feedback requested and the feedback received. The sheet scored "not connected" if feedback was provided but was not connected to the request. The sheet scored "connected" if the feedback provided was directly related to the feedback requested. The results were that nine of the sixteen sheets showed no connection between the feedback the author requested and the feedback received. This, I decided, was extremely problematic because it meant that the author was not receiving feedback on the aspects of the writing that he or she was having the most difficulty with.

In coding the ratio of positive to negative feedback, I found that it was evenly balanced. I was pleased with this finding because before implementing the conferencing sheet, almost all of the feedback provided was positive.

Dialoguing with Oneself: A Push for Self-Reflection

For the author follow-up question, I coded the written responses as "yes" or "no." I was frustrated to find that ten of the sixteen authors did not complete the author follow-up section at all. Of all the sections on the conferencing sheet, I felt that this section was the most important because it involved self-reflection. This was where the author synthesized the information provided by his or her peers and decided which suggestion would be used to revise the writing—a critical component of writing workshop!

As we continued to use the conferencing sheets in writing workshop, I discovered that I only saw results when I circulated the room and continuously reminded them to complete the author follow-up section. When I did not remind them, more often than not this section remained blank. It was not until close to the end of the study that I asked some of the repeat offenders why they often left the author follow-up section blank. What I learned was that because this section was printed at the bottom on the back of the conferencing sheet, many of my students "forgot" that it was something they were supposed to do (out of sight, out of mind). As a result, I redesigned the conferencing sheet so that the author follow-up was more visible and the page was now one-sided instead of two-sided (see Table 17.1). Unfortunately, I did not make this change until the end of my inquiry, so I was unable to determine whether it made any significant difference in the amount of response to this section.

I did determine, however, that it was this process of self-reflection that would become important for my students in the revision process. I decided that the focus of my inquiry would now center on my students' ability to synthesize their peers' comments, determine which comments were useful and which were not, and then decide which suggestions to try to implement in their revisions. I was curious to find out if there would be a noticeable improvement in their writing if they tried to implement their peers' suggestions in their revised writing.

Talking Back: Encouraging Effective Oral Feedback

I had already observed my students shift from providing various methods of written feedback: Post-it notes, written comments on the draft, and written comments on slips of paper to using the conferencing sheet. It was now time for me to listen to what they were talking about during the writing workshop. I gathered data by taking fieldnotes as I moved from group to group while they were participating in writing workshop. Although one group always appeared to be engaged in discussion about the writing that they were reviewing, I noticed that it really was only two of the group members who were doing the critical analysis. The others listened and agreed, but let the two of the members take charge. This group responded to a story titled "The Golden Staff," which was written by a classmate in another group. It was not typical practice for a group to analyze the writing of someone outside of their writing group; however, in this case, George, who was frustrated by the quality of feedback he was receiving from his group members, asked this group to comment on his work so that he could get a different perspective than what he got from his usual writing group, and its members agreed to do this.

Betty: I really liked the excitement of the story. He has a lot of good ideas here.

Sally: Yeah, I agree.

Melanie: I think so too. There's a lot of suspense. How does he do that?

Betty: I think that he does it really well at the beginning, but there's a problem at the end.

Melanie: Yeah, like there's a lot of detail at the beginning, but it's like he didn't know how to end it.

Sally: I know what you mean.

Jane: [She nods in agreement, but doesn't contribute to the discussion. She is distracted by someone sitting nearby and strikes up an unrelated conversation with her.]

Betty: I'm going to say that he needs to work on the ending. It just doesn't feel like it's finished.

Melanie: You could also say that he needs to add more detail to lead up to the climax of the story. I don't get why Charles wants the staff in the first place.

Betty: Yeah, I know. That is kind of weird.

Sally: I don't get it either.

In analyzing this conversation, I found it obvious that Betty and Melanie were leading the discussion. Sally was willing to agree with whatever her two peers said and Jane was completely disengaged. However, in their written comments all students seemed to participate equally. The quality and effectiveness of oral feedback is something that needs further investigation. In fact, one limitation of this inquiry was the amount of time I had to collect and analyze the oral feedback of the students participating in workshop. In analyzing student conversations, I was left with more questions than I originally started with. Is it worthwhile for students to talk through their ideas rather than just writing them down? Does this help some students more than others? Is it a waste of time for those students who choose to disengage?

The benefits of oral feedback versus written feedback would be a worthy topic for further investigation. By listening to my students, I discovered that they felt it important for the student author to indicate what kind of specific feedback he or she wanted. They also felt upset when a group member did not provide specific suggestions about what they should do to improve their writing or reasons why they liked or disliked their writing.

Second-Take: Another Look at Revised Writing

The central question of my inquiry was whether or not the feedback that my students were receiving in the writing workshop sessions was helping them to write better revisions. In order to determine if this was the case, I collected samples of student work including conferencing sheets, the original writing, the revised writing, and a self-evaluation sheet. I selected one group of four girls to focus on for the analysis of the revised writing. These four girls, Anne, Tessa, Veronica, and Benita, were all juniors and "regular-level" students. They produced average work, but exhibited the most on-task writing-workshop behavior (that is, they provided both verbal and written feedback, used the conferencing sheets and self-evaluation sheets, limited their talk about unrelated subjects, etc.).

Three of the four girls in this group did fill out the author follow-up section on the conferencing sheet. As I mentioned before, I feel that self-reflection is a key component of the revision process. As I anticipated, I found that the girls who did fill out the author follow-up section did demonstrate more improvement in their revisions.

Anne wrote, "I plan to work on the expression when I read and make my characters come to life and elaborate more on the actions." I noticed that she did add a considerable amount of dialogue to her revision, which did help to make the characters come to life. On the conferencing sheet, one of her peer reviewers suggested that she should "make the dialogue more clear." I think this reviewer meant that the writer should use quotation marks and structure the dialogue in paragraphs correctly, because it was mixed into the rest of the story's prose. However, I did not see that the writer changed this in the revision. Maybe she was unclear about what the reviewer was telling her to do, or maybe she did not understand how to structure dialogue.

Tessa wrote that she was going to address "the resolution of my story, to extend it to make more sense—elaborate with detail on the whole story, expand it—give the story more background and more meaning so that the story doesn't become confusing." I did see a dramatic difference in the amount of detail used in the revision in comparison to the original. In the original version she wrote that her main character was "raised by her grandmother when an unfortunate accident let to the death of both of her parents." In comparison, in the revised version she wrote, "As a child, Nia went through some difficult times. One night, at the age of 9, she was at home alone sleeping while her parents went out on their occasional dates to spice up their marriage. It had been a bad storm and the weather was just getting worse. On their way home, Nia's parents went over a pothole and skidded into a nearby lake where they drowned. Their bodies were found the next morning. Nia then had to go through three years of a custody battle between her maternal and paternal grandparents, who lived on either sides of the country. She ended up going to live with her favorite grandmother by the name of Nana Jean." This example demonstrates that Tessa truly worked on using her peers' suggestions to incorporate more detail in her revision.

Veronica wrote, "I plan to work on the grammar. I also want to put more work into this piece of writing. I want to extend my ending and make it longer and more interesting. I'm also going to extend the conflict." I did notice that she had made corrections to the grammar. For example, in the original writing she wrote, "She was gorgeous her name, Cherri Mitchel." In the revision she wrote, "She was gorgeous. Her name was Cherri Mitchell." The student also added a twist to the story to make it more interesting. In the original version, she just described how one character helped another get rid of the hiccups by telling her to hold her breath for 30 seconds. However, in the revision she explained that the character was afraid to hold her breath, so the other character held his breath with her, which in turn gave him the hiccups. The main character then made a joke and told him that her advice was for him to hold his breath for 30 seconds. This revision shows intentional character and plot development in the revision.

Although Benita did not complete the author follow-up question on the conferencing sheet, there was evidence that she used her peers' suggestions in her revision. The peer reviews indicated that she should use more detail, elaborate on the resolution of the story, and extend the conclusion. I noticed that Benita had paid attention to these suggestions and had intentionally tried to make these changes in the revision. I concluded that although Bianca did not record her intentions for revision in writing, she still must have internalized her peers' comments and gone through the self-reflection process.

However, Benita's ability to internalize her intentions about her revision was not typical for many of my students. After taking a look at other student samples, I found that, in general, students who did not take the time to complete the author follow-up section tended not to implement their peers' suggestions for improvement in their revisions. In contrast, students who *did* complete the author follow-up section produced revisions that were more developed, descriptive, and grammatically correct. I attribute this to the fact that those students who completed that section had consciously gone through a synthesis of their peers' comments and a reflective period in which they made concrete decisions about how they would revise their writing.

Is Writing Workshop Worth It? Students' Perspectives

Towards the end of my inquiry, I decided to conduct a focus-group interview with several students to find out what their perspectives on the writing workshop sessions were. I asked four students, all from different workshop groups, to voluntarily participate. I conducted the interview more like a discussion. The students remained after class and sat down alone with me to answer my questions. My objective for this interview was to try to find out their general impressions of writing workshop, whether or not they felt the addition of the peer conferencing sheets was beneficial, and whether or not they felt that their peers' suggestions helped them with revising their writing. To begin my interview, I asked these students if they thought that writing workshop was worthwhile.

Sally: Yes, it helped me to do my papers better. I learned, like, how to use certain techniques and what not to do.

Anne: At first yes, but then people kept doing the same thing. Like, they were writing the same comments and so it wasn't as useful.

George: No, not everyone in my group was prepared. I didn't always get quality responses.

Keisha: The same [as George]. They did it as an assignment. You know, just for a grade, just because they had to. I don't feel that I got quality feedback from them most of the time.

234

After talking to these students, I felt that perhaps I had made a mistake by not making them change groups at the beginning of the study. It seemed obvious after talking to George that the members of his group were not treating the workshop sessions seriously and that they might have benefited from being moved to other groups. Keisha also confirmed George's response about group members' lack of participation and inability to provide quality feedback. I do wonder whether or not changing the group dynamics would have helped shake some of these students out of the routine that they had seemingly developed with each other. After receiving this negative feedback, I was curious to hear the positive things they had to say about workshop. The next question I asked the students was what they liked best about writing workshop.

Keisha: Reading aloud.
Anne: Yeah, reading aloud was the best part.
Sally: Reading aloud and hearing the good feedback, the useful feedback I should say.
George: Just showing people my work.
Mrs. D: What didn't you like?
Sally: All the unnecessary talk.
Keisha: When one person would write the same thing that somebody else already did, because they were lazy and didn't want to think about it.
Sally: I think our groups were too big. At least I know mine was.
Mrs. D: Your group seemed to grow over a period of time, didn't it?
Sally: Yeah [laughs].
Mrs. D: How many people per group do you think would have been a good number?
Sally: Three.
Anne: Yeah, three is good.

Again, it was extremely useful to receive this feedback from the students about how they felt groups should be arranged. As a result, I would definitely pay more attention to this issue in using writing workshop conferences in the future.

One major intervention that I made during the inquiry was instituting a uniform method for students to provide feedback to their peers. It was important to me to find out whether or not students found the conferencing sheets helpful, and whether or not completing the feedback request and author follow-up sections on the conferencing sheet helped students to produce better revised work. First, I asked my students if they thought that the incorporation of the conferencing sheets helped with giving and receiving feedback.

Keisha: Yeah, it helped organize the comments instead of writing on the paper and you can't decipher who wrote what.
George: No, even with the sheet, they still didn't write good comments, even when you told them what to look for.
Mrs. D: Did you do the feedback request and the author follow-up sections on the conferencing sheet?
Anne: Yeah, I did both.
Sally: No, well, yeah the feedback request, but not the other part. I forgot.

Keisha: No, I never did the author part. I never knew I had to. I mean I knew, but I never saw it, so I didn't do it.

Mrs. D: When you say that you didn't see it, do you mean that you didn't see it because it was on the backside of the sheet?

Keisha: Yeah, I would forget that it was there.

Sally: It helps how you have it on the front now, because I would forget to do it when it was on the back.

This discussion helped me confirm the validity of my decision to redesign the conferencing sheet so that the author follow-up section was on the same side as the rest of the paper. According to Keisha and Sally, this was the main reason why they "forgot" to fill out this section. I think that this was the case for many students. Anne's remark that filling out this part was useful in helping her decide what to revise also validates my hypothesis that self-reflections plays a critical role in the writing workshop process.

Mrs. D: Anne, since you did the author follow-up section on a regular basis, do you think that it helped you focus your ideas for your revision?

Anne: It helped me decide what to do for the revision.

Mrs. D: Did you use your peers' suggestions in your revisions?

Sally: Yep.

George: The ones worth looking at; I mean the ones that were serious.

Mrs. D: How could you tell if the comments were worth looking at?

George: I mean you can tell if someone just wrote something down or if they actually care and are serious. I don't know. You can just tell.

Sally: The ones [comments] that are specific are the good ones.

Anne: Everything that they wrote was stuff that I already knew I needed to do, so I would just do it for the revision.

Keisha: I didn't really use them [peer suggestions]. I'm a better critiquer than my group members, so I felt better just doing what I knew I needed to do.

Although Sally and George mentioned that the "good" or "specific" comments their peers provided were useful for them, I got the impression that receiving good feedback was not typical for them. Keisha and Anne also echoed this sentiment, but took it a step further by citing their own expertise as writers as the reason why they rarely took their peers' suggestions.

The Good, the Bad, and the Ugly

So, after survey, observation, implementation of a new method for providing feedback, additional observation, and a focus-group interview, what did I learn about how writing workshop affects revision and how to get kids to provide more thoughtful feedback to each other? I wish I could answer those questions definitively and neatly tie the knot on a perfectly wrapped package, but I would be kidding myself if I even attempted to do so. This inquiry ultimately sparked more questions for me than it was able to answer.

However, I did conclude this study with some very useful information about the connection between self-reflection and revision.

One of my most important findings was that self-reflection is essential if students are to produce a revision that is of higher quality than the draft. In all cases that I examined, students who took the time to read their peers' comments and the effort to try to incorporate some of these suggestions into their writing produced higher-quality revisions than students who did not. Students who requested specific feedback from their peers and completed the author follow-up section on the peer conferencing sheet also produced higher-quality revisions than those who did not.

I cannot conclusively say that it was the implementation of the peer conferencing sheet that sparked this critical self-reflection. The students whom I interviewed at the end of the inquiry had mixed feelings about how useful they felt the sheet was. However, I do think that completing this sheet forced my students to think about their writing when they otherwise might not have done so of their own accord. I also am unable to determine the benefits of oral feedback versus written feedback. Due to time constraints and interference of background noise when I tried to audiotape student conversations, I was unable to collect the oral data necessary to compare the effectiveness of the two feedback methods. This is definitely an area that I feel would be worth exploring in a future study.

I also leave this inquiry armed with new knowledge about students' preferences for establishing and maintaining workshop groups. Positive group dynamics are extremely important in order to make writing workshop an effective method for revision. I did not pay enough attention to this when I began my inquiry, and it was not until I interviewed students at the end of the inquiry that I discovered that a couple of the groups were not working to their potential because of the lack of effort on the part of several group members. I will certainly think about group assignments and changes more carefully the next time that I use writing workshop in the classroom.

Even with several unanswered questions, I do feel successful. Taking time to assess my practice and talk to my students about how my teaching methods were affecting their learning and growth was an invaluable experience. I learned more about my students as individuals and as writers than I ever would have if I had not embarked on this investigative journey.

Appendix: Writing Workshop Survey

1 How often are you prepared to participate in workshop? ("Prepared" means that you come to class with a copy of your weekly writing assignment ready to read to your workshop group.)
2 How often are the other members of your group prepared to participate in workshop?
3 How confident do you feel when you critique (make comments about) your group members' writing?
4 How often do you read the comments that your group members write on your stories or poems?
5 How helpful are the comments that your group members make in workshop about your writing?
6 How often do you use your group members' suggestions when revising your writing?
7 When participating in workshop, do you read your writing aloud to your group members?
8 When participating in workshop, do you make verbal comments about your group members' writing?
9 When participating in workshop, do you make written comments on your group members' writing?
10 In general, how useful do you feel the writing workshop sessions are?
11 If you were allowed to change workshop groups for second semester, would you want to?
12 Do you prefer for the teacher to assign students to workshop groups?
13 Do you prefer to choose the students in your workshop group yourself?
14 Do you feel that you are in a group with people who perform at the same level as you do?
15 What suggestions do you have for improving the weekly writing workshop sessions?
16 What do you feel is currently working and/or not working with the weekly writing workshop sessions?

References

Atwell, N. (1998). *In the middle*. Hempstead, TX: Sagebrush.

Krogness, M. (1994). *Just teach me, Mrs. K*. Portsmouth, NH: Heinemann.

Larson, J., & Maier, M. (2000). Co-authoring classroom texts: Shifting participant roles in writing activity. *Research in the Teaching of English, 34*, 468–497.

Street, C. (2005). A reluctant writer's entry into a community of writers. *Journal of Adolescent and Adult Literacy, 48*(8), 636–641.

Vygotsky, L. S. (1962). *Thought and language*. Cambridge, MA: Cambridge University Press.

Table 17.1 Final version of the peer conferencing sheet

WRITING WORKSHOP CONFERENCING SHEET

Date: _____   Students participating: _____

Author/Title of piece shared: _____

What kind of feedback are you asking for? _____

_____

_____

_____

Responder(s): Summarize (and initial) the feedback give to the author.

STRENGTHS OR POSITIVE ASPECTS	QUESTIONS, COMMENTS, OR SUGGESTIONS FOR IMPROVEMENT
_____	_____
_____	_____
_____	_____
_____	_____
_____	_____
_____	_____

Author: What do you plan to work on as a result of this conference?

Chapter 18

Nicole Perez's Inquiry Paper

INTRODUCTORY HIGHLIGHTS

- Used a case study of two kindergartner bilingual teachers.
- Used a survey with teachers early in her study.
- Created a Peer Observation Form (PEF) for coaching experiences.
- Employed English translations for Spanish wordings.
- Used quotes in running text.
- Used interesting headings.

Coaching as a Collaborative Process

Nicole Perez

Teachers are some of the most challenging people to work with. We work in an environment that is unique and where no one knows what it is like to be a teacher unless they are one. Today public schools are under a lot of pressure to achieve high test scores and therefore many schools have hired literacy coaches to help support teachers with their instruction. I am one of those people. I have been a literacy coach for almost two years and at the beginning of this school year I asked myself several questions: What makes an effective literacy coach? How can teachers warm to the idea of having someone analyze and discuss their instruction? What do I know that others do not know? I then thought about the role of a coach and how he or she could help teachers improve their instruction. Is the model of planning, observing, follow-up, and implementation beneficial to instructional improvement? Would teachers begin to trust me more if they saw me as a peer rather than as an authority? How could I change the role of the literacy coach to peer collaborator?

The Coaching Process

Teachers who need support with a specific area of instruction may engage in a four-step process with a coach: planning, observing, analyzing and reflecting, and conferring (Bean, 2004). During the planning time the coach and teachers(s) may come together to discuss goals the teacher(s) would like to set for instructional improvement. They may also plan a lesson the coach would model based on a goal the teacher has set. During the observing time, the teacher observes the lesson the coach models. After the observation, the teacher and coach have time to reflect on the lesson and jot down ideas or questions they would like to share during their follow-up session. The last step of conferring involves the coach and teacher meeting again to discuss their comments, questions, and thoughts about the previous lesson. They may also discuss future steps to take, including a plan for the coach to observe the teacher's implementation of these new strategies.

The Art of Communication

How could I begin to investigate the benefits of the coaching process with teachers if I could not communicate effectively? Knowing how to work with adults is rarely mentioned or learned about in teacher preparation classes, yet an effective coach must know how to communicate with others in order for him or her to be successful. Because one part of the coach's role is giving feedback, the coach must know how to say things to adults in a sensitive manner. Teaching is a very humbling experience and many are not comfortable being observed, and therefore the coach must be as tactful as possible. "Coaches must be good listeners, be able to empathize with the teachers, and provide balanced feedback that reinforces excellent teaching behavior and provides ideas for improvement" (Bean, 2004, p. 98).

Toll (2005) offers a lot of ideas on effective communication. There are a variety of ways to respond to teachers' comments or questions that actually allow teachers to think more about their own instruction. When coaches provide time for teachers to reflect on their own teaching, the whole coaching process becomes more valuable for the teacher. Asking teachers, "What do you think?" helps teachers discover that they might know the answers to their own questions, giving them the confidence they might need. Taking time to find answers is part of the coaching process anyway. When coaches admit they do not know something, a teacher may feel assured that the coach does not have all the answers, and this could be an opening for building a partnership between teacher and coach.

Getting My Feet Wet

I am fortunate to work in a small public school that has fifteen classrooms from kindergarten through sixth grade. Situated in a predominantly Mexican community, my school has a dual language program that aims for all students to be biliterate in English and Spanish by the time they graduate. This model emphasizes heavy instruction in Spanish in kindergarten through second grade and then is balanced between 50% Spanish and English in third through sixth grade. Additionally, I work with a diverse staff of teachers, some of whom have taught for less than five years and others who are nearing retirement.

Because our staff have a variety of experiences under their belts, I decided to begin my investigation by using a teacher survey that asked staff their opinions about the role of coaching and peer collaboration. Teachers were to either agree or disagree with statements about collaborating and how teachers learn best about improving instruction. At the end, teachers had the opportunity to write how they felt they were supported with instruction and what areas they would like more help with. The purpose of beginning my inquiry this way was to get an overall sense of how people felt about peer collaboration. Were they comfortable working with others? Many work in grade-level groups but most have been reluctant to work with a coach. Overall, most teachers said they were interested in collaborating with teachers and/or a literacy coach. They also agreed that they were interested in getting and giving feedback about their instruction. However, only a few teachers took the time to answer the open-ended response at the end of the survey. Those that did respond to how they had received support in their instruction answered positively.

For example, I asked in the survey, "Do you feel supported with your instruction? How have you been supported and/or what do you need more help with?" One teacher responded, "Talking through lessons and making changes in how I teach after these discussions has helped me a great deal. Using what I learn in other areas during other lessons helps me reach more children." Although she exemplified the success of peer collaboration, I wondered why so few teachers took time to reflect on this question. Had they previously had bad experiences with instructional support? Were they opposed to peer collaboration or just uninterested?

The Kindergarten Connection

I decided to begin my collaboration project with the kindergarten team, Marcia and Marta. I had developed a strong rapport previously with these teachers and knew they were interested in learning new literacy strategies because this year [the year of the project] they both had many students learning how to read and write early in the year. These teachers were also eager to learn new methods and had collaborated with other teachers in the past on various projects. However, each classroom had about thirty students, so their classrooms were cluttered and needed a bit of reorganization. Something I wanted them to think about was how they could provide the opportunity for students to use the room as a resource to help students read and write. The teachers needed to think about what was hung on the walls; what was the purpose? Was there student work that students could practice reading, and was it at their eye level?

The three of us began our first meeting discussing how to incorporate interactive writing into the kindergarten classroom. Interactive writing involves the teacher and students "sharing the pen." Students and teachers write a message together on a topic everyone can contribute to. For example, in both classrooms students had studied heroes. The teachers had taught them about characteristics of heroes and gave examples of American heroes from history. Therefore, we planned that our first lesson would be to help students create a message about what a hero was.

I continued to explain to the teachers how I would model interactive writing and they would take notes using a Peer Observation Form (PEF). The PEF was a document I created to help teachers stay focused during an observation. Teachers were to write what they noticed during the observation in regard to teacher instruction and student learning, as well as questions or comments they had about the lesson. My intention for the use of this form was for teachers to have something in their hands they could use for our follow-up sessions, to be specific about what they observed so they could reflect on their own instruction and student learning, to cite specific examples of what they observed, and to explain how these strategies could be used to improve instruction and student learning. I was very explicit in describing the purpose of the modeling process and how the PEF would be used during modeling and follow-up meetings. I explained that this form would be used by them and me so we would each have the opportunity to observe and be observed. I wanted to make the teachers feel comfortable and for them to understand that we would all be learning from each other during this collaborative process. My goal was for teachers to understand my role as a peer rather than evaluator, someone who is closely related to an administrator—something I clearly am not. After each observation, the teacher and I would meet together for a follow-up meeting, preferably the same day as the observation so our thoughts were fresh in our minds and we were ready to discuss the lesson.

Taking First Steps

How does the coaching process impact instructional improvement? One thing that always gets in the way of effective instruction is time. There is little time for planning and reflection; a forty-five-minute preparation period a day is not sufficient. That is why I wanted to plan lessons with teachers that were short and concise. Interactive writing usually lasts about twenty minutes. Students are reading, writing, and thinking during this time and my goal was to help teachers stay focused and set specific purposes for instruction. During our first meeting, I explained that I would model specific strategies used during an interactive writing lesson and these strategies would be discussed in our follow-up meeting. I wanted them to think about specific strategies I was using and how I was supporting students with reading and writing. I would model how reading and writing were connected while at the same time students would be engaged in meaningful, authentic writing activities.

During my first lesson, I asked students about characteristics of heroes. Students replied, *"Alguien que te puede cuidar"* ("Someone who can take care of you"). We counted out the words so that students understood we would be writing five words that day. Counting out words helps students understand the concept of spacing and making new words. The first word was *alguien* ("someone"). I modeled how to stretch the word out so students could hear the individual letters and write them down. This strategy is helpful for students so they can think about letter–sound relationships while writing. Students began stretching the word and discovered that "ah" is the first sound in *alguien*, so many began to write the letter *a*. Also, the strategy of stretching out words helps students include all letters while writing the word. We continued to write the word together, paying close attention to individual sounds that students could connect letters to. When finished writing the word, we read it together, modeling for teachers how to connect writing with reading.

They were also encouraged to look at the word wall, a list of words in alphabetic order that students had previously learned such as high-frequency words or sight words. In kindergarten, students' names are posted on the word wall, creating anchor words for students to build new words. For example, before writing *alguien*, I asked students if there was a name on the word wall that began with the letter *a*. Several students mentioned classmates' names. I told them that names they know how to read can help them read and write new words. The word wall also helps teachers create a resource for students, something I had initially emphasized in our first meetings.

During our follow-up meetings, I began by asking teachers what they noticed about the lessons. I always began meetings in this fashion because I wanted teachers to make comments about observations before I did. Their reflections were what mattered because they wanted to improve their instruction. After they had finished, I would add additional comments if necessary. When I modeled lessons, we discussed specific strategies I had implemented. When I modeled interactive writing, teachers were intrigued by the concept of counting words, stretching words, and repeated reading. Marcia commented, "I loved the idea of counting out words. I never realized how important that is for students to better understand writing and spacing."

Impact on Student Learning

One of the first strategies I modeled for interactive writing was how to use dry erase boards with students. While students and I are making a message together, they are thinking about sounds, letters, syllables, and building new words from words they already know. For example, the first message we wrote together was *¿Que es un héroe?* ("What is a hero?") *Que* is a very common word in Spanish and I wanted to see if students knew what letter(s) stand for the *q* sound. I looked to see if students were looking at the word wall for clues and observed them begin to write letters on their dry erase boards. By using the dry erase boards, teachers can see how students are thinking. What letters are they writing? Are they looking around the room for clues, at others' writings? Are they making any connections from previous letters or words already learned?

Thus, the dry erase board has become an excellent resource for student assessment. Marta noted, "I noticed kids who are not always paying attention are now catching up. I do like interactive writing because of that. Because it engages them a little bit better." Students who were daydreaming before had become more focused because they had a tool to help them learn how to read and write better. They had become active participants in the learning process. Both teachers could clearly see who was getting it and who needed more support. During whole-group instruction, they were able to place students who needed support closer to them to provide more opportunities to help them.

For example, during one observation, Marcia was using the dry erase boards to help students write words from the calendar. She was incorporating reading and math into her daily routine. This day the students were writing *jueves* ("Thursday"). I noticed some students wrote the word quickly while others were thinking about beginning sounds. In our follow-up meeting she noted how surprised she was to see who was sounding out the word before writing it while others needed to look at their classmates' boards for support. She asked, "How can I give them [her advanced students] more freedom in their writing without me?" She had not realized how much her students had learned before using the dry erase boards. She could *see* the progress individual students were making during whole-group instruction. A previous concern she had mentioned was not having enough time to meet with small groups on a daily basis. That is where I reminded her of how much she would learn about her students through interactive writing.

Marta commented about her students using dry erase boards, "Students were engaged. Students were discussing sounds amongst themselves. Reluctant Spanish speakers were looking for support from other students and volunteered to participate. My constant walkers and wanderers were engaged in writing and sharing with others." Thus, while the teacher is sitting in front of the class at the easel modeling writing, students have the tools in their hands to support them with their writing. After extensive use of the dry erase boards, both teachers began planning more activities that would provide for authentic writing experiences. They could not believe how much their students had learned and were capable of learning. Their students were writers and they wanted to continue to keep them engaged and enthusiastic about writing.

Ready to Get Their Hands Dirty

I had modeled two interactive writing lessons for Marcia and Marta and now they were ready for me to observe them. Both teachers were going to continue writing about characteristics of heroes with their students. I was happy to see that these teachers had taken specific strategies I had modeled under their wings. For example, after deciding on what sentence to write together, Marcia held her fingers out ready to count the words in the phrase. She also reminded them to stretch the word *cuidar* ("to take care of") so that students could hear the individual sounds clearly. She said, "Think of the first sound you hear and write the letter that makes that sound." When writing the high-frequency word *que* ("what"), Marta directed students to look around the room to see where it was written in different places. She also reread the words they had written several times before beginning to write a new word.

A few days later, Marcia excitedly asked me to observe a final activity using students' writing about heroes. Interactive writing is so powerful because teachers can incorporate students' writing into several rereading activities. Students love reading their own writing because it comes from them; it is in their own language and voice. Marcia cut up a sentence into individual words and the students had to put them back into order and glue them on a large piece of paper. Her students had spent several days reading these sentences about heroes and had become very familiar with many of the words. Therefore, they had to decide as a group what each word said, where to put blank squares representing spaces, and where to put the proper punctuation. This was quite a bit of problem solving for kindergarten students! I was pleasantly surprised to see success among each group. It was obvious they had read the words several times previously, understood the concept of spacing to make new words, and that the period or question mark went at the end of the sentence.

After my observation of this lesson, it was clear to me that Marcia had a strong concept of the instructional benefits of interactive writing. She understood its purpose and strengths for incorporating problem solving, reading, and writing.

A Second Pair of Eyes

I discovered that when teachers began to implement strategies learned in their own lessons they were more reflective. They were able to think about their instruction and its impact on student learning. After Marcia's final activity about heroes, we discussed what she noticed in our follow-up meeting. She commented, "They [her students] were focused. Everyone grabbed a word or a space card. Everyone had a way to contribute to the paper. Jon could find where the spaces go. Omar knew that the period went at the end of the sentence. I liked the way children helped each other." She was able to assess her students during this activity. She was learning specific skills students were grasping the concept of, and could say more than "he is learning to read." Assessments like these are valuable not only for teachers but for parents, too.

Marcia was also able to reflect on her instruction. She was aware of what she was saying to students while they were deciding the order the words went in the sentence. "I found myself going, 'No. Let's look at it again. Don't paste yet. What comes next—a space or a word?'" Marta also reflected on her practice by thinking about her students' seating arrangements on the rug after observing what her students were capable of or needed help with. "I guess the ones [students] I put up in front are exactly the ones I wanted to see."

Marta and Marcia responded positively toward the modeling and observation process. Marta felt that using the PEF made her "more organized and prepared for meetings." Marcia felt the PEF helped them reflect on their teaching, knowing exactly where improvements needed to be made. "I have something to look back on and see myself without taping myself. I also get a second pair of eyes that can catch things that I didn't necessarily see. I get to see how to reteach or change my practice." She appreciated having someone to share her instruction with. After several weeks of working together, they felt comfortable admitting sometimes they had felt very lost in their instruction. Marta said, "I've noticed how this [interactive writing] really fits in here [in her literacy instruction]." I replied, "Things are making sense?" She answered, "Yeah, I see how they connect [the lessons with the purpose]." Through our collaboration, she was able to see the big picture of how reading and writing could look in her classroom. She was engaging her students in meaningful literacy practices on a daily basis.

What Does this All Mean?

What have I learned through this whole coaching process? The most powerful tool for me was taking the time to reflect on my modeling and instruction, and giving comments during follow-up meetings. Taking the time to jot down thoughts about coaching helped me consolidate feelings about working with teachers and its effectiveness. After meetings, I would always ask myself, was I clear with comments and suggestions to teachers? Was my modeling of specific instructional strategies effective? Did my lessons make sense?

A new approach for teacher meetings this year was to say less and listen more. Throughout this inquiry I stuck to this format and discovered that discussions were more meaningful if teachers were leading them. Marcia and Marta were the first ones to make comments about students' needs and difficulties. They saw the need for change in their instruction because observations were made by them, not by someone coming into their rooms and telling them they needed to change something.

One suggestion I make to teachers now is to always make time for reflections. For example, currently a fifth grade teacher is trying out literature circles with her students and is taking small steps to ensure they learn how to engage in meaningful conversations about what they are reading. When I chat with her about how things are going, I always remind her to take notes about what worked and did not work so that she can learn from her teaching and apply these strategies with her students next year. Thus, I would like to take all that I have learned about collaborating with teachers and apply these strategies for teacher meetings next year. I think what helped make this process successful was choosing to work with willing and interested teachers. Having a trusting relationship previous to the project helped us all feel more comfortable with trying out new instructional strategies and being honest with comments and questions. What makes collaboration possible is for all members to admit they do not know something and want to work together to figure something out.

Potholes

Teachers' lives are so hectic, and although Marcia and Marta were interested in this collaboration project, they could only make time to meet, plan, observe, and discuss once a week. Only meeting once a week weakened the opportunity to try things out and practice them several times. For example, at first the only interactive writing the students were engaging in was through my instruction. Then both teachers felt comfortable enough to take the reins and incorporate interactive writing into their literacy block daily.

I would like to take what I have learned about collaborating with teachers and use these methods with more reluctant teachers. Although I work with a small number of teachers, some are still hesitant to work with outside sources. They are comfortable maintaining the same routines and style of teaching they have used for many years. I do believe that many are concerned about students' progress, and that will be my avenue into forming new collaborations. I have to be more persistent with teachers, as many of our students are struggling and teachers owe their students the chance to try out new strategies that address their needs.

References

Bean, R. (2004). *The reading specialist: Leadership for the classroom, school, and community*. New York: Guilford Press.

Toll, C. (2005). *The literacy coach's survival guide*. Newark, DE: International Reading Association.

Chapter 19

Catherine Plocher's Inquiry Paper

INTRODUCTORY HIGHLIGHTS

- Employed vignettes to describe different types of coaching.
- Used quotations in running text and in separate sections.
- Used interesting headings.

Coaching for Change in a K-8 Urban Elementary School: Building Cultures of Collaboration and Reflective Practices

Catherine Plocher

Many educators recognize the power of literacy and the critical role of conversations with children in classrooms. We are often reminded that conversations and collaboration with colleagues are important as well. We think about our literate lives as teachers in ways that make us stronger and smarter teachers of children. We study the experts and what they say about literacy development, and we reinvent our own strategies as learners and teachers.

Literacy coaches need to have a high respect for their teachers. Instead of seeing themselves as the "literacy experts," they need to be colleagues, sounding boards, friends, and resources for the teachers in their school. Coaches must not see their job as one in which they tell teachers the "right way" to do things. Instead, they need to realize the challenges that teachers face, and find ways to support them as they figure out how best to meet the needs of their students.

In-depth thinking and study are important to learning. Literacy coaches and their colleagues need to attain new understandings together. A coach needs to balance his or her role as a listener, partner, and agent of change. They need to understand that teachers need opportunities to direct their own learning, and that the coach is there to support them. Coaches need to base their work on research and best practices, but also understand what teachers face from their own experiences in the classroom. Coaches cannot present a program that magically meets the needs of children and teachers. Instead, they need to share their beliefs and passions about teachers and learners and types of change that can happen with strong leadership.

A literacy coach's journey is an awakening. Literacy coaches' roles are defined by what they have learned from working with talented and dedicated teachers. They understand that teachers never stop learning, and that coaches can support their attempts to develop new skills and expertise in many different ways. A literacy coach needs to meld collaboration and conversation, as teachers move towards new understandings and insight. Together they will come to recognize the power of literacy and shared learning.

Professional development gives teachers the power to make effective decisions. It is most strongly supported when a teacher reflects on his or her own craft with the support of another teacher who has more experience and training in assisting or "coaching" colleagues, and when observation and reflection take place during and after the classroom experience on a regular basis (Dole & Donaldson, 2006; Lyons & Pinnell, 2001).

Literacy coaches have a powerful opportunity to assist teachers in the difficult and challenging work of improving student learning. Many educators agree that a literacy coach can be a critical component of the teaching profession; but to be effective, coaches need to have a clear focus for their work (Killion, 2003). Literacy coaches need to remember that their first duty is always to their teachers, literacy instruction, and student learning. Coaches have to present themselves as collaborators to support teachers in achieving their goal in increased student learning (Killion, 2003). They also need to establish themselves as someone that teachers can appreciate and trust.

This form of staff development means "working *with*" colleagues to support their learning. Working with a colleague involves supporting and coaching the teacher in his or her interactions with students, and engaging in active learning and reflection. Coaches provide personalized support and development, working side by side with individuals to increase their instructional efficacy and improve student learning. Coaches will not be involved in the supervision or evaluation of any teachers. Their role is to provide support and to enhance the development of the instructional skills and strategies of their colleagues. Every year takes on its own rhythm, and the job of a literacy coach is circular and never-ending.

Learner-Centered Professional Development and Coaching

In my first year of teaching, the only professional development or coaching I received was occasional in-service training provided by the district. Usually these in-services failed to address what I was facing with my own students, and as a new teacher in a tough school, I needed more. The planners of these in-services usually did not understand that there is more to adult learning than an expert at an overhead projector with a marker at the right hand and a graphic organizer in the other hand. They didn't consider the learners in the darkened auditorium. Just as good teaching must meet diverse needs in a classroom, effective professional development must meet the individual needs of teachers. We know learning takes time; it isn't neat and tidy. So why don't we believe it should be that way for teachers? Loucks-Horsley et al. (1987) write, "To be successful, professional development must be seen as a process, not an event" (p. 59). We would never base student learning upon a single experience, claiming, "I will teach all my students to read today with one, really great lesson." Learning is gradual and incremental, and one-shot in-services do not provide teachers with the necessary time or scaffolding to learn.

Adults learn in much the same way as children do. Pearson and Gallagher's (1983) gradual release of responsibility model demonstrates this for children, but it can be easily adapted to adult learners as well. Miller (2002) writes, "If you think back to a time when you learned how to do something new, the gradual release of responsibility model comes into play" (p. 48). I agree with Miller and wonder why professional development has failed for so long to consider the phases all learners move through toward new thinking. As educators, we are accustomed to taking into account the diverse needs in a classroom of children, but the needs of adult learners are quickly forgotten. Adult learning is too often reduced to pulling together a number of teachers to listen to an expert lecture on a given subject.

According to Pearson and Gallagher (1983), children begin the learning process by watching a teacher model a strategy. Then, students practice, using the strategy with scaffolding, such as working in pairs, in small groups, or with a teacher. Finally, with time and practice, students begin to use the strategy independently and in a variety of contexts.

In contrast to the more traditional forms of teacher in-service, learner-centered professional development moves through the same gradual release continuum, which begins with modeling and demonstration from a literacy coach. In this stage, the teacher watches how to enact quality instruction by participating in classroom observations, receiving coaching, watching professional development videos, and reading and discussing descriptions of effective instruction. The goal in this phase is to offer a visual picture of high-quality instruction.

Next, the teacher practices the approach that was previously modeled. In this phase, an instructional coach may teach alongside the teacher to offer feedback. Or teachers may participate in peer observations and informal walkthroughs, meet in teams to discuss implementation of new teaching strategies, examine student work, or determine next steps in instruction. Without this phase, one will not improve, because feedback is essential for all learning.

When independence is reached, the teacher successfully integrates the new approach into his or her own learning. Depending on the teacher, independence may take several attempts in the early stages, because it depends on the teacher's current knowledge base and the complexity of the new learning.

One-shot in-services and limited coaching fail to give teachers the time and support they need to learn. In contrast, the gradual release continuum embeds the essential elements for successful and long-term learning.

Changing My Practice

For two years I have been the literacy coach for a kindergarten through eighth-grade elementary school in the Chicago public school system after being a classroom teacher for five years in the third and fourth grades. As I began my sixth year, my school offered me the chance to become a literacy coach. This gave me the opportunity to focus my attention on an area in which I had always been interested: adult learners.

The school sits in a low-income neighborhood with a high population of English language learners and refugees. Somewhere between 750 and 800 students are at this school on any given day, many of whom come and go as their families struggle to find housing or employment, or travel between countries.

One of the reasons that I decided to become my school's literacy coach was to provide aid to teachers by supporting their learning. I have realized that I provide different levels of support to teachers at my school. I noticed that I reserve most of my time for staff development and supporting teachers in their classrooms. I try to keep paperwork, data analysis, and the development of local assessments to a minimum so that it doesn't interrupt and interfere with my classroom work. During this time I facilitate internal walkthroughs, support teachers in their classrooms, and serve as a sounding board through collegial conversations. I also develop new resources and find materials for teachers.

The past three months, I have noticed that the support I provide teachers falls into three main categories: going deep with coaching by supporting teachers in ongoing coaching cycles, providing what I call "dibble-dabble" coaching, which is short-term, informal coaching/modeling and observing to gain entry for longer-term coaching in the future, and engaging in collegial conversations, where I am more of a sounding board and/or resource for finding books and materials for teachers to use for their instruction. I have noticed that many teachers participate in the above experiences, based on the collegial relationships, trust, and rapport that I have with them. I have found that many of the teachers that I go deep with in long-term coaching not only value my content knowledge, but also have formed a stronger collegial relationship with me as a member of a community of learners. The teachers with whom I dibble-dabble request my support sporadically, seeking my assistance through hearing about me from other teachers with whom they have a relationship. Or, they might indicate a desire to work with me because of an idea they derived from professional development. The teachers with whom I have limited collegial conversations and serve only as a resource are the same teachers whom I have not built a collegial relationship with yet; they don't view me as an important part of their learning community.

In reflecting on these different activities that I undertake with teachers, I posed the following inquiry questions: "What are the different levels of support that I provide to my teachers?" and "How do different needs of teachers impact these different levels of support and the kinds of relationships I have with individual teachers?"

Supporting Teachers at Different Levels

Going Deep

Going deep consisted of sustained, ongoing, intensive support by modeling and was participant driven. The coach and teacher plan in pre-conferences before going into the classroom. Following the pre-conference, either the coach or the teacher observes to provide feedback, the coach models to demonstrate lessons, or they might co-teach as part of the model of gradual release of responsibility. Following the work in the classroom, they debrief in the post-conferences to determine strengths and next steps. Pre-conferences for planning and post-conferences for debriefing are valued and vital. Support at this level includes the collective solving between the teacher and coach regarding specific problems of practice that emerge from teachers' work with their students. The coach schedules the sessions, frequently allowing instructional sessions to take hold. Sessions can be scheduled in a strand—for example, five days in a row—and are ongoing throughout the year.

I find that in the long term, going-deep coaching, where teachers are involved in ongoing coaching cycles, works best for teachers who are looking to make major structural and organizational changes to their literacy programs. My work in their room might span a one- or two-year period to be able to ground our work in inquiry, reflection, and experimentation. Below are several examples of how this type of coaching arrangement works.

Example 1: Supporting Nancy's efforts to implement book clubs. Nancy, a fifth-grade teacher, was looking for an opportunity for collaboration and shared thinking. She knew that she could use me as a resource and that I would model new strategies in her classroom, even though she would set the course for her learning. Nancy had read *Book Club* (Raphael, 2002) and was interested in trying literature discussion groups with her students and wanted my support in implementing them.

Before working in Nancy's classroom, we had a pre-conference to plan for enacting of literature discussion groups. We looked at how we could adapt the concepts outlined in *Book Club* to meet the needs of her fifth-grade students. We decided to incorporate content and management mini-lessons to enable her students to have high-level conversations about a shared text over the next five weeks. In the content sessions, we wanted to teach her students explicit comprehension strategies that would deepen their understanding of the text they read; in the management lessons, we wanted to help students develop norms for exploring a text together.

During the first two weeks, I introduced and modeled book club mini-lessons with her students. As the classroom teacher, Nancy always stayed in the room and participated in the lesson. We always let the students know we were trying out some new ideas. We wanted students to see this as a collaborative effort and that I was actually teaming with their teacher. During the third week, Nancy and I co-taught the mini-lessons and instruction together, and during the last two weeks, I observed Nancy's instruction and provided feedback and support where needed.

Nancy and I debriefed every day on our implementation of literature discussions. This was an informal meeting, usually in her room at the end of the day. I always asked if the format was working for her. I encouraged her to personalize the implementation of literature discussions and make it her own. In the beginning we found that students had trouble transferring their thinking from Post-it notes to their reading logs, so we modeled the process and scaffolded the instruction until the students grasped the task more successfully. We also noticed that students were creating a "laundry list" of vocabulary words from the chapters in the text and spent a large amount of time in their discussions talking about these words and very little time conversing about deeper thinking about the text. We experimented with a variety of reading logs and ways to use them until we found a format that we are satisfied with. At the end of the unit of the book club experience, we asked students to reflect on the reading logs and explain the strengths and weaknesses of them. We also asked the students to design a reading log that they thought would be effective, adding their explanations about their thinking behind it.

I found that long-term coaching and the continual debriefing between Nancy and me prompted us to keep refining the delivery of instruction to students and empowered Nancy to make the implementation of literature discussions her own. I also found that because of Nancy's and my collegial relationship, we were able to jump right into coaching and planning. Often when we were in the classroom together, we worked as a team, which caused the instruction to continue when I wasn't there. Nancy had structures for authentic instruction, so mostly Nancy needed a supportive and a reflective partner to try out a new approach. I was able to be a partner in the learning process along with Nancy.

It is important that adequate modeling and guided practice occur if a lasting change in classroom instruction is going to take place. Teachers, like students, need practice and repetition of new strategies to acquire fluency and automaticity to ensure that the changes in classroom practice will be lasting. Practice needs to be part of their professional development. Research by Joyce and Showers (as cited in Dole, 2004) shows that it took twenty-five trials in the classroom before new instructional practices became part of a teacher's routine. By the end of my five weeks with Nancy, she was the one leading the lessons and organizing the student discussions, and I was the one lending the extra set of hands in the background.

Example 2: Working with seventh-grade teachers on extended response. My principal normally supports instructional coaching on a volunteer basis, but the state testing was approaching and my principal was becoming concerned with a few teachers' outcomes and asked me to add specific teachers to my coaching schedule up to when ISATs (Illinois Standards Achievement Tests) were given. Therefore, my principal "mandated" me to coach three teachers (Peter, sixth grade; Faith, seventh grade; and Debra, seventh grade) for this period. This was uncomfortable for me because I had yet to establish trust and rapport with these three teachers. I was very hesitant to add these teachers to my schedule for a few reasons: the mandated teachers did not want me there; they felt as if they were being "put on the spot" by their principal; and they felt that they had been deemed to be below-par teachers. Although this was an uncomfortable situation and one that was out of my control, I decided to make the best of things and use this opportunity to attempt to establish trust and rapport with these teachers.

Since my mandated focus was on the ISAT test, I met with Faith and Debra, the seventh-grade teachers, and asked them what they wanted support in. Although I was mandated to work with them, I wanted to try to build some type of common understanding by providing choice and valuing what they considered important. Also, the teachers wanted to sit down and spend some time talking during their planning time together.

This example covers my experience with Debra and Faith (see Example 3 for information on my coaching activities with Peter, the sixth-grade teacher). Debra and Faith said they have been having trouble with their students writing extended responses to texts. They both had been recently transferred, from first and fourth grade respectively. Faith and Debra both had over twenty-five years of teaching experience, but they were nervous and frustrated working at this new grade level. They told me they were finding it difficult to adjust to the different curriculum and instructional demands for older children.

After further discussion and planning with Faith and Debra, we decided that I would model a strand of lessons focused on extended response, because when I asked them how much coaching support they would like, they said that one day of coaching would not help much. I sat down with Faith and Debra in a pre-conference and asked them what they had done already on the topic, and asked for more clarification if I was not clear. Through our conversation, we developed a plan regarding the details of what I would model.

Our initial interactions told me a lot about the teachers that I was about to work with. Debra and Faith felt comfortable enough to collaborate with me about a struggle they were having in their classroom instruction and wanted support. When I asked them what was frustrating about extended response during this pre-conference, Debra and Faith shared their concerns. Debra remarked, "Many of my students don't write very much no matter what I tell them." Faith said that "we write every day, but they don't understand the interpretations." The following conversation occurred when I asked how they had been teaching extended response:

Faith: I give them a passage to read and the question, then I have them write the response. After they write, I collect it and grade it by giving them feedback, but they don't pay any attention to my comments because they do the same thing the next time they write.

Coach: Have you walked them through the process of writing an extended response? What I mean by that is have you modeled each step and performed think-alouds about your thinking process for them? The reason I ask this is because I often experienced in my own teaching that often the students don't understand the thinking process. Once I was explicit about the process through my own modeling, the students were much more metacognitive.

Debra: No. I don't really know how to do that.

Faith: Me either.

Coach: That's OK. I had to learn this the hard way, but I would love to show you guys a strategy that has worked well for me.

Faith: That would be nice. What do we need to do?

Coach: Well, first of all, I want you two to choose a passage and extended response question that is similar to something that would be on the ISAT. You have two choices, a narrative or expository passage. The students will encounter both on different sections of the test. Do you have a preference?

Debra: No.

Faith: No.

Coach: What have you worked more with?

Faith: I worked only with narrative passages so far.

Debra: So have I.

Coach: OK. Well, do you want me to introduce an expository passage so they can start becoming familiar with that genre?

Faith: Yes. That sounds good. How long will you work with us?

We continued the conversation with my outlining my ideas on teaching the facets of extended response during a four- or five-day period. We also set up how we would work together. They would be next to me when at my side so that students would know that we were working together, and we would get together every evening after school to debrief on the day's lesson and plan the next day's lesson.

Looking at this conversation, I found that it was a collaborative one that began to establish trust and rapport, and that going deep by coaching for a solid week instead of just one day was the key to gaining future access with these teachers. Faith and Debra needed more than feedback on one lesson: they needed support in putting together and implementing a chain of lessons. Modeling lessons on writing extended response was needed before the teachers were ready to take on these practices themselves. Building trust with the teachers enabled them to be open and honest with me. Even early on in the conversation above, I could see that Faith and Debra were comfortable enough with me to be honest with their struggles. The questions that I asked helped to identify what the teachers had already done with the students. Through our discussion, I could see that Faith and Debra have been having the students write a lot, but with no guidance or direction. I also identified a need for more content knowledge regarding the extended response. I could tell by their responses that they were not familiar with the process themselves, so they seemed comfortable for me to offer a way to teach extended response in ways that they could take on subsequently.

I followed up with modeling a four-day strand and met in a post-conference to debrief. Both teachers told me that they learned a lot and we set up a plan for them to follow for more instruction in writing. As I look back, my regret is that I didn't include a day or two of follow-up observation to support them going on their own (gradual release of responsibility). I think if I had considered it, the coaching would have been more powerful because teaching extended response was something new to them, and they might have had questions or concerns while they implemented instruction on their own. I was unable to support the teachers for another strand of lessons immediately, but I did provide continued support by giving them another set of lessons. Nevertheless, I felt that the coaching was successful because I was able to get an "in" with them and have continued pedagogical conversations. I built a trust with them and assisted in instruction that they found beneficial and valuable. Faith and Debra continued to request me to model lessons with their students, but they do not implement the instruction when I am not there. Initially, I thought modeling this approach of instruction would allow them to apply the same approach themselves, but throughout follow-up conversations and observations it became clear that they have not picked up where I left off. They just wait for me to come back. Sometimes, teachers resist moving out of the modeling phase. The reason behind this is because the modeling phase involves less risk taking for teachers because most of the responsibility lies with the coach. In the guided practice phase, more responsibility lies with the teacher, which can be scary because some teachers prefer for their practice to remain private, don't like to hear constructive criticism, and don't want anyone to see what they are doing until they are doing it perfectly. Moving into the guided practice phase means the teacher has to take on new risks, an essential part of learning.

Example 3: Trying to work with Peter. As indicated above, Peter was a sixth-grade teacher who was also mandated by the principal to be coached for the ISAT. Peter was unhappy and uncomfortable about the situation because he had taught at the school for a number of years and felt that the principal was implying that he was a below-par teacher. I wanted to try to build rapport and trust with Peter by coaching him on his goals for student learning. This situation started off much differently than with Faith and Debra. Faith and Debra were open to the support and were happy for me to address an area of need, but Peter was not. I asked him if we could informally sit down and talk about his goals for coaching and he said he didn't have time, but we could talk about it for one minute in the hall. When I tried to reschedule to a different time, he said that he was too busy to reschedule and he didn't need my help, but he knew that the principal hadn't given me an option. I told him that we could make the best out of the situation and I would be happy to support him in any way possible. He finally replied that he had been working on the extended response and his students were pretty good at it, but it didn't hurt to have a review. I told him that I would be happy to model and I was looking forward to working with him and his students.

I realized that this coaching strand was going to be a challenge because his lack of interest and unwillingness to plan, but I was determined to build a rapport with Peter and hopefully be able to continue support after the sessions were over. His students were very engaged (were eager, asked clarifying questions, participated enthusiastically during talk, etc.). Peter continued to look at me as "the teacher" and took my presence in his class as a break (one week, he left the room for a while; another time, he took a sick day and left in his plans a note that I would be teaching his kids that day for an hour; and so on). One week he spent part of the time sitting in back talking with some students who were on a time-out from their classes because of problems they had had and had been asked to sit in his. Needless to say, I don't think he got much out of the experience of my teaching. I didn't want to get upset, because how I handled a situation like this could determine any possibilities for working with him in the future. On the last day I worked in his class he asked the students to thank me for everything and tell me how much they had learned from me. I took this opportunity to remind the students—and Peter indirectly—that we are all learners and that I needed to thank them too. I explained that every time I coach, I learn new things from the teachers I work with and their students. I am lucky because I get to work with many different people, and each time I work with a class, I become better and smarter. That's what learning is. I emphasized that they were all so smart and had so many different ideas, and that sharing them with a partner made them even smarter. As I was walking out the door, four or five of the students personally came up to me and thanked me individually for the time and help I had given them.

I have reflected on this situation in a number of ways. First, I thought that I should have been more explicit about my role as a coach, but I intentionally was not with Peter because I already felt that I was unwelcome and tried to make the sessions as comfortable as possible. I do not think this situation with Peter could have been much better, because he already had prior convictions about the mandated assignment. So, what I found out in this situation in Peter's class is that if the coach does not have a collegial relationship and rapport, coaching cannot be forced.

Dibble-Dabble Coaching

Dibble-dabble coaching support is short-term informal coaching, modeling, and observing. The coach goes into the teacher's classroom for a one-shot session. Often, the teacher is interested in the coach modeling a strategy that they heard about from another teacher or in a professional development that perked their interest. Other times, the teachers do not want to go deep into an area of study and support, but want only feedback on one lesson. Sometimes the dibble-dabble session provides entry for longer-term coaching in the future with the teacher.

Example 4: Helping Jane on running records. Jane was a fourth-grade teacher who had been teaching at the school for a number of years and did not always look for opportunities for collaboration and coaching. Jane is very analytical and slow to try new structures in instruction. Many whole-staff professional development meetings have been spent on differentiating instruction to address the needs of all students in the classroom and to come up with assessments that inform this instruction. A few weeks after the last professional development, Jane approached me to ask if I would take one or two days to explain how to administer running records on some of her low readers, as well model an assessment with one of her students. I was very excited because Jane was a teacher who not very responsive unless she herself had asked for assistance. I eagerly agreed and made immediate changes in my schedule so I would not lose her. I sat down with Jane in a pre-conference and explained the process with the materials available. Then we went to her classroom and I conducted two running records on two students' reading while she watched and asked questions. Once she felt comfortable enough to try it herself, we conducted the next two running records together and compared our data and discussed questions that Jane had. Then Jane tried the next one on her own and responded that she was comfortable to do the rest without support. I was happy to release responsibility to her.

When I asked Jane if there was anything else she would like support on for future coaching, she was hesitant to respond. Jane said she wanted a little time to get comfortable with the running records and if she needed anything else she would ask. About a month later she asked me to come in for one day and model a strategy with a group of her low readers. This experience was also a success.

I found that this coaching experience to be a success because Jane valued the support and asked me to come back later for more support. Jane is a teacher who needs to think through changes that she is going to make, but once she decides to make those changes, she will come to me. When I tried to push a little more on, adding her to more of a longer-term coaching schedule, she resisted.

I see my relationship with teachers who request dibble-dabble coaching as positive. I have found that they still want as much support as the teachers who go deep when I am working with them. This is OK because these teachers know what they want to learn, and when they are ready, they come to me. I still informally approached these teachers once in a while and asked if they would like support in specific areas of interest, with hopes of moving them towards going for deep coaching, but often they preferred to come to me on a short-time basis. I have found that dibble-dabble coaching is not as beneficial as long-term coaching because it is hard to build new structures and make larger instructional shifts. However, dibble-dabble coaching offers a means to indicate to teachers that they can be part of the collegial community at the school.

Example 5: Supporting Linsey on critical thinking. Linsey was a language arts teacher in a departmentalized eighth grade. She recently had been trying to improve her instruction related around student questioning and critical thinking. Linsey came to me and asked if I could come to her classroom and observe a lesson because she felt that her instruction had been unsuccessful and would like feedback. Linsey told me that she had come to me because she had heard from others that I had modeled lessons on this topic with teachers in other classrooms and the teachers said that they were successful. I immediately agreed and made room in my coaching schedule right away.

After observing Linsey's lesson, we sat down and I provided feedback consisting of strengths and wonderings. I debriefed with her about the lesson and asked if she would like me to continue working with her on this topic. She said that she wanted to try the suggestions first and then would see. On further follow-up, Linsey said that she felt she had a better grasp on her practice on the topic, but would seek me out for support when she felt she needed it. Linsey continued to ask for dibble-dabble short-term support, but it occurred only when she initiated it.

My dibble-dabble coaching experiences with teachers such as Jane and Linsey have enabled me to gain collegial relationships with many teachers in the school. I do not carry out the same kind of coaching with them as I do with teachers where we go deep. Most of this coaching tends to be observational on the part of the teacher. I feel that this is the hardest type of coaching to do because I always have the pressure to have an exemplar lesson or conversation or I might lose them.

"I Have A Question . . . ": Coach as Resource and Partner in Collegial Conversation

Support doesn't always come in the form of working in a teacher's classroom. Sometimes, supporting classroom instruction comes in the format of offering my time behind the scenes of the classroom. One example of a way how this was done was by having myself available for collegial conversation before and after school where teachers dropped by to talk through their thinking or an idea. This is a more informal way for teachers to pose just a quick question when they might feel comfortable enough to schedule a conference to receive some support. Also, sometimes teachers just need help finding resources to support a lesson. In this case, they might be looking for a book recommendation or inquiring about the location of resources. Other teachers might request my help redesigning a layout for their classroom or reorganizing classroom libraries. It also involves helping teachers with opportunities for reflection with me as sounding board for their idea. Setting up and maintaining the organization of the school book room or making transparencies of student work for instruction are additional ways that the coach can lend a helping hand. Sometimes a teacher just needs an extra hand to access materials more easily. Thus, the coach can play a vital role of support for teachers by merely helping them manage small tasks more efficiently and quickly.

Example 6: Developing a positive relationship with Susan. Susan was a seventh-grade teacher who had one of the strongest personalities at the school. She did not hesitate to tell me that she had been teaching much longer than me, so she should have my job. Our relationship did not get off to a very good start, but through social conversations about adult book clubs that we participate in and our similar interest in books, our relationship has grown tremendously.

Initially, Susan would talk through every professional development that I led, sometimes making sarcastic and rude comments about it. I tried sitting down with her and having a conversation about our situation, but she proceeded to tell me that it was not personal and that her feelings were not going to change. However, as time went by, we had informal chats about books we liked, and we found that we had a lot in common pertaining to literacy philosophy. This seemed to be an "in" with Susan. After that, she participated in professional developments and even recommended other literature to read by putting it in my mailbox for me to read.

I tried extremely hard to build a positive relationship with Susan initially, but it failed time after time until I was able to change the conversations from school-related to personal connections. I didn't expect ever to be valued by her; I just wanted her to be civil. However, once I was able to build a personal relationship, the school relationship soon followed.

Susan still did not want me to support her in her classroom with coaching, but she often came to me for book recommendations for units that she was working on with her students. She was also the first to share great books for instruction that she had found in the bookroom. I have found through this experience with Susan and the experience I had with Peter that if I do not attempt to have a collegial relationship with teachers, I will never be effective as a coach no matter what I could share regarding my content knowledge or my intentions to help.

Example 7: Helping Kay on students' work as instructional tools. Kay was a fourth-grade teacher who did not want any of my coaching support but came to me for support with her classroom environment. Although Kay was a teacher I had not built a collegial relationship with yet, she had told me that she wanted some resource support. In a school-wide professional development, we had talked about displaying student work as "instructional tools" and not as "museum pieces" (which are student work found all over the walls with no purpose except just to hang something up). Students do not often benefit from this latter type of display, but instructional tools are student work that is displayed in a way that students can observe the posted work and receive instructional guidance in areas they might need support in. One way to do this is to highlight specific areas in the work that are exemplar examples and attach comments next to these areas explaining explicitly why this work is good. Students can use these as examples and model after them.

Although Kay had been clear that she did not want coaching support, she used me as a resource once in a while. She told me that because she knew I had seen a lot of classrooms, she thought I could offer some recommendations of teachers who were presenting their students' work as instructional tools. I told her that I would be happy to take her to one of the rooms, so we visited Nancy because I knew Nancy would engage in a collegial dialogue. Nancy and I showed Kay this type of student work, and Nancy was able to explain the concept and answer Kay's questions. I was careful to let Nancy lead the discussion because I did not want Kay to feel that I was being too dominating.

I have found that I need to be strategic with teachers with whom I am trying to build a relationship if I want to be able to provide coaching support for them in the future. Kay was able to get the information she needed and has continued to use me as a resource when she needs something or has an idea for instruction. She is not comfortable enough with me yet to go any further, but I am still able to provide support.

Wrapping It Up

I have found that conversations and collaboration are critical components of coaching. There are many different layers to the support I provide teachers. This support falls into three main categories: going deep with coaching by supporting teachers in ongoing coaching cycles; dibble-dabble coaching—that is, short-term informal modeling or observing that might lead to longer-term coaching in the future; and collegial conversations coaching where teachers see me as a resource and sounding board. I have also found that the kind of trust and rapport I have with them depends on the kind of coaching I can offer. Teachers with whom I go deep in long-term coaching practices not only value my content knowledge but also see me as a member of a community of learners. Dibble-dabble and collegial conversation coaching offers fewer opportunities to create such a relationship with teachers. I have also found that no matter what type of coaching is involved, the most effective coaching and support occurs when teachers receive support on their own goals, not the goals of the coach. Coaches need to guide learning, not push it.

Through this inquiry, I have realized the importance of collegial relationships to make strides with teachers. I have only begun to tap into this aspect of coaching, but questions have arisen for a future inquiry based on this topic. In what ways can coaches foster a collegial community in their schools? Prior to my inquiry, I "kind of" knew that I entered into different types of coaching with different teachers, but are there other ones than the three I found in my inquiry? I saw that teachers were starting to build stronger relationships with me as their coach, but I am only one person. A limitation to coaching is that I cannot "go deep" with everyone at the same time. I need to try to figure out ways to help provide an environment where teachers can rely more on each other, go to each other for feedback and support, and start trying to "open their doors" more for each other. Another limitation is that there are some teachers who don't seem to want to be part of the school community at all. But what else can a coach do in such circumstances?

References

Dole, J. A. (2004). The changing role of the reading specialist in school reform. *The Reading Teacher, 57,* 462–471.

Dole, J. A., & Donaldson, R. (2006). "What am I supposed to do all day?" Three big ideas for the reading coach. *The Reading Teacher, 59*(5), 486–488.

Killion, J. (2003). Design staff development with student needs in mind. National Staff Development Council, www.nsdc.org (2003), 1–9.

Loucks-Horsley, S., Harding, S. K., Arbuckle, M. A., Murray, L. B., Dubea, C., & Williams, M. K. (1987). *Continuing to learn: A guidebook for teacher development.* Andover, MA: Regional Laboratory for Educational Improvement of the Northeast and Islands.

Lyons, C. A., & Pinnell, G. S. (2001). *Systems for change in literacy education: A guide to professional development.* Portsmouth, NH: Heinemann.

Miller, D. (2002). *Reading with meaning: Teaching comprehension in the primary grades.* Portland, ME: Stenhouse.

Pearson, P. D., & Gallagher, M. C. (1983). The instruction of reading comprehension. *Contemporary Educational Psychology, 8,* 317–344.

Raphael, T. (2002). *Book club: A literature-based curriculum.* Lawrence, MA: Small Planet Communications.

Epilogue: Further Reflections and Possibilities

In this book, we have attempted to provide strategies for teacher researchers in conducting *and* writing up their inquiries on literacy topics. We have described teacher research as *systematic, intentional inquiry by teachers* about their own school and classroom work (Cochran-Smith & Lytle, 1993). It entails *mindfulness* on your part: paying attention, consciously looking for what is new and different, reconsidering what you know by questioning preconceived ideas. Becoming a teacher researcher is the onset of a journey where you begin to develop *inquiry as stance*—a new worldview and habit of mind (Cochran-Smith & Lytle, 2009). Teacher research strengthens your *voice* so that you are heard at your school and district, as well as by wider audiences if you take the step of "publishing" your insights and understandings.

According to Zeichner and Noffke (2001), there are three major interrelated dimensions that characterize teacher research: personal, professional, and political. The *personal dimension* focuses on your own search for understanding and improving your own practice, which necessarily involves figuring out how and what children learn from your practice. Having a heightened awareness of your practice causes you to question underlying assumptions and helps you rethink classroom experiences, seeing them in a new light. Theories-in-action developed through teacher inquiry enable you to be more explicit about the what and why of your pedagogical decisions. Also, teacher research can often prevent "burnout" by keeping teaching an exciting and vitalized venture. Moreover, it reminds you of your intellectual capabilities as you become more knowledgeable about topics that you study.

The *professional dimension* concerns the ways in which you increase your knowledge base, which contributes to the overall educational profession. Your teacher research represents a distinctive way of knowing about teaching and student learning, and can add to and alter what we know in the field (Cochran-Smith & Lytle, 1993). As a professional who conducts inquiry, you are able to challenge current assumptions about literacy theory and practice.

Finally, the *political dimension* of teacher research has to do with your efforts to develop an agenda for more social justice. How can you change and transform literacy education to challenge existing structures of power and privilege so that literacy education, and the world, are fairer and more just? How can teacher research help to improve classroom interaction for *all* students so that all students have ample generative opportunities to learn?

When the personal, professional, and political dimensions of teaching interact through teacher research, the result can often be more humanizing learning conditions for teachers and their students. Through research, teachers are more intentional about student learning in their classroom. That intentionality helps to disrupt social constructions of teachers as technocrats who take knowledge from one place (e.g., the curriculum) and plant it in another (students). It locates at the center of schooling the everyday classroom practices of teachers and students. Teacher research gives teachers a tool, an organizational structure for thinking about and talking about learning in their classrooms, and possibly beyond. Because teachers have an empirical basis, born from the data they have systematically collected, they have a warrant for evocative educational arguments that speak to the core of educational theory, practice, and policy. The structure of teacher research works as a megaphone for teachers' voices, amplifying the role of teachers as public intellectuals (Giroux, 1988). Moreover, teachers' systematic, focused attention to learning—their own and that of their students—often helps teachers to see students in new ways and to recognize strengths or approaches to learning that were previously obscured.

Teacher research is not easy. But it gets easier. As you become more familiar with an inquiry stance, methods of research, and the kinds of questions you want answered, you will be more able to seamlessly integrate your research into your practice. The objective of teacher research, whether it's your first project or your fiftieth, is not to "get it right"—to find the "best practices" once and for all. Rather, teacher research is about seeking a deeper understanding of the literacy practices in your classroom so that possibilities for your professional learning and your students' learning are expanded in a context of mindful attention. It is a continual process of searching and discovering—a difficult, but joyful, pursuit of something better.

WHAT ARE THE POSSIBILITIES?

The aim of this book has been to support and scaffold novice teacher researchers. But as the above discussion suggests, conducting your *first* inquiry opens many further possibilities. We hope that you continue to teach through your inquiry stance. We hope that your inquiry has helped you take ownership of the theories underlying your practice—that you see yourself as a professional who can be continually refreshed and revitalized though teacher research.

If you have conducted a teacher inquiry as part of a course, what happens when the course is finished? Where can you find the support to continue your journey as a teacher researcher? Here are some possibilities:

- See whether you can initiate teacher researcher groups at your school or district. Teachers want schools to become intellectual environments (Tafel & Fischer, 2001), so you might be able to find some partners among your immediate colleagues (maybe there are interested teachers in the course you took) to propose such a research group. Some districts have small grants for teacher research.
- Think about sharing your research at annual meetings of professional organizations such as National Council of Teachers of English (NCTE) or the International Reading Association (IRA). These organizations also have research grants you could apply for. Finding like-minded teachers at these conventions, who are also doing inquiry, will stimulate your continual

interest in inquiry. You might even identify some teachers to develop a long-distance research group. (Most schools and districts are proud to have their teachers presenting at conferences and provide substitutes while you are gone.)

■ Look up faculty members at a local college or university to see whether they might be interested in studying a common literacy topic. Collaborative school–university inquiry projects have become more widespread.

■ Consider various websites to connect with teachers. You might try the NCTE "Conversations" entry page of the National Council of Teachers of English (http://www.ncte2008.ning.com) or the site of the National Writing Project (NWP) Virtual Institute (http://www.nwp.org/cs/public/print/resource_topic/teacher_research_inquiry).

Good luck and happy researching!

REFERENCES

Cochran-Smith, M., & Lytle, S. L. (1993). *Inside/outside: Teacher research and knowledge.* New York: Teachers College Press.

Cochran-Smith, M., & Lytle, S. L. (2009). *Inquiry as stance: Practitioner research for the next generation.* New York: Teachers College Press.

Giroux, H. A. (1988). *Teachers as intellectuals: Toward a critical pedagogy of learning.* Westport, CT: Bergin & Garvey.

Tafel, L. S., & Fischer, J. C. (2001). Teacher action research and professional development: Foundations for educational renewal. In G. Burnaford, J. Fischer, & D. Hobson (Eds.). *Teachers doing research: The power of action through inquiry* (pp. 221–235). Mahwah, NJ: Lawrence Erlbaum.

Zeichner, K. M., & Noffke, S. E. (2001). Practitioner research. In V. Richardson (Ed.), *Handbook of research on teaching* (pp. 298–330). Washington, DC: American Educational Research Association.

General Peer Conferencing Form

Date: _____ Persons at conference: _____

Author/Title of piece shared: _____

What are you sharing? (outline, draft of a section, draft of full paper, etc.) _____

_____

What kind of feedback are you asking for? _____

_____

Responders(s):

Summarize (and initial, if more than one person is responding) the feedback given to author:

STRENGTHS OR POSITIVE ASPECTS/ PARTS OF PAPER	QUESTIONS, SUGGESTIONS, COMMENTS, FOR MAKING PAPER BETTER

Author: What do you plan to work on as a result of the conference?

Common APA (American Psychological Association) Citing Conventions

Note: authors cited here are fictitious.

These are only *some* examples. Details can be found in the *Publication Manual of the American Psychological Association* (6th edition, second printing, 2009).

TEXT CITATIONS

Citing One Work

Type of citation	Running text format: first citation in text	Running text format: subsequent citations in text	Parenthetical format: first citation in text	Parenthetical format: subsequent citation in text
Single author	Jones (1978)	Jones (1978)	(Jones, 1978)	(Jones, 1978)
Two authors	Jones and Smith (1999)	Jones and Smith (1999)	(Jones & Smith, 1999)	(Jones & Smith, 1999)
Three to five authors	Jones, Smith, and Brown (2002)	Jones et al., (2002)	(Jones, Warren, Smith, & Brown, 2003)	(Jones et al., 2003)
Six or more authors	Smith et al., (2007)	Smith et al., (2007)	(Smith et al., 2007)	(Smith et al., 2007)

Citing Two or More Works within the Same Parenthesis

Order the citations of two or more works with the same parenthesis *alphabetically* (including citations that might be shortened to *et al.*).

Two or more works by the same author: separate with commas
(Jones, 1987, 1989)

(Smith, 2002a, 2002b)—use *a*, *b*, etc., for same year, same author citations

Two or more works by two or more different authors: separate with semicolons
(Jones, 2002; Smith, 1997; Warren, 1990)

(Jones et al. 2000; Smith & Warren, 1999; Zones, Peters, & Smith, 2008)

REFERENCES

- All work that is cited in the manuscript must appear in the reference list.
- Alphabetize the reference list using the surname of the author (first author for multiple authors).
- Multiple entries by the same author are listed by date of publication, earliest first.
- References are double-spaced.
- The first line of each reference entry should be flush left; subsequent lines should be indented five spaces (use "Control t" on your computer at the second line to create a hanging line).
- Use an ampersand (&) between two authors. Separate three or more authors by commas; separate the last author with an ampersand (&).
- Capitalize only the first word (and proper nouns) in the title and subtitle of a journal article or book.
- Capitalize all important words in the titles of journals.
- Italicize titles of journals and books.
- Italicize the volume number of journals.

General form for journal references:
Author, A. A., Author B. B., & Author C. C. (year). Title of article. *Title of Journal, xx*, pp–pp.

General form for book reference, where "location" is city and state (e.g., Portsmouth, NH):
Author, A. A. (year). *Title of book*. Location: Publisher.

General form for book chapter reference:
Author, A. A., & Author, B. B. (year). Title of chapter. In A. Editor (Ed.), *Title of book* (pp. xx–xx). Location: Publisher.

Author, A. A., & Author, B. B. (year). Title of chapter. In A. Editor & B. Editor (Eds.), *Title of book* (pp. xx–xx). Location: Publisher.

Author, A. A., & Author, B. B. (year). Title of chapter. In A. Editor, B. Editor, & C. Editor (Eds.), *Title of book* (pp. xx–xx). Location: Publisher.

Reminders Regarding Grammatical and Other Language Usage

The following are some of the areas of language use that teacher researchers might need reminders on. (For some more details, refer to: Strunk, W. Jr., & White, E. B. (2000). *The elements of style: The fiftieth American edition*. New York: Longman.)

■ The word *data* is a plural noun. Thus, verbs and adjectives have to agree (e.g., *data are*, NOT *data is; these data*, NOT *this data*).

■ In general, be sure that your subjects and verbs agree (that is, they are all singular or plural). Violations of this usage rule sometimes occur in long, complex sentences, so recheck them.

■ If possible, write in the plural when talking about children, students, teachers, instead of using the single form (e.g., *the child, the student*, or *the teacher*). This avoids your having to constantly using *he or she* or *his or her* pronouns in sentences. Moreover, using "short-cut" versions of pronouns (e.g., *his/her* or *he/she*) is not appropriate. The use of *he* or *she* to refer to *the child* (as a class, not a particular child) is considered to be sexist language and should be avoided.

■ Watch your use of the definite article *the* before *students* or *teachers*. Most of the time you can do without using it (e.g., *students wrote in their journals*, NOT *the students wrote in their journals*).

■ Be sure to use *who* to refer to humans (e.g., *the students who*, NOT *the students that*).

■ In U.S. usage, use commas to separate three or more terms in a series. Use *books, paper, and pencils*, NOT *books, paper and pencils; children opened their books, read several pages, and wrote in the journals*, NOT *children opened their books, read several pages and wrote in the journals*.

■ Try to not use the same words over and over; try using synonyms to make the text more interesting.

■ In U.S. usage, place commas and periods *within* quotation marks. For example: "Sentence."; . . . "phrase," "phrase," and "phrase." Even if a single word, at the end of a sentence, is in quotes, the period must be placed within the quotation.

■ Use parallel constructions (similar form) to express coordinate ideas (in phrases, clauses, etc.). Violations of this principle occur a lot when a lot of ideas are being expressed in the same sentence. For example, use a past-tense verb for each phrase: *children opened their books, read several pages, and wrote in the journals* (NOT *children opened their books, read several pages, and journals were used*). Similar forms—parallel constructions—should be used expressing the clauses of compound sentences, series of participial phrases, and so forth. Here are some examples:

- I also applied Vygotsky's principles to my writing workshop sessions by modeling a process for writing workshop in which students would take turns reading their writing aloud, making verbal comments about each other's work, and marking written comments either on Post-it notes or directly on the drafts.
- In my data collection, I looked for signs that students were engaged in their independent reading, that they were excited about choosing and reading books, that they came prepared for and participated in independent reading, and that they saw themselves as an active participant in the meaning making process of reading.

- If *not only* . . . is used, then *but also* . . . is needed in the next clause.
- Use *which* for including a nonrestrictive clause (one that embellishes the sentence but could be deleted, leaving the grammatical structure and the meaning of the sentence intact [e.g., *The books, which were organized alphabetically, were found on the shelves.*]).
- If you find a sentence that is several lines long, take a look at it again. It is likely to be ungrammatical and hard to understand. Think of making the sentence into two or more sentences.

Index

Titles of children's books used in classrooms are indexed together by title under the heading 'children's books'.